Good Guys

Good

How Men Can Be
Better Allies for Women
in the Workplace

Guys

DAVID G. SMITH
W. BRAD JOHNSON

Harvard Business Review Press
Boston, Massachusetts

Library of Congress Cataloging-in-Publication Data
Names: Smith, David (David Glenn), 1965- author. | Johnson, W. Brad, author.
Title: Good guys : how men can be better allies for women in the workplace / David G. Smith, W. Brad Johnson.
    Description: Boston, Massachusetts : Harvard Business Review Press, [2020] | Includes index.
    Identifiers: LCCN 2020012277 (print) | LCCN 2020012278 (ebook) | ISBN 9781633698727 (hardcover) | ISBN 9781633698734 (ebook)
    Subjects: LCSH: Sex discrimination in employment. | Sex discrimination against women. | Women employees—Public opinion. | Helping behavior. | Male employees—Attitudes. | Male feminists. | Male domination (Social structure)
    Classification: LCC HD6060 .S554 2020 (print) | LCC HD6060 (ebook) | DDC 650.1/3—dc23
    LC record available at https://lccn.loc.gov/2020012277
    LC ebook record available at https://lccn.loc.gov/2020012278
ISBN: 978-1-63369-872-7
eISBN: 978-1-63369-873-4

Dedication

*With admiration and gratitude for the hope you
inspire in us as the next generation of allies,
this book is dedicated to four remarkable men:*

*David's son, Jacob Smith
Brad's sons, Jacob Johnson, Daniel Johnson, and Stanton Johnson*

Contents

PART THREE

Systemic Allyship

Becoming an Advocate for Organizational Change

Preface

In 2016, following the release of our first book, *Athena Rising: How and Why Men Should Mentor Women*, we were busy giving talks and workshops on engaging men to become more inclusive mentors. The conversations were rich and the work was rewarding, but it became increasingly clear that gender-based inequalities in society and our workplaces were more pernicious and pervasive than we'd imagined. Yes, men needed to get better and more deliberate at mentoring women, but in order to become full conspirators in addressing bias, sexism, pay inequities, and poor representation of women in leadership, men also needed to become better colleagues, advocates, and accomplices with women. Women were looking for more. They were looking for men to show up as genuine allies for gender equality.

Most of the men we encountered in our public conversations about inclusive mentoring and sponsoring of women understood on some level that exclusion of women from full workplace parity was kryptonite when it came to the corporate bottom line and organizational flourishing. They recognized the toll that gender bias and codified sexism in the workplace extracted from their mothers, sisters, daughters, and female friends. Many of these men were eager to learn how to really move the dial on inclusion. In other words, they were *good guys*. They just didn't know what to *do*, what their role in leveling the playing field for women at work might be, or how to get started on their own ally journey. We wondered how we could leverage this genuine interest and good intent, how we could lure more guys to climb down off the fence and venture into bold conversations about gender in the workplace. Most of all, we wondered if these guys could be effectively equipped with the gender intelligence and action strategies necessary to become real collaborators with women in creating a workplace for everyone.

The year 2017 ushered in the #MeToo movement, the post-#MeToo workplace, and our own effort to help men step into allyship for women at work. Although we'd hoped—naively perhaps—that #MeToo might be a catalyst to move men to action in their organizations, evidence reveals it has merely heightened the proclivity for men to avoid and segregate women, exacerbating gender inequalities while further isolating women. We were so perplexed by men's reactions that we wrote our first HBR.org digital article on October 13, 2017, about men stepping up as allies entitled, "Lots of Men Are Gender-Equality Allies in Private. Why Not in Public?" Three years—and one major qualitative study on what excellent male allyship looks like in practice—later, we are delighted to offer *Good Guys*, the product of our research and journey toward helping men be better allies to women. Before diving in, we thought you might be interested in a few data points from our own ally journeys.

David Smith

I entered the US Naval Academy in 1983, as part of the Class of 1987. Our class was the eighth to include women, and it was my introduction to a world in which women were not on a level playing field. I just didn't fully comprehend how and why. Having gone through high school with some of the smartest women I know (who outnumbered the guys in our honors and AP courses), it was strange being in an environment where women were outnumbered by more than ten to one and, in so many ways, were treated as second-class citizens. Being an ally in that culture was treacherous.

My thirty years serving in the navy was filled with personal and professional experiences that influenced my thinking on fairness, equity, and inclusion. While many men point to the influence of their daughters on their understanding of gender inequities and motivation for change (something we'll discuss later in this book), the relationship that really started to personally develop my awareness and tug at my inner sense of justice was with my wife—also an officer in the navy. Many long conversations about her experiences at work over the years recalibrated my awareness in ways that I am only now beginning to appreciate. But it wasn't until my second squadron tour and later assignments that I began to put this awareness to work as women were allowed to join combat squadrons and ships. Gender integration in the military was prefaced by training about the rules and regulations for what not to do and setting clear expectations for good order and discipline. Glaringly missing was any training or education on cross-gender relationships in the workplace. There was an assumption that the traditional workplace would remain the same despite shifting social and cultural gender norms and that women would adapt to the workplace.

Fast forward to 2006 when I began my doctoral graduate work in sociology. There were two key takeaways during my graduate work that shaped my perspective. First, I began to understand how systemic inequalities such as sexism and racism are perpetuated by social and cultural processes within social institutions—work and family. For me, that meant that in order to understand how to begin eliminating gender inequities, I needed to study women's and men's experiences together at home and work. Dual-career couples were the perfect place to start, and my original research on dual military couples continues to inform my research.

Second, my mentor and dissertation adviser, Mady Segal helped me to better understand my own role in perpetuating inequities. At that time, the term *ally* was unfamiliar to me, but looking back, I would have considered myself an ally and certainly part of the solution, not the problem. She challenged me and opened my eyes to various ways that I was unknowingly reinforcing the system that creates gender inequities. I still remember thinking, "What? Me? How is that possible?"

The wonderful thing about grad school is that you have time to really reflect, which I desperately needed to do. Our dissertation research meetings served a dual purpose of mentoring me through the dissertation process and mentoring me as a person. While I'm proud of the research, I think I learned just as much about how to be a better ally, for which I am grateful.

Brad Johnson

Three salient themes emerged as I reflected on the journey to writing this book and—I hope—becoming a better ally for women in the process.

First, any ally chops I might have originated with my father. My dad was a full-on partner at home. Most nights, he made dinner, did the dishes, folded laundry, and helped with homework. He championed my mother's career at every turn and prioritized family time. My father could also be fierce when it came to confronting injustice. I carry vivid memories of Dad calling out men who belittled or harassed women. Dad was a big guy, and if size is privilege, he used his to shut down a lot of misogynist nonsense. I have no doubt that my dad's modeling made it easier for me to step comfortably into collaborative relationships with women while keeping my antennae tuned for evidence of inequity.

Second, my relationship with my only sibling, my younger sister, Shannon, has been essential in building my empathy for the experience of women at work. Shannon and I are both clinical psychologists and we both entered the navy following graduate school to serve as officers and clinicians. One thing has become crystal clear over the years: as a woman, Shannon's experiences in the workplace have been markedly different from my own. Despite the fact that Shannon and I have rather similar approaches to relationships, leadership, and emotional presentation, she is often told that she should smile more. She has been dinged on evaluations for not being "emotionally available," and when she has given men under her command clear constructive performance feedback, she has been told she is "emasculating." She has even been made to feel bad for "running too fast" and outshining junior men on physical fitness tests. Needless to say, I have not encountered similar obstacles. Watching my remarkable sister weather these gendered headwinds at work has sharpened my attention to the challenges women confront daily in the male-centric workplace.

Finally, my nearly thirty-year journey as a researcher and writer on the topic of mentoring relationships in the workplace has afforded me the opportunity to become immersed in the research evidence bearing on the many ways gender influences access to quality mentoring. Women are less likely to find mentors, and when they do, the quality of the relationship and the career benefits accruing to them don't measure up to the mentorships men experience. There are several reasons for this, but chief among them is men's reluctance to wholeheartedly engage with women at work. If mentoring, sponsorship, and intentional friendship are key ingredients in achieving gender equality in the workplace, then men have a crucial role in making life and career-altering developmental relationships available to everyone, especially in male-centric workplaces featuring few senior women.

About the Book

We've incorporated these experiences and our own research in crafting this book. As social scientists, we rely on evidence-based practices to provide the foundation for everything you read about being a *good guy*. We've distilled the latest social science research to help you understand the science behind action-oriented strategies. And to make these strategies relatable, we provide examples from men and women across industries to see what allyship looks and feels like in the context of their lived workplace experiences. We use their voices throughout the book, so you can hear directly from men and woman who are partners and allies. We interviewed fifty-nine women, all thought leaders and luminaries in their professions and organizations. They generously contributed their experiences and recommendations for men on stepping up to the plate as allies. They tell stories about how they were held back, where they faced bias, and also where they found support and were lifted up by male allies who came alongside at important moments.

One of the many things we learned in doing the research for this book is that a growing community of men in every walk of life and industry is taking ownership of our gender inequality problem and personally leading with conviction and humility. The women you work with know who they are. We also interviewed twenty-nine men in preparing to write this book. Without exception, every man we interviewed was identified as an ally by one of the women we interviewed. These are stand-up guys who don't just talk the talk—they walk the talk, too. You see their commitment in the intentionality and action-oriented way they approach solving gender inequities in their organizations. Their firsthand reflections on the practice of allyship are also included throughout *Good Guys*.

To ensure broad applicability, we included interviewees from a wide range of industries in the corporate, nonprofit, and government sectors. By design, you'll also find that our interviewees represent a diversity of race/ethnicity, sexual orientation, and family type. This provides a rich set of experiences and examples that will resonate with anyone looking to hone their allyship skills.

Those are a few of the elements that shaped our learning and thinking along the ally journey. We share our stories and research because transparency and purpose are foundational to the work in this book. We hope that you will take this to heart as you read and learn how you can be a courageous leader and better ally for women in the workplace.

1

Men: The Missing Ingredient in Gender Equity

What does it mean to be a good guy to women at work? A few things probably come to mind. Don't harass women. (That one should be obvious.) Mentor women when you can. Encourage gender equality programs in the workplace, and as a manager, make sure women have the opportunity to participate. Offer fair pay and, when available, flexible work arrangements, especially for working moms.

You can do more.

That women struggle with gender inequality is well known. They feel invisible, unheard, and disrespected in the workplace. They face inappropriate comments, sexual harassment, and in worst cases, assault. They miss out on career opportunities and promotions, and face motherhood penalties if they have children.

On a broader scale, workplace inequities in recruitment, hiring, and compensation create disadvantage not only for individual workers, but also for their families and broader national and global economies. The gender wage gap is the most widely recognized workplace inequity and is a particularly useful example in understanding how these issues affect society and the economy at large. In 2018, the gender wage gap in the United States was 81.1 percent and has remained nearly unchanged, with less than a 1 percent improvement since 2008.[1] As with other disparities at work, the gender wage gap is amplified for women of color. Beyond race and ethnicity, the gap is particularly crushing for single mothers and women below the poverty line. Eliminating the gap has the potential to increase the pay for 60 percent of women, reduce poverty for women by half, and add 2.8 percent to the national gross domestic product (GDP).[2] On a global level, there is more reason to achieve gender parity sooner than later, as it could add up to $28 *trillion* to annual global GDP.[3] With this kind of economic prosperity, many of the world's enduring social problems aren't quite as daunting.

Despite these worldwide benefits, gender equality is largely seen as a women's issue. Organizations and their male leaders see gender inequities as something women need to solve, and men are historically missing in efforts to address these problems. And because most men are not meaningfully engaged in addressing gender inequities, it may take another 202 years to create gender parity, according to 2019 World Economic Forum estimates.[4]

Gender inequities are not women's issues—they are leadership issues. Framing gender inequities as "women's issues" gives men a free pass—"we're not women; it's not our problem." If gender equity is perceived to be a women's issue, men are more likely to believe they have no psychological standing or ownership to support taking action. The perception that men lack legitimacy because they aren't women, don't share women's experiences, or don't have the expertise keeps men silent.

Men need to do more to be a good guy in the workplace and pave the way for gender equality. The truth is that in most organizations—especially those that are traditionally male-dominated—men are more likely to occupy key stakeholder positions. Men have the influence and power to create change, and they are crucial to altering the status quo.

So, why is it that so many men don't see or understand women's experiences at work? The simple answer is that it's hard to see problems we don't encounter.

It's Good to Be a Man in the Workplace

The workplace was created by men, for men, to do men's work. Because men are the workplace norm, the entire business and workplace environment is based on men, with a few exceptions (e.g., women's restrooms). The ideal room temperature for offices, conferences, and work activities is set at a lower temperature based on men's work wear—business suits—and their higher metabolic rates.[5] Wherever you may work, the workspace and job-related equipment are probably based on men's average height, weight, and build. For example, aircraft cockpits, commercial vehicles, carpentry tools, safety protective equipment, body armor, and so on are all geared to men. In one recent example, NASA had to cancel a scheduled space walk with two astronauts because it had only one spacesuit available that was designed for a woman, but both astronauts were female.[6] Male as the default gender also extends to many areas of research, most importantly, safety, health, and medical research, making the world a safer and healthier place for men to live and work.[7]

One of the primary roadblocks to male awareness of gender disparities relates to our *mis*perceptions of women at work. As one illustration, men often presume that women leave their companies at higher rates than men because they want to pause their careers to have children. In fact, McKinsey & Company's annual *Women in the Workplace* report in 2017 revealed that women are *not* leaving the workforce to have children—80 percent of the women planning to leave their company in the next two years were *staying* in the workforce.[8] Instead, they're leaving a workplace that doesn't treat them fairly, hoping to find one that might. Like men, less than 2 percent of women say that they are leaving the workforce for reasons related to family.[9]

Male misperception extends to how men and women perceive opportunity and equity in today's workplace. CNBC's "Close the Gap" research on the finance industry indicated that male senior leaders generally believed that gender discrimination had significantly declined.[10] In the survey, it found that 56 percent of male participants believed that men and women were just as likely to become leaders in their industry, while only 37 percent of women said the same. Similarly, 75 percent of men indicated that men and women working at similar levels of management were paid equally, while only 40 percent of women agreed.[11] Clearly, many men don't perceive gender inequities in the traditional workplace. It's hard to fix what you can't see.

Obstacles to Male Engagement

Men have told us that they don't know how to get started in the fight for gender equity, and some encounter obstacles when they do. These obstacles include unclear rationales for inclusion, lack of support from senior leadership, or fear of making mistakes. Who wants to inadvertently offend someone or hurt their feelings when you have good intentions? It's easier for you to avoid taking action, so you don't engage. If you're not comfortable talking about gender, women's work experiences, harassment, discrimination, or emotions, then you'll probably avoid those conversations.

Another challenge to solving gender inequities and making real change in the workplace is *zero-sum beliefs*. People who hold a zero-sum perspective believe that gains for a nondominant group (women) are a loss for their own dominant group (men). In the case of gender, men are more likely to hold zero-sum beliefs related to gender equality and are therefore less likely to engage in action that reduces inequality for fear of losing in some way. Men who are older and have stronger beliefs in social hierarchies, more sexist beliefs, and less awareness of gender inequality are more likely to hold this perspective.[12] Zero-sum thinking is one of the many stumbling blocks for diversity and inclusion initiatives. Diversity is a tough sell in organizations where many people see diversity as a threat to their identity, job, or advancement opportunities.

No one is blaming men for inheriting a workplace that fits us so perfectly that we don't even notice, but that doesn't mean we can ignore the negative effects on women's lives and careers. It's time to focus on fixing the systems within our workplace that reinforce and normalize the institutional sexism that creates gender inequities. The only way to drive significant long-term change is to fix our organizations' behavior and culture and to engage men in partnering with women to make this change.

Traditional Workplace Gender Rules

When the workplace rules are designed for workers based on specific gender roles, it's hard to see why there's a problem if you fit into those roles and follow the rules. *Gender rules* are expectations derived from social beliefs we share about appropriate behavior for men and women.[13] In the traditional workplace, they look like the following rules:

- Men work outside the home and women work inside the home.

- Work that women perform is inherently less important than the work men perform.

- Women are not competent at performing men's work.

- There is something fundamentally aberrant about a woman who performs men's work, and the corollary, men should not perform women's work.

Almost every gender bias and norm in the workplace flows from one of these traditional gender rules. While we may disagree with these rules—and we do—they still tacitly operate, shaping workplace behavior. Let's see how these gender rules operate in our everyday lives.

When women are visible in the workplace, they are expected to occupy roles that are appropriate for women's work—administrative, support, or caregiving. In the workplace, this can take many forms, but "office housework" (i.e., taking notes, planning social events, bringing coffee or snacks) is particularly prevalent and challenging to overcome—if you're a woman.

Even less visible to men are gendered expectations for work roles when men and women become parents. Because we see women as caregivers, they are often perceived to be less committed at work and evaluated similarly. You might assume that actual performance should help overcome this discrimination against mothers. Testing this hypothesis, researchers found that even when presented with unambiguous performance information, evaluators rated mothers lower than single women or men based on perceived deficiencies in interpersonal qualities. Successful women with children were specifically evaluated as less warm and likable, resulting in poorer organizational employment outcomes.[14]

These same gender rules also reinforce behavior for men in terms of what they *do* see. Men receive signals and messages that there is something wrong with them if they want to devote time away from work to care for children. One father with two young boys was asked by skeptical coworkers about his decision to take paternity leave: "Why would you want to be home with a baby for that long?" Reinforcing the perception that childcare is women's work, other coworkers quipped, "I bet your wife appreciates what you are doing."[15]

It might seem easy to dismiss this kind of workplace banter as harmless, but it has a real and measurable impact on men's perceptions and decisions about workplace flexibility and parental leave. While men and women are just as likely to espouse attitudes of support for flexible work schedules and parental leave, men are less likely to actually use the benefits.

Traditional gender rules also lead to implicit bias in the way men see their female colleagues.[16] For example, when men are asked anonymously how they feel about women, they offer a list of positive traits (e.g., "Women are great. I love women. They are kind, caring, and gentle."). This is the well-researched *women are wonderful effect*.[17] Yet, we still find widespread biases against women in the workplace. Men's "wonderful" assessments of women serve to mask the things they *don't* say about them: that she's a brilliant leader, she has innovative ideas, she's ambitious, and so on. In other instances, they hold women back from career or growth opportunities as a form of protection—"She wouldn't want to travel now that she has kids" or "This project will take a lot of time, and she is already so busy"—what's known as *benevolent sexism*.

It's important to recognize how we label sexist and harassing behavior in the workplace. Too often, harassment is considered another women's issue, yet men are the people most likely to harass women. Labeling harassment as a women's issue is a form of hostile sexism that evokes a negative reaction toward them. There's also the issue of ownership of the problem. As Gretchen Carlson, TV commentator and author of *Be Fierce* who ignited the latest cultural revolution regarding harassment in the workplace with her lawsuit against Chairman and CEO of Fox News Roger Ailes, told us in an interview, "When men hear something is a women's issue, they tune out. Not because they don't care; they just assume they don't have to pay attention because it's for women. Let's start calling harassment exactly what it is—a men's issue."

Male Allies as the Missing Piece of the Puzzle

How do we solve our problem? Men need to get involved. We need to learn to work together as gender partners and allies for each other. We define allyship as:

> Actively promoting gender fairness and equity in the workplace through supportive and collaborative personal relationships and public acts of sponsorship and advocacy intended to drive systemic improvements to the workplace culture.

Allies exhibit both affirmation and informed action. We use the terms *partner* and *ally* because they conjure images of women and men as equals in the workplace, working together to achieve their mission. Allies in an alliance acknowledge the power of relationship and prize interdependence and responsibility to each other.

Debra Meyerson and Megan Tompkins would frame male allies for equality as "tempered radicals."[18] Allies are cultural insiders who understand the dominant culture, but have an outsider's (nondominant) perspective. They understand the behaviors and characteristics of traditional workplace culture and are aware of and understand how gender inequality works and have the courage to change it.

Allies aren't *saving* women. They don't see an opportunity to take control of gender initiatives and rescue women from inequality, reinforcing the heroic, masculine stereotype and strengthening the status quo. Instead, allies emphasize humility and gender partnership—men and women working together in complementary roles—to create and support inclusive workplaces.

In their work with men as advocates and accomplices for women in the global development sector, Sahana Dharmapuri and Jolynn Shoemaker concluded that "when men are involved, it's a sign that gender equality benefits all of society, not just a certain portion of the population."[19] Effectively, this demonstrates to the women these men work with that we're all in this together. And when men speak out on gender equity issues, they're also influencing their male colleagues—and junior men are watching and listening.[20]

When you're getting started, allyship can feel complex, with competing expectations. Allyship demands that you simultaneously become attuned to women's experiences and enter into conversations about gender equity. As an ally, you must learn when to speak up, listen, ask questions, and sometimes become invisible. Then you must go bigger. Involve men directly in gender equity work.[21] Ask men to participate, volunteer, and contribute ideas, and give them a role in changing policy. Integrate gender diversity initiatives into operational business outcomes and then hold managers and leaders accountable. Make it clear that women are not the only beneficiaries of gender equity, and more men will act. That takes being a "good guy" to the next level. (See the sidebar "Note to Men: There's a Lot in This for You, Too.")

Note to Men: There's a Lot in This for You, Too

The benefits to men of partnering with and supporting women are significant but may not always be obvious. Kimberley Doyle, director of corporate engagement at Catalyst, commented about benefits accruing to male allies: "One of the things holding men back from being better allies is they don't often understand what they have to gain from being an ally. Some of the benefits include better physical and mental health, more rewarding and intimate relationships, not to mention the business case for making more money and being more influential leaders at work."

There's more, especially for white men. Developing allyship with women brings the added bonus of developing allyship skills that are transportable to other groups in the workplace. Rachel Thomas, co-founder and president of LeanIn.Org and OptionB.Org, said, "Men who are good at working with women also learn skills that make them more effective working with people of color. By getting better at allyship with women, you are going to be better at working with a substantial and growing slice of the workplace population. This is a competitive advantage for men that delivers real value to your organization."

Allyship also crosses over from the workplace to the home front when we support each other in our roles as caregivers. Josh Levs, author of *All In*, elaborated that men need women's support, too: "Just as women need help from everyone to ensure true equal opportunity in the workplace, men need help from everyone to ensure equal opportunity as caregivers—it's the big unknown half of gender equality. If the message to guys is 'be one of the good guys, help women,' it's nice but it fails to address the fact that men have challenges too." It can be difficult even for the most courageous man to talk about caregiving challenges or flexible work-family roles when facing the resistance of the status quo norms in the workplace. Lev's research finds that it helps when men can acknowledge that we don't have all the answers and that we can learn something from our female colleagues.

One of the true paradoxes of male allyship is the consistent social psychological research evidence showing that when men advocate for women or call out gender inequities, they are perceived to be more credible because they are not acting in self-interest.[22] The research shows that when men advocate for gender equity initiatives, their voice and message are given more weight because they are supporting initiatives that benefit women. Women are all too familiar with these double standards. It's time for men to open their eyes to this opportunity and privilege and use it. As apparent outsiders to the cause, our voices on the topic of gender equity carry considerable weight.

Engaging men at every level of the organization is critical to changing the traditional workplace culture. Rachel Thomas of LeanIn.Org and OptionB.Org warned that "junior men fall into the trap of thinking there is nothing they can do. Junior men can actually do a great deal to partner with women for equality and inclusion. Some of these allyship acts are small but still bring a lot of impact."

As it turns out, men can do so much more because of their innate privilege—even at the junior levels. Being members of the dominant gender at work, we are free to navigate the system through our knowledge of the culture and use our understanding of women's experiences to disrupt the status quo. To develop our sense of being allies, we learn to see the world through others' experiences. This requires being more aware, challenging assumptions, reading, learning, asking questions, and listening. Without this effort, we risk falling into the trap of silence—doing nothing. We can do better.

Fortunately, over the past several decades, more men have been willing to speak out publicly and act to level the playing field for women. The research evidence is clear: when men are actively engaged in gender diversity, both women and men have a more positive outlook about their organization's progress toward eliminating gender inequities. One international study asked women and men if they agreed that their company had made significant progress in the last three years in improving gender diversity at all levels of the company. These responses were correlated with whether they agreed that men in their company were involved in championing gender diversity. The results show that in companies where men are actively involved in gender diversity, 96 percent of people report progress, whereas where men are not engaged, only 30 percent see progress.[23]

Allyship and support for gender equity must be public, too. It's not enough that we hold ourselves individually accountable—we must be advocating for gender equity in public spaces, even when women aren't in the room, *especially* when women aren't in the room. Marine Corps Colonel Maria Pallotta's advice for men is: "You've got to be out there saying this organization is better for the contributions of the women on our team. If you don't, her male peers will undermine her. It's not enough to be neutral. The entire organization has to know you are a proactive advocate for women."

There are lots of ways that men can deliberately involve themselves in increasing gender diversity. Some include supporting flexible work policies, modeling the right behaviors, communicating fairly, sponsoring high-potential women, and getting involved with company-specific initiatives.[24] This book aims to help you get started with just that.

The Allyship Journey

There are three types of male allies. In our conversation with Subha Barry, President of Working Mother Media, she described them as "a small group of men who are already allies, know what they have to do, and do it all the time. A large middle group who are aware of the inequities, but watching the lay of the land, deciding if it is politically smart to act or use political capital. Finally, there is a small group of misogynists with very strong views who aren't going to change."

In this guide to male allyship, we focus on the first two groups: first, leveraging and reinforcing all-in allies into leadership roles; second, motivating the large middle group of men to lean in to the good work of inclusion and equality. Whether you are a leader, manager, or a junior employee looking to support your female colleagues, this book will give you practical tips and advice to help you be a male ally—to learn from the women around you, to get over your fears and hesitancies, and to make real change in the workplace and beyond.

The skills you need to be a better ally for women at work will also make you a better ally for everyone. Think of them as gateway skills. What makes you an ally to women also applies to being a better ally to someone of a different race, sexual orientation, military veteran status, or generation. This will become clear as you learn how to develop these important skills for today's workplace.

The book is organized into three parts: *interpersonal allyship*, *public allyship*, and *systemic allyship*. The chapters comprise sixty action-oriented strategies that will guide your skill development and personalized ally action plan.

Part one, Interpersonal Allyship, examines how you show up in workplace relationships with women. Chapter 2 encourages reflection on your gender intelligence (GQ) and employs strategies to expand your knowledge about how women experience the workplace. Of course, you can't be an all-in ally at work unless you're an ally at home, so strategies in chapter 3 will arm you with actions to make you a world-class ally for your own partner and children. Chapter 4 is loaded with strategies to ensure your everyday interactions with women at work are creating a work environment that tells women that they are included, valued, and respected. Part one ends with the importance of developing friendships with women based on trust and reciprocity. The strategies in chapter 5 equip men for the relational aspects that are key to forging a network of women colleagues who are part of your personal board of advisers.

After mastering crucial ally relational strategies, part two prepares you for public allyship by offering strategies on how to be a proactive ally despite the occasional anxiety and some obstacles you will likely face. Chapter 6 is full of strategies and best practices to help you navigate the prickliest of scenarios. Many of these challenging scenarios happen in meetings. Chapter 7 gives you specific strategies to handle these ubiquitous inequities. Being a public ally requires advocacy, and the final chapter in part two outfits you with ways to boldly sponsor women and promote their excellent contributions.

Finally, part three addresses systemic allyship and equips you with strategies to advocate for allyship and organizational change at any level. Chapter 9 explores the multitude of organizational processes in which systemic inequities are perpetuated and the strategies you can apply to vanquish them. Allies need support too, and we know there's strength in numbers. Chapter 10 contains strategies for growing a robust community of allies and developing a rich culture of allyship.

Whether you work for, alongside, or manage women, deliberately engaging with them in the workplace is the only real solution to overcoming the systemic sexism and inequality that keep all of us from maximizing potential and our organization from thriving.

Making Mistakes Is Part of the Journey

Allyship is a continuous learning process—a journey on which we will need to leverage and learn from each other—men and women in partnership. As Karen Catlin explains in her book, *Better Allies*, even seasoned allies with wide-open minds are constantly learning and absorbing new information about how to support less privileged people around them. Maintaining a learning orientation, a growth mindset, and a healthy dose of humility goes a long way toward being better allies. This is a marathon, not a sprint.

There are no perfect allies. As you work to become a better ally for the women around you, you will undoubtedly make a mistake. You'll be stepping out of your comfort zone and you'll be putting yourself on display as a partner and supporter. Brené Brown, author of *Dare to Lead*, research professor, and Huffington Foundation–Brené Brown Endowed Chair at The Graduate College of Social Work at the University of Houston said, "You can choose courage or you can choose comfort. You can not have both." In many ways, allyship is a test of courage. If it were easy, we wouldn't be talking about it. Allyship requires us to enter spaces and conversations that can make us feel uncomfortable and take the occasional misstep.

Many men have never been in a space where they were a minority; they can find this both uncomfortable and powerful. (Take it from two guys who routinely speak and work in female-dominated spaces.) Most people don't want to unintentionally offend someone or hurt their feelings. And others worry that they'll experience resistance, backlash, or the dreaded *wimp penalty.*[25] They fear they'll be stigmatized through association with women's initiatives at work.[26] When faced with these uncertainties and fears, they naturally want to step back, rather than push forward.

But men need to get comfortable with these situations and conversations. Allies must immerse themselves in spaces where they can use their curiosity and learning orientation to ask questions and just listen. They must change the prevailing discourse from a wimp penalty. Instead, recognize that it actually takes a stronger, more secure man to support women's initiatives. This requires showing up in spaces where you don't think to venture and in ways you are unaccustomed to, and speaking up when you see backlash behavior. And in the process, make mistakes, learn from them, and figure out ways to improve.

In our experience, we find that when we make a mistake, we benefit from the honest relationships we've developed with women who trust our good intentions. As Catlin said, "[T]he best allies are willing to make mistakes and keep trying. As allies, we must acknowledge when we're wrong or could do better, and correct our course. We resist getting defensive and insisting that we're already doing enough. We listen and learn. We iterate."[27]

Speaking out isn't easy, and no one expects perfection. But becoming a partner and ally to women is a crucial element of helping them reach equity in the workplace. If you think you're doing enough, you're probably not. Push further.

Jennifer Brown, CEO of Jennifer Brown Consulting, a true inclusion thought leader, provided her insight on diversity and allyship: "I think the work of allyship needs to be sustained and over time—and you're only an ally when someone says you are. The caution there is that being an ally is a journey and not a destination. Allyship is something you can aspire to, but you have to be careful when you claim it. Acknowledge we have our own work to do. Let's both go together."

Part One

Interpersonal Allyship

How to Show Up in Workplace
Relationships with Women

2

Expand Your GQ (Gender Intelligence)

As you launch on your mission and start developing the knowledge you'll need to fight for gender equity and fairness, we want to furnish you with the gender intelligence you'll need to be successful. In this chapter are seven ally strategies designed to sharpen your *gender intelligence* (GQ).

Ally work starts with developing a keen sense of awareness of self and others. Sharpening your situational awareness and becoming more vigilant to the gender dynamics operating all around you is an essential first step. We'll then encourage you to tackle any lingering anxiety you might have about boldly and deliberately interacting with women as colleagues, accomplices, mentors, or sponsors. As an ally, you'll ask women about their experiences to better understand the stressors, roadblocks, and dilemmas they encounter. Then, you'll listen and learn, considering how you might strategically deploy your own privilege as a man in the workplace to make things more equitable for women. We'll urge you to deliberately seek and welcome feedback from women about your ally behaviors. You'll also learn to appreciate that not all women's experiences are the same by

A Glossary of Ally Slang

Bropropriation (aka, hepeating): When a woman's good suggestion or creative idea is co-opted by a man so that he receives credit for her work.

Gaslighting: A form of psychological manipulation that sows seeds of doubt in members of a targeted group, making them question their own memory, perception, and sanity.

Gender rules: Expectations derived from social beliefs we share about appropriate behavior for men and women in important roles.

Manel: A nondiverse (all-male) conference panel.

Mansplaining: An explanation of something by a man, typically to a woman, in a manner that is regarded as condescending or patronizing.

Manspaces: Settings such as meetings where men assume they'll have a seat at the table, be able to speak up, expect to be heard, aren't interrupted, and expect full credit for their ideas.

considering how women of color and people with other intersectional identities experience the workplace. Then, we'll challenge you to become vigilant for those—sometimes subtle, yet always pernicious—sexist words and comments that dishearten and undermine female colleagues, and we'll ask you to intervene when you hear them. (See the sidebar "A Glossary of Ally Slang.")

Although this chapter will give you a running start on expanding and sharpening your GQ, there are many sources for gender intelligence. Beyond this guide, seek out current books, articles, presentations, and conferences. The preponderance of research shows that personal experiences and education heighten awareness of gender inequities, reduce sexist attitudes, and increase participation in gender equity initiatives.[1] Ask curious questions of women you've worked

Manterruption: When a man interrupts a woman who is speaking, communicating disrespect for her and disregarding her perspective, often resulting in a gender imbalance in the amount of time men and women speak in venues such as meetings.

Office housework: Administrative work (e.g., taking meeting notes, bringing refreshments, planning social events) that is necessary but undervalued, unlikely to lead to promotion, and disproportionately assigned to women.

Tempered radicals: Cultural insiders who understand the dominant culture, but have an outsider's (nondominant) perspective.

Wimp penalty: Fear of being penalized for speaking up on behalf of someone leads to concerns about negative perceptions and a backlash that is often related to unproductive behaviors such as isolating women and avoiding gender equity initiatives.

with to form trusting relationships. Maintain a learning orientation and a healthy dose of gender humility to foster a growth mindset and challenge status quo thinking. Dismantling the inner workings of systemic sexism will require reflection on what you are learning, always refreshing and updating your GQ to amplify the impact of your ally actions.

Sharpen Your Situational Awareness

Your gender intelligence relies on situational awareness (SA) that starts with knowledge of others and what they are experiencing. Just like motivations, factors such as apathy or lack of awareness can keep well-intentioned men on the sidelines when it comes to gender partnership.[2] When men don't understand that women have different experiences and why it matters or that they have the ability to serve as potent accomplices for change, they don't engage.

Men have some hurdles to overcome here. Although most of us support increasing female leadership in our organizations and broadly recognize that they face barriers to senior leadership that men don't, we are not as aware of or able to recognize gender discrimination or harassment.[3] Despite recent emphasis on harassment and assault by the #MeToo movement, research in 2018 shows that 42 percent of women still experienced gender discrimination and 38 percent reported sexual harassment.[4] Yet, 77 percent of men didn't see sexual harassment as a problem in the workplace.[5] Situationally aware men become more acutely attuned to gender inequities and harassment and then more willing to address them in real time.[6]

Several of the women we interviewed promoted the value of a male ally for SA. Amy Orlov, vice president for programs, Forté Foundation, recommended that men "look for patterns and begin to notice workplace behavior and dynamics they didn't even see before. What is happening in the room? How are your female colleagues experiencing this moment? Try to objectively observe these dynamics." In a similar vein, Annie Rogaski, COO of Avegant Corp., encouraged men to be attentive to what's going on around them: "It's hard for men to identify these gender issues; it's like trying to pay attention to the air around you. If you're in your natural state and things seem normal to you, it's harder to notice when something that seems normal is negatively impacting someone else."

We are big fans of Rogaski's air metaphor. Let's extend it to water. As men, we've long been the big fish, hardly noticing the other fish in the sea. We are so used to swimming through the male-centric work world, it never occurs to us that other fish might find the water dangerous, even toxic, at times. It takes some real effort for a big fish to slow down, look around, and observe how other fish are experiencing the water.

So, what's a guy to focus on? Start with the following questions and go from there:

- Who is in the room and who's not?

- Given the topic of discussion, who really should be in the room discussing her work or serving as a subject-matter expert?

- Who's sitting at the table and who's standing or sitting in an outer ring?

- Who's got a nameplate at the table?

- Who is taking up maximum physical space and who is folded in on themselves?

- Who appears to be comfortable?

- Who is speaking most of the time and who has barely contributed?

- Who is getting interrupted?

- Has someone been dismissed or belittled?

- Are there any sexual innuendos or inappropriate humor being transmitted in the context of bro banter?

- Are women in the room visibly uncomfortable with the topic or something that's been said?

- How would you describe the mood in the room (e.g., good-natured, energized, icy, angry, anxious)?

- Whose input has not been solicited or ignored once offered?

You get the idea. GQ competency number one is to focus, watch, and listen. Make mental and physical checklists, use sticky notes—whatever it takes to keep your SA sharp. If your SA is acute and accurate, chances are that no bro will slip any harassing, sexist, or egregiously biased comment or behavior by you.

Cure Your Gynophobia

But wait a minute, isn't the post-#MeToo workplace a scary world for men? Guys are asking, "How do I approach and communicate with women?" "How do I differentiate between appropriate and inappropriate behavior?" "What do women think of men?"

Despite the importance of the #MeToo movement in empowering women to come forward and hold perpetrators accountable for their crimes, the movement also triggered a marked shift in the way people approached everyday interactions at work. Sometimes these changes led to productive conversations about what was acceptable and unacceptable behavior—everything from hugs and opening doors to closed-door meetings and calling women bossy.

However, in this post-#MeToo era, a steady stream of data reveals that men are more anxious about engaging openly with women at work. *Gynophobia* is an abnormal fear of women, and more and more men are reacting to this feeling in counterproductive ways.[7] For instance, national representative surveys by LeanIn.Org indicate that 60 percent of male managers feel less comfortable mentoring, working alone, or socializing with women.[8] And across the corporate world, senior-level men are more hesitant to spend time with junior women across a range of basic work activities such as one-on-one meetings, travel, and work dinners.[9] Some men have responded to #MeToo by segregating and isolating themselves from women entirely.

Let's pause, take a deep breath, and remember the truth about #MeToo, which is fundamentally about women—quite appropriately—demanding to come to work each day without facing assault or sexual harassment. That's a pretty low bar. The false narrative—perpetuated by men—that women are more "dangerous," "scary," and can't be trusted because they feel empowered to call out male predators and serial harassers is nonsense. Every man reading this needs to push back on the post-#MeToo myths about the risks of engaging with our female colleagues. Men's claims about women's frequent false accusations of harassment are without evidence. Next time you hear this from a guy, ask him to furnish some credible data to prove it. You'll usually get a response beginning with, "I heard about a guy . . ." Here is the truth: if you are a well-meaning and admittedly imperfect dude (much like your authors), someone who sometimes makes a mistake but generally wants to get better and be part of the equality solution at work and in society, then you've got absolutely nothing to fear.

We think most guys are self-aware enough to keep themselves out of hot water at work. Kim Elsesser, author of *Sex and the Office* and *Forbes* columnist, had these words of wisdom for men at work: "Most men are not going to inadvertently do something like ask a woman to get into the shower with him! The average guy might worry about whether a comment will be misinterpreted, but this has nothing to do with sexual assault and harassment. If you're a guy and you're worried about whether a compliment will be misinterpreted, you've got nothing to worry about." The #MeToo movement should be a catalyst for change in the workplace that spurs more conversations between men and women. Let's not allow it to become a siren for men to avoid women. It's time for men to double down in supporting our female colleagues. Allies speak up, ask questions, and listen—even when it's uncomfortable.

If you are a man in any sort of leadership role, intentional interaction with women is a non-negotiable job requirement. In our interview with a female executive in the technology sector, she offered two recommendations for men in the post-#MeToo era: "First, don't harass anyone! Second, don't ignore women. You cannot lead or manage women if you are not willing to have a one-on-one meeting with a woman. Full stop." We concur. If you are unwilling to meet or have coffee or lunch alone with a woman, you probably should resign your leadership role. Let a woman, or a more confident and inclusive man, take your place.

Still anxious about engaging with women at work? Here is the good news: there is a safe, effective, evidence-based treatment for any phobia, including gynophobia. The cure is called *exposure therapy*.[10] It is side effect–free and guaranteed to reduce your distress if you practice it diligently. Exposure therapy requires that you actively and frequently seek out collegial conversations and interactions with women. Sit down and chat with them, invite them to coffee or lunch, ask them for help, and ask about their career interests. Look for a senior woman who might mentor you and initiate mentoring conversations with some of those high-potential junior women around you. These interactions also have the added benefit of developing trust and respect. A female executive in the technology sector said, "I think men and women should be able to have regular interactions and everyone should behave appropriately. But, if you're afraid for whatever reason, just make access equal. If you're not comfortable having dinner with women, don't have dinner with men!" Exposure therapy will certainly cause you anxiety at first. The more you tolerate it and keep interacting with women, the less anxiety you'll experience.

JPMorgan Chase provides a nice example of structured exposure called the 30-5-1 approach. We think it is a perfect way to get started leaning in as an ally:

- For 30 minutes each week, have coffee with a high potential woman.

- For 5 minutes each week, congratulate a female coworker on an accomplishment.

- For 1 minute each week, highlight that woman's accomplishment with other coworkers.

Some guys reading this are wondering, yeah, but how do I get started talking to women and engaging as an ally? First, don't be vague (e.g., "Hey, want to have lunch sometime?" Or, "I'd like to mentor you"). Such context-less overtures may leave women wondering what exactly you have in mind. Instead, start with something very specific you've observed or are curious about (e.g., "Shaunda, I saw you give that presentation yesterday. You knocked it out of the park. I hope we can keep you here at ___ Inc. Stop by my office anytime if you'd like to chat about next steps in the company. I'd be interested to hear about your career plan." Or, "Hey, Stacy, I noticed you've got experience negotiating IT contracts. I'm doing it for the first time. Can I get on your calendar to pick your brain? I'll buy the coffee").

See, not so daunting! Greet your female colleagues when you see them, ask how they are doing, initiate friendly conversations, invite them to collaborate on projects that might benefit them. Avoid pretense and just be yourself. Admit what you don't know and spare the bravado. Authenticity and vulnerability demonstrate that you trust her, and as she begins to see you as an ally, she will trust you. If you are comfortable interacting with women, they will (probably) be comfortable interacting with you.

Ask Women about Their Experiences— and Learn from Them

Some men hate asking for directions. We want to project an aura of knowing everything. Perhaps the only thing more averse for some guys than asking for directions is asking a woman for directions. Here is the problem: men don't know what they don't know about the experiences of women in the workplace.

Asking women what it's like for them to show up to work with the goal of understanding and learning is a hallmark practice of strong allyship. Asking women about their experiences also requires honest-to-goodness humility. We've got to check our egos at the door, demonstrate transparency about what we don't know, and express real curiosity about our female colleagues' experiences in the workplace.

A humble question is the first step toward building our empathy and wisdom. Many women we spoke with emphasized the importance of asking. Ipek Serifsoy, president of the Deep Coaching Institute, said, "Men have a terrible time fathoming the things women experience daily. Women are reluctant to share negative experiences with men because they know on some level that men don't share those experiences. So, men need to be humble and acknowledge there's a lot they don't understand." Not only do women intuit that men have very different experiences at work because men rarely show interest in really understanding the obstacles and challenges their female co-workers encounter, women also may not bother sharing these experiences with men. Of course, women can also be reluctant when invited to share for fear of coming across as whining or complaining. For all these reasons, allies need to develop relationships with women at work, ask good questions, and build their gender awareness.

Here's some good news: the more you give yourself permission not to know everything, the more you will enjoy learning about the women around you. Embracing humility is an antidote for anxiety about your performance and perfection as an ally. Julie Kratz, founder of Next Pivot Point, put it this way: "You don't have to know what it's like to be a woman. Just ask a woman what it's like for her at work." And don't forget that expressing interest and asking women good questions is a crucial way for them to discover who the genuine allies in the workplace are (see the sidebar "Questions for Building Gender Awareness").[11]

Two important caveats about asking women about their experiences are: first, don't come off as an interrogator. No one responds well to being peppered with unexpected questions about personal experiences. As the relationship evolves, ask curious questions that fit seamlessly within your collegial conversations. Second, be clear about why you are asking, give some context for your questions, and don't cross appropriate boundaries so that your questions make her consider a restraining order—nothing too personal. For instance, if you're asking about her experiences in the workplace, be sure to give the context about your commitment to improve as an ally for equity or your interest in sponsoring her for the right opportunities. Get to know her, show your heart is in the right place, and maybe begin with questions about her career aspirations. Stephanie Vander Zanden, director of diversity and inclusion at Schreiber Foods, reflected, "I've had men ask me about where I'd like to go in my career. It opens

Questions for Building Gender Awareness

- I'm curious about some of the things women in this organization find most challenging day to day, things that I—as a man—might not notice. Would you feel comfortable sharing some of the challenges you encounter most often?

- If there was one thing you wish men who work here were more aware of, something men could do, stop doing, or do more of that would improve the experience of women, what would that be?

- If there was one thing I could become more aware of, perhaps one thing I could start doing every day that might make the workplace better for you and other women, what would that be?

- I've been reading a book about becoming a better ally for women in the workplace. If you were giving a guy advice on how to really show up as a male colleague to make the workplace more fair and welcoming for women, what would you tell him?

a door—very comfortably—to mentoring/sponsoring conversations. I so appreciated having someone ask me directly."

Kendrick Brown, academic dean of the University of Redlands, also recommends that men establish some basic trust with women before asking directly about their experiences in the workplace, especially when a woman's intersectional identities (e.g., gender, race, sexual orientation) are in play. Brown suggests, "I might frame it this way: 'I want to be the most effective mentor, supervisor, colleague, that I can for you and I want you to know that I'm interested and open to having conversations about the identities you bring to the workplace, your experiences, and what you'd like me to understand about them.' This frames the conversation as an invitation. It's then in her court to decide whether to share her experiences with you."

Are you unsure if it's okay to ask a woman about her experience? Just ask her, especially if you are in a position of power.[12]

An extension of allies' skill in questioning is crucially important from the perspective of women. It involves asking your female colleagues what is happening when you observe indicators—verbal or nonverbal—about something bad. Perhaps the best example comes from our conversation with Gretchen Carlson. In one of her first jobs as a reporter, she was sexually harassed by a photographer assigned with her on a news story. When she returned to the station, she was emotionally rattled and shaken. She recalled, "The news director at the time saw that I was distressed and having trouble focusing on the story I was writing. He kept coming up to me and asking, 'What's wrong?'" At first, she was reluctant to say anything. Women are often afraid of being blamed for the incident in situations like this. She continued, "He was perceptive enough to notice something was wrong, kind enough to care about it, and I eventually told him what had happened. He made me feel comfortable with it and I immediately felt better." Shortly thereafter, the photographer who harassed her was relieved of his duties. This is a prime example of a man in a power position noticing that something had happened to a woman, and that it wasn't right. Most important, he cared enough to check in with her and then—in collaboration with her—address the source of the problem.

Sometimes, asking involves things that may appear mundane to men but are critical to making female colleagues feel like part of the team. Our favorite example came from Dr. Regan Lyon, air force major and special operations surgeon. We interviewed Lyon while she was on deployment in Afghanistan. As the only woman on a forward deployed base, she told us, she is often out on patrol in armored vehicles with all-male crews. Initially, when it was time for a bathroom break, the vehicles pulled over and the dudes hopped out and relieved themselves right on the vehicle's tires. She said, "As a woman, I actually have to 'drop trow' and worry about whether I'm exposing myself to the entire unit. I can't leave the road for fear of an IED."

So, the guys observed the problem and then asked her how they could make peeing equal and comfortable for her. "They figured out quickly how to make it easy for me. Now, when it's bathroom break time, our convoys pull two vehicles up to create a V so I can pee between the vehicles. They respect my privacy, and it's become no big deal. I so appreciate that they just normalize it." Not all workplaces have the unique challenges of military field conditions, but the more mundane scenarios are just as important.

When understanding more about the workplace experience of a female colleague and your role in getting started as an ally, simply ask: "What's one thing I could do to better support you?" Corollaries include: "What's one thing I could do to make your job easier?" "What's one thing we could do as an organization to remove obstacles to your advancement?"

Before asking a woman to relate her experiences, however, consider that as an ally you have to do your own work in preparing for these conversations. Routinely build your GQ by reading about gender in the workplace, attending gender inclusion events, and so on. Too often, people in the majority (white men) reach out to women or people of color to ask about their experiences without also self-educating. Simply asking may be efficient, but it also places the burden on women and other minorities to do the educating. Jennifer Brown of Jennifer Brown Consulting reminded us that "emotional labor is part of allyship, because an ally takes the time to do their homework in reading, listening, understanding, without burdening women or people of color to do more of the labor they've been doing for so long." The takeaway? As an ally, do your homework first; then ask to ask about others' experiences.

Be aware that developing a deeper understanding of the experiences of the women around you will inevitably and irrevocably transform your perspective. Asking, listening, and learning in this way will benefit everything you do as an ally, as a leader, and as a man—both at work and at home. A guy who took the time to really ask about the experiences of his female colleagues reflected: "Once you put on that lens, you can't take it off. The world never looks the same."[13] Gender empathy changes everything.

All Women Are *Not* the Same: Expose Bias at the Intersections

As with men, not all women's experiences are the same at work. In developing GQ, allies learn to appreciate *intersectional identities*. Allies seek to understand the experiences of women of color related to double jeopardy or invisibility. Some intersectional identities allow people to choose how they present themselves at work. Aware of "covering" behavior (choosing to hide an identity fearing a negative perception) and how it can create challenges with authenticity, allies create interactions and an environment where people are valued for bringing their whole selves to work.

While our focus is on gender allyship, people and their multiple identities are more complex. Our intent is not to oversimplify allyship, but rather to highlight one set of workplace inequities that is limiting the full capacity to thrive. As we progress through the conversation, we'll address the many ways that allyship applies more broadly, and we can expand ally behavior beyond gender. Let's start by considering how we can be allies for women of color.

First, meet people where they are and use your SA, learning orientation, humility, and listening skills to understand unique experiences—without making assumptions. Women of color often report that they have to work twice as hard to get half as far—*double jeopardy*.[14] The intersection of race and gender also causes many women of color to feel invisible because they are the dominant group for neither their gender nor their race.[15] Hence, they feel they have to work twice as hard to be noticed. In the workplace, this appears in the form of feeling devalued, demeaned, disrespected, excluded, and isolated.[16] The American Bar Association's Commission on Women in the Profession and the Minority Corporate Counsel Association's 2018 study of female lawyers of color reported some bleak findings: women of color work harder for recognition and respect, are held to higher standards, are paid less, receive fewer promotion opportunities, and are more often mistaken for administrative or janitorial staff.[17]

Second, before giving advice, consider how your approach may not work for a woman of color. Enlightenment comes in many forms, and when a female colleague provides the gift of feedback, be willing to listen and have the humility to recognize that she is right, and you are wrong. For example, Sean Vogel, program director at Lockheed Martin, shared a personal experience and aha moment when he realized how his approach didn't necessarily work for others. Vogel was telling a black woman who was preparing to give a software proposal that she needed to "approach the audience with a little bit of a swagger, have a little bit of an attitude," so that people would notice that she was in charge of software development. At some point during his mini lecture, the woman looked at Vogel and said, "I can't do that." He then realized she was exactly right. She couldn't act the way he could as a white man. Owing to racial and gender biases about black women, people might not respond well. As allies, we need that level of awareness.

Third, push back against racial bias that undermines women. In 2016, a photo of the graduating black women from the US Military Academy West Point—fists raised in a show of solidarity—circulated and quickly received national news attention and a visceral negative reaction from conservative news outlets that framed the photo as a Black Lives Matter protest. In fact, it was a long-standing tradition called the "Old Corps" photo. Graduating West Point cadets pose together to celebrate camaraderie and their upcoming graduation. Their solidarity was especially poignant considering there were only sixteen black women among the nearly one thousand graduating cadets that year. Ordinarily, such a photo would scarcely be noticed. Yet because the participants—black women—represented two distinct and highly visible minorities at a service academy, the backlash was enormous. In our interview with former Army Lieutenant General Robert Caslen, who was the superintendent of the US Military Academy at the time of the photo, he related, "I interviewed every one of these women and was convinced this was purely their solidarity with one another and their celebration at graduating from West Point. I retained all of them, they graduated, and there was a great outcry from many conservative sources. It was important to stand up to this heat and not let this group of women be tarnished by a biased interpretation of their intent."

Fourth, be ready to adapt—one-size allyship does not fit all. As an ally, you are in an alliance with women, but that doesn't mean that they all will react to your allyship in the same way. You have to respect everyone's receptiveness to your support.

Finally, show her that you value her unique identities and perspectives so she avoids covering and fully engages in her work relationships. We all have hidden identities that we choose to reveal—or not. In the case of stigmatized identities, people may choose to hide these identities as a coping strategy to avoid prejudice, discrimination, or bias that can have serious implications in the workplace for employment outcomes.[18] "Covering" is a coping strategy often employed by LGBTQ people, people with disabilities, and even military veterans, and it has a negative impact on employees, their work relationships, and the organization. While covering may increase feelings of belonging and acceptance, it also causes fear of discovery. Feelings of inauthenticity lead to less connection in relationships and ultimately greater disengagement from others at work.[19] People covering stigmatized identities often report sadness or loss, isolation, loneliness, and anxiety about being outed.[20]

As allies, we can help create a workplace climate where people can bring their whole selves to work and thrive in their authenticity. Show that you value their unique identities and perspectives so they can avoid covering and fully engage in their work relationships.

Own and Strategically Deploy Your Privilege

It's time for some tough love and straight talk to our male colleagues. *Privilege* has become a loaded word, invoking all kinds of defensiveness, anger, and blame among some men. However, we are going to address it head-on because it is important for allies to wrestle with and understand in creating gender equity and fairness.

Privilege is a systematically unearned advantage, in the form of resources and power, simply by belonging to a dominant group.[21] No matter your role in your organization, as a man, you have an "invisible knapsack" of privilege, conferred by society and the male-centric workplace.[22] It's part of your everyday lived experience to the point where you don't have to think about it. There are literally hundreds of examples of these everyday invisible man-perks. Here are a few: you're less likely to be interrupted when speaking; you're not automatically assumed to *not* know what you're talking about; common vocabulary refers to your gender as the default; people don't expect you to smile all the time; you can forgo grooming during travel without being judged; you are praised for performing ordinary parental duties.[23]

If you're a guy who identifies with the dominant groups in our society (white, heterosexual, middle or upper class, etc.), and you're still not sure whether you have privilege in some way, check in with one of your guy friends who doesn't identify with all of these demographic groups. Does he experience privilege and power relations differently at work? We often find that minority men are some of the most prominent and vocal allies for women.[24] Their own experiences contending with systemic workplace inequities provide insight into how the traditional workplace rules shape behavior and outcomes.

Regardless of how you experience privilege, you need to acknowledge it. You can develop your GQ through acknowledging your privilege and using it for good.

First, be open-minded and ready to accept and truly own your male privilege. Think about the last time you made a career decision. You were probably never asked, "How does that decision affect your wife or kids (whether you have them or not)?" or "Why are you focusing on your career instead of your family?" In many ways, that would seem like a weird conversation even in the twenty-first century. Not so much for women. These sorts of questions surrounding career choices are far too common and impact their decision making.

At work and in life, men rarely think about the benefits conferred by their gender. So, when guys hear that they are privileged, they'll often argue that they've had to work their butt off to reach their position. Did they work hard? Certainly, but it doesn't mean that there wasn't a tailwind pushing them along. Privilege is akin to a tailwind. Cruising along with our male tailwind, we scarcely notice the gendered headwinds buffeting our female colleagues.[25] We are not blaming or shaming here—it's just hard to see our own dude privilege.

Second, engaging in ally work is not about making yourself look better—don't signal your virtue.[26] This is not about you, no matter the accolades, attention, or positive feelings that come from being an ally. Do the work for the right reasons, not to make yourself look or feel better.

Third, as an ally, doing or saying nothing is not an option. Silence is *not* one of your options—allyship demands you deliberately deploy male privilege in a consistent way. Once you own your privilege, that invisible knapsack of opportunity and social capital, it should seem unconscionable not to open it and use its contents for the benefit of women and other less privileged groups around you.

Finally, use your privilege to change systemic problems. The act of using your privilege to dismantle the very system that confers your privilege can feel unnatural. Relinquishing power, sharing resources, calling out inequities, and giving up the spotlight are all part of the job. For example, when you turn down participation in a nondiverse conference panel ("manel"), recommend some diverse panelists.

Sahana Dharmapuri, director of Our Secure Future, shared with us how men who were identified as allies in the global development sector understood and used their privilege for good: "These men recognized their privileged role that allowed them to act differently to support women. The issue of gender equality is so transformative, because once the person starts to grapple with these questions, you can't go back, which is what many of these men said. Once they had this experience, they couldn't go back to looking at the world the way they did before. They couldn't ignore their privilege." We know you're ready to take on the challenge of understanding and learning about your own privilege so that you can embrace the work of becoming an ally.

Deliberately Seek Feedback from Women

We've noticed a pattern among dudes who often offend women (and male allies) with clueless sexist or harassing behavior at work: they have failed to consciously and consistently elicit feedback from women.

We're all human, and there's not a guy we know who hasn't occasionally committed a gender faux pas in the workplace. Maybe you've told (or laughed at) a joke that demeans women, maybe you struggle with "manterruptions" or "mansplaining" in meetings, or perhaps you've commented on a woman's appearance in a way that made her visibly uncomfortable. Join the club. In chapter 1, we warned you that allyship is a journey. If making mistakes in this space comes with being a male human being, learning from those mistakes and getting better makes you an evolving ally. The question is not if you will err; it's how to ensure that when you do, you get quick and reliable feedback from women you've developed trusting reciprocal relationships with.

Surround yourself with a tribe of female friends and confidants. Then, be sure to check in with them about how you are doing in both your interpersonal allyship for them and your public allyship for women more generally. For the best feedback, it's crucial to have a diverse network of friends. Ask for constructive feedback; when you are lucky enough to receive it, accept it without being defensive. The women you forge trusting friendships with will notice your sincere intention. J. T. Metzger, president, SmartStreet Consultants, said, "Women I count on will speak up when I am doing something dumb or showing my blind spots. Often, they do it in a playful or joking way, but it helps me to really understand something boneheaded I did. There are also women who recognize me publicly for good behavior. It feels great to have it called out when I'm getting it right too."

To earn A-team status as an ally seeking input from women, have at least one female colleague who agrees to be your gender confidant. This will be a woman, often a mentor or a peer, who consents to hold you accountable for the way you interact with women and your inclusive allyship broadly. Look for a woman with these qualities: she's no-nonsense in calling you out; she's given you feedback in the past; and she's perceptive and astute in noticing gender dynamics, bias, sexism, as well as good allyship. This relationship must be based on mutual trust and will be most effective when it includes good humor. Deliberately empower your confidant to call you out; then don't get defensive when she does.

Kendrick Brown explained the importance of signaling genuine receptiveness to feedback from women: "When a woman takes the time to tell us that we've messed up, we can't take it as an attack. It is an opportunity to learn, to look more closely, to question our own behavior. If someone takes the time to express that to you, you have to receive that as a gift. The person who doesn't get angry anymore about sexist behavior, that person is dismissing you and no longer invested."

If you assume people are taking the time to provide feedback because they care, want you to learn, and become aware of a blind spot, then it will be easier to embrace the feedback. While it can be painful to your ego to endure this feedback, think about the courage it took them to give it. US Navy Master Chief Petty Officer Nate Warren worked in a mixed-gender special operations unit and explained his approach to being receptive to criticism and other perspectives: "I stay open to the possibility that something isn't equitable. If women tell me they aren't getting the same opportunities, then I take a step back and see what I'm doing. Some men don't like to be challenged like that, but I'm always open to the possibility that something isn't fair—and then I act to make it right. If she's got the courage to bring that to my attention, there has to be something to it."

Genuine presence, openness to learning, and determination to remain in the moment when receiving feedback from women is an

Appropriate Responses to Feedback for Allies

- I apologize; I'm going to do better.

- I recognize that I have work to do.

- I'm going to take some time to reflect on this.

- I appreciate the labor you've put in.

- How can I make this right?

- Thank you.

- I believe you.

essential commitment of an ally. Shelley Correll, Stanford sociology professor and director of the Stanford VMware Women's Leadership Innovation Lab, advises that "if you really care and someone blows up at you, you can run off and say [you] tried, or you can listen, learn, and go back to the table. I don't think anybody who's an ally hasn't had the experience of doing something where they meant to do good and it didn't go well and it's painful—it's not the time to run away." If you feel threatened, your body will respond to the threat by pumping adrenaline, not listening, and accelerating a response to the threat. Your body is working against you and requires you to take a deep breath, slow down, and recenter your focus on what the other person is saying and doing. This isn't natural for most of us and is something you'll need to practice and develop. Have practiced responses ready to employ, like the ones in the sidebar "Appropriate Responses to Feedback for Allies." This not only ensures you respond in an open-minded and empathic way, but also buys you some time to slow down your mind and body.

Another recommendation has to do with how you respond to light-bulb moments. These epiphanies are when you suddenly get it about something women experience at work or the way gender disparities manifest in your workplace. When the light bulb goes on for you, share that awareness with women in your network and ask if it resonates with their experience. If they confirm it, use the new insight to sharpen your ally behavior and share it with other male allies.

For instance, several years ago when we were writing our book *Athena Rising*, our working manuscript title was "Guiding Athena," which seemed perfectly logical to us. After all, guiding is often a synonym for mentoring. Then, our publisher, a woman whose judgment we had grown to admire, called us out: "Gentlemen, have you really thought about how that whole 'guiding' thing might land with women? Did you think about the implicit message that women must be guided?" Today, we still cringe at that blind spot and feel genuine gratitude to her for shining a spotlight on it—something we're now sharing with you.

Notice Sexist Words and Phrases—and Intervene

Now that your SA is switched on and you're attending to gendered dynamics in the workplace, it's time to start genuinely paying attention to words. Listen carefully. Sift the ambient noise, the banter, the side conversations, and of course, the dialogue in both formal meetings and informal office interactions. What's an ally listening for? Be attuned to those everyday microaggressions directed at women. These include subtly sexist comments, biased language, and even overt, leering harassment. Strain to hear those daily slights, objectifying comments, and stereotypes that leave many women feeling inferior and unsafe. Some common types and examples are listed in table 2-1.

When you do hear a gender-biased or egregiously sexist comment made at your meeting, what do you do? Later in this guide, we're going to equip you with several action strategies for addressing it. But you have to *do* something. Make responding part of your brand as an ally. Annie Rogaski described a senior male attorney at her firm who

TABLE 2-1

Subtle and not so subtle sexist language

Common type	Examples
Noninclusive and patronizing language Language that prioritizes men or downplays women.	• *"guys"* • *"girls"* • *"man-hours"* • *"man-up"* • *"he/his"* (when referring to a profession, such as referring to physicians as "he" and nurses as "she") • *"it takes balls"*
Sexism and gender bias Prejudicial and discriminatory comments and behaviors that play on stereotypes and rigid gender roles	• *"You're taking notes, right?"* (Assuming the only woman in the meeting will take notes) • *"Could you grab me a cup of coffee before the meeting?"* (Never asks a male colleague to do this; she's not his assistant) • *"You should smile more!"* (Implies that a woman's appearance and emotions ought to be controlled and that she exists for others' pleasure) • *"What are you girls gossiping about?"* (Infantilizes women and implies they are caddy gossips, unlikely to be discussing a weighty or work-related topic) • *"What she's trying to say is . . ."* (Mansplaining for a woman) • *"Whoa, I think you might be a little oversensitive; you're coming across as shrill."* (Dismisses her concern, frustration, or passion on a topic with a reference to her poorly modulated emotions) • *"When are you going to have kids?"* (Clear boundary violation designed to undermine her professional status; implies all women are ticking time bombs of maternity and, therefore, a flight risk, a risky investment, and perhaps not as committed as her male counterparts)
Flat-out misogyny Comments that are nearly always designed to denigrate, demean, and sexually objectify women	• *"Whoa! Someone's grouchy! That time of the month, is it?"* • *"Is it just me or is she crazy/hysterical!?"* • *"If she used a little makeup, she'd be datable."* • *"Yeah, that's nice, but I'd like to hear what your (male) colleague/ boss has to say about that."*
Benevolent sexism Statements that may sound merely traditional or chivalrous on the surface, but ultimately serve to keep women in a box and imply that women should be protected	• *"She's nice but not really leadership material."* (Implies that the two are exclusive of one another and reinforces that she can't be a leader) • *She's really articulate/smart!"* (Implies that most women are not) • *"We'd invite you to join us at ___ (social event), but you wouldn't enjoy yourself anyway, and besides it's at night."* (Implies she can't decide this for herself) • *"It would be great to have you be the point person on the presentation in Europe, but we understand that you have kids, and we know you're already too busy."* (Think that they're "helping" but actually excluding her) • *"She is a caring, compassionate manager."* (Neglect agentic performance phrases such as "exceptionally competent" and "accomplished leader," stemming from the perception that men are "bad but bold" and women are "wonderful but weak.")

Source: P. Glick & S. T. Fiske, "Ambivalent Sexism," in *Advances in Experimental Social Psychology* vol. 33, (Cambridge, MA: Academic Press, 2001), 115–188.

would consistently correct anyone who referred to women as "girls." She said, "I remember being so surprised by it, that he would care enough to speak up. It didn't matter who had said 'girls.' It could be a man, a woman, someone junior, or someone senior to him and he would still call it out. It was like he was the 'girls' police. Every time he did that, he signaled that we are in a profession, that we need to treat people with respect, and that referring to women as 'girls' was not respectful." Well done, ally!

Think of your ally mission here as having two distinct elements. First, you need to debug conversations. Remember, if the water is saturated with bias and sexism, the workplace fish—men in partic-ular—may hardly notice when someone says something disrespect-ful. Think about what was wrong with a word or phrase and how—if unchecked—it could become one of those thousand cuts your female colleagues experience daily. Second, you've got to become a bias inter-rupter. Use humor; use a good old-fashioned Socratic question (e.g., "Excuse me, Tom, but did I just hear you say ___? Can you explain what you mean by that? Was that a joke? If so, I didn't get it. That's not who we are here at ___. I don't want to hear that again."). Call it out by saying something—anything!

Be especially attuned to a dude who prefaces something he says with, "I'm not sexist, *but* (some derogatory sexist comment follows)." This guy is probably sexist. He may have some dawning insight about bias and sexism, but he's still working through the denial stage. Have some empathy for this guy, but don't let him off the hook. Also, be alert for the classic sexist rescue maneuver. We see this at times from men *and* women. Call out a harassing comment or sexist joke, and sure enough, someone swoops in and says, "Oh, I'm sure he didn't mean to offend anyone." Well, he did. He offended you. Don't back off your standards for dignity and respect. Tell him why you were offended and ask him to be more respectful moving forward. And by the way, there's no space for "boys just being boys" or "locker room talk" in a community of male allies—don't allow sexism and harass-ment to go unchecked in dudes-only gatherings.

A final option if guys in the workplace resist your interventions or just don't seem to get the message about language is to hand them a copy of Jessica Bennett's awesome book, *Feminist Fight Club*.[27] In it, she addresses word usage advice directly to the average dude. A sample passage is: "Don't call us 'nags,' or 'crazy,' or 'bossy,' or 'aggressive.' We are nags and bossy for exhibiting the same behavior you do, except that when you do it, you're simply 'reminding' or being 'stern' . . . even when you're being 'redundant.' While you're at it, please refrain from infantilizing language too: We're not your 'kiddo' or your 'sweetie' and especially not 'sugar.' We may be cute, but our ideas are killer!"[28]

Sharpen and then deploy GQ skills that see through subtle (and not so subtle) forms of sexism to reinforce gender inequities. By noticing these behaviors and saying something, allies have the power to effect change—one dude at a time.

Ally Actions

- **Sharpen your situational awareness.** Be vigilant in observing how your female colleagues are experiencing meetings and other gatherings and be alert to inequities and disparities in these contexts.

- **Cure your gynophobia.** Publicly push back on false narratives about the risks of engaging with women at work, while deliberately and transparently initiating conversations, friendships, and mentorships with female colleagues.

- **Ask about women's experiences.** With humility and genuine curiosity, strengthen your GQ by learning about the uniquely gendered workplace experiences of some of the women you work with.

- **Recognize that all women are not the same.** Be attuned to the unique experiences and intersectional identities (e.g., race, ethnicity, gender identity, sexual orientation, generation, religion) of the women you work with.

- **Own and strategically deploy your privilege.** Recognize and fully own your privilege as a man—your opportunities, advantages, resources, and power—while leveraging it for the benefit of women and other marginalized groups.

- **Deliberately seek feedback from women.** Establish trust with a network of women who will give you unvarnished feedback about how they perceive your workplace attitudes and behaviors and receive this feedback as a gift.

- **Notice sexist words and phrases—and intervene.** Watch and listen for noninclusive language, sexist comments, overt misogyny, and harassing behavior; then, say something to disrupt it.

3

To Be Legit as an Ally, Start at Home

Ally Rule #1: You don't get to pass "go" on the ally journey until you intentionally and consistently step up as an ally at home (if you have no partner or children, you're not off the hook here; the way you role-model self-care, work-life integration, and meeting obligations to family and friends remains vitally important). Nothing delegitimizes your ally brand so quickly as slinging on the ally cape to impress women at work while not fully supporting your partner at home. To that hollow form of allyship, we call foul. The same is true for failing to model real domestic allyship for children, keeping your own family obligations secret in the workplace, and missing opportunities to role-model full domestic partnership for other men.

Here is the real problem: despite the prevalence of traditional family gender role norms, the families that these norms apply to—families with children, a father as the sole breadwinner, and a stay-at-home mother—are now a minority in the United States. Less than 30 percent of families with children have a father as the sole breadwinner and a stay-at-home mother.[1] Today, children are more likely to grow up in a family with two employed parents or a single working parent.

Yet, mothers continue to do the majority of unpaid domestic work, even in families where they are the sole breadwinner or make more than their husbands.[2] And when there is a sick child, ailing relative, or household emergency, women are still expected to take time off from work to handle these domestic and caregiving responsibilities. Tied to this traditional gender norm is the assumption that women's earnings are not vital to the healthy functioning of the family household or to our national economy. Mothers comprise 41 percent of the sole or primary breadwinners in society.[3] Interestingly, for dual-earner married couples with children where the mother is the primary breadwinner, their combined family income is, on average, higher than all other earner combinations.[4] In addition to their breadwinner status, women make up more than 50 percent of US workers and account for a majority of consumer spending.[5] The devaluing of women's paid work (gender pay gap and motherhood penalty) and unpaid work (unequal division of household labor) perpetuates gender inequities and torpedoes corporate outcomes. If you are a male ally with a partner, you've got to demonstrate real allyship at home first, no matter what "home" looks like.

To balance economic need and professional desire for employment, while avoiding the motherhood penalty, women with partners often report employing the strategy of *intentional invisibility*, meaning that to feel authentic as a spouse or parent, to manage competing expectations in the office, and to balance work and family responsibilities, she is more likely than a man to employ risk-averse, conflict-avoidant strategies.[6] This means women are more likely to stay behind the scenes, work under the radar, and perhaps miss out on career advancement, all to avoid unwanted attention to the fact that they are mothers, caregivers, or spouses. This doesn't happen so often for guys, largely because we haven't always been pulling our fair share at home and nobody at work has expected us to. For the women we care about to thrive, this obviously has to change.

There are glimmers of good news on the horizon. More men are stepping up at home. New survey findings show that one in three fathers have turned down opportunities for leadership in the work-place because of family responsibilities.[7] Research shows that the "ideal man" today is not only a good employee working to be suc-cessful as a breadwinner, but also a nurturing husband or partner, father, and son.[8] Finding new models of work-life integration that re-duce inhumane work hours and role overload improves marriages and parent-child relationship quality.[9] New evidence from Ernst & Young reveals that the percentage of fathers who chose three or more weeks of parental leave rose from 45 percent in 2016 to 60 percent in 2018.[10] As more dads lean in to parental leave, publicly signaling their parenting commitments and leveling the domestic playing field for women, Ernst & Young has seen a sharp decline in turnover among women. There is evidence that when these fathers return to work, they are more supportive of women's employment; these men are more inclined to challenge traditional gendered divisions of labor and roles in the organization.[11]

Before we go any further, let us acknowledge the focus on hetero-sexual families and relationships. Much of the research focuses on these families, and in this chapter, we sometimes default to heterosex-ual language for simplicity. Nonetheless, we attempt to use inclusive language (e.g., partner) when possible, and the ally strategies covered herein are equally applicable for LGBTQ families and relationships.

In this short chapter, you'll find four ally strategies designed to help you achieve congruence between your ally brand at home and at work. If, in reading any of these strategies, you discover a certain gnawing sense of unease—perhaps a symptom of *ally dissonance*, an awareness of incongruence between what you believe is right and what you actually *do* as an ally on the home front—we've got your cure. Ask your partner for a domestic-partner performance review, step up and do the dishes (without being asked), champion your partner's career, deliberately model domestic allyship for children, become transpar-ent about your family/life obligations at work, and be attuned to how domestic allyship extends to parents, siblings, relatives, and even com-munity initiatives.

Pull Your Weight at Home

There is a disconnect between the way men and women perceive fairness in domestic work. Long the exclusive responsibility of women, we guys are still quite comfortable deferring housework and childcare to women, often telling ourselves things like: "I can't do it the way she likes." "She prefers it that way." Yet, recent evidence tells a different story. Nearly half of mothers report that the proportion of household chores their partner does is unfair to them.[12] This is especially true for new mothers who expect that their male partner will take on half of the new-parent duties and responsibilities, only to find that these dads adhere to more traditional family roles.[13] This leaves new moms to take up the slack in household labor and childcare while having to decrease their paid work. Needless to say, this leaves these mothers feeling more stress, understandably resentful, and snubbed when it comes to their professional identities.

When you ask women's male partners about how fairly household labor is divided, less than a quarter think the balance is unfair. A significant proportion of women report that men don't fully appreciate the physical and mental labor that goes on in the background to keep a household running smoothly. The majority of women living with male partners wish for more help with household chores, childcare, and even emotional support.[14] Many express frustration at having to anticipate the needs of others, assuming the role of project manager—explicitly delegating tasks to their male partners, and then having to track completion of those tasks.[15] This invisible, yet taxing cognitive labor takes a toll over time. Scott Behson, author of *The Working Dad's Survival Guide*, explained that when he was at a department store and saw several items of clothing on sale that his son probably needed for the winter, "He didn't know what his son was growing out of, what he needed, and what size pants, shoes and jackets he was now wearing."[16] He had to call his wife and have her bail him out. Men have to take on half the emotional load and track these things, too.

Daily Actions for Domestic Allies

- Do your fair share of food shopping and keep track of what foods are running low so the grocery list isn't just for your partner to create.

- Do more scheduling of the day-to-day family and kids' events (doctors' appointments, sports activities, school functions, and family outings).

- Do the dishes, dust, vacuum, clean the toilets, and get a load of laundry started. If they're old enough, enlist the kids to help out. It'll be good for them.

- Get school-age kids going on homework, spend quality time with them while they work, and check it over with them. Respond to any notes from teachers and both schedule and attend parent-teacher conferences.

- Pay attention to your partner's work schedule, including travel, deadlines, or big events. Pitch in more when their work tempo is especially demanding, to reduce their stress level.

- Check in with your partner often. Ask how their day was. Notice changes in their mood, and set time aside daily for a conversation in which you focus on listening, understanding, and inquiring about how you can help.

So, what's an ally to do? Author Jessica Bennett puts it succinctly: "[D]o the dishes!"[17] Bennett reminds us that men who help out more with household chores and childcare have overall higher marital relationship satisfaction.[18] Face it, if she's doing the majority of the domestic work—perhaps despite being a primary or co-breadwinner—she'll probably be feeling burned out and resentful. Of course, this domestic work sharing can't stop with dishes. The sidebar "Daily Actions for Domestic Allies" offers several suggestions for stepping up immediately as a male ally at home.

Note to all heterosexual mankind: on the whole, in the year 2020, your wives and partners continue to bear the gendered burden of maintaining family stability by being constantly available to deal with caretaking and family contingencies—whether they are employed full-time or not.[19] Gentlemen, you may *think* you're sharing fifty-fifty with your partner at home, but how do you know? When was the last time you asked her for a *partner performance review* in the areas of housework, childcare, and emotional support? The evidence shows we guys think we're allies at home when, in fact, the women we're supposed to be partnering with aren't feeling any ally love. Take a deep breath, ask her to sit down with you (after you've cleaned the kitchen and put the kids to bed), and ask how she sees the household chore ratio, your contribution to it, and what you could do to be a more wholehearted ally, doing your part at home so she feels supported both in and outside the home.

Asking for a partner performance review is only the first step. The second step is to just listen and take notes when she tells you the truth. Thank her, and if you have work to do, ask her if there are specific things you can do right away to step up. If you can be nondefensive when your partner gives you feedback, you'll be better at receiving feedback from women at work. Now that you've received some initial feedback, check in with your partner periodically for an update. Routine communication and considerable flexibility are key ingredients to terrific allyship at home.

Rachana Bhide of Bloomberg Radio News often captures invaluable illustrations of ally excellence.[20] Bhide provides this example of a man stepping up as an ally at home. Megan Anderson, founder of #GoSponsorHer, said, "Sharing the pie fifty-fifty is tricky given that the proportions are always shifting and someone always ends up needing to do more of the grunt work at any given time. Mike and I are explicit about those shifts and explicit about who is taking the lead on the home front at any given time. If we are going to make real change, we have to allow men to change too—they needn't carry the traditional pressures being the sole partner with a career."

Take Time Away from Work and Leave Loudly

Men can do a profound service for their partners, their children, themselves, and their organizations by deliberately maximizing their parental leave time. In societies where men take longer parental leave time, more women stay in the workforce, the wage gap is smaller, and more women occupy senior leadership positions on boards.[21] Several things happen when men lean in to maximize leave time: children thrive through maximum attention and stimulation from both parents; we better support our partners; we embolden women in our workplaces by leveling the leave-taking field; we strengthen our ties to the organization, leading to higher wages; and we model for junior men that this is what real men and good dads do. This is why broadcast journalist and author Josh Levs and Dove Men+Care grooming products recently announced a Pledge for Paternity Leave, calling all dudes to stand up against the stigma of men as caregivers and exert their right to full parental leave.[22]

But staying home to help out when our kids are born is only the start. Make time and give full attention to the small moments with your partner and children. The myriad day-to-day interactions really matter. Trips to the doctor, walks around the neighborhood, morning drives to school—these moments often yield the most important memories.

James Sudakow, author and work-life consultant, recommends the following three quick ways that you can prioritize work-related tasks in order to make the most of being an ally at home:[23]

- *Know what's truly urgent.* Work can be urgent, and often for good reason. But most of it can wait, with no dire business consequences. This "artificial urgency" is a significant barrier to achieving balance. Ask yourself what makes something urgent? If there isn't a clear deadline or reason for a high priority, it really isn't urgent.

- *Set boundaries.* Be intentional. Be clear with your colleagues and ensure that there are consistent times when work and family do not intersect. This is "ruthless compartmentalization." It might mean blocking out half-day segments during the week that are for family and you do not take work calls or check email.

- *Set goals.* At work, setting clear objectives means leading and managing your team in a consistent way, meeting your stated business goals and commitments, and hitting your key performance indicators. Most families don't have performance metrics. But you can create them for yourself to ensure that you're a better dad to your kids and a better co-parent to your spouse. It could be as simple as clarifying how many family dinners you are going to have each week, or how many school drop-offs you are going to do.

You also need to make these domestic commitments transparent to colleagues at work. When you need to come in late, leave early, or take time off to care for a child, support your partner, or attend a school event, do this boldly—versus sheepishly or reluctantly. We call this ally behavior "leaving loudly." Our good friend Karen Catlin, author, coach, and former executive at Adobe Systems, reminds aspiring male allies not to go slinking out the side exit, tiptoeing like a cat burglar when one of the everyday exigencies of life crop up, requiring you to leave work early.[24] Maybe it's meeting the plumber, taking a kid to the doctor, chaperoning a field trip, or taking your turn as "story reading parent" for your child's third-grade class. Whatever the life obligation that causes you to leave work, prioritizing a family obligation, talk about it! Show your team, female colleagues, and every junior guy watching you that you have a life and a family, you care about your health, and that you're not timid about giving these priorities top billing. Leave loudly with head held high. Let your colleagues know *why* you're taking the time off or working from home. Leave an email out-of-office reply celebrating your absence when on paternity leave. Such transparency, normalizing, and honoring of family obligations are powerful acts of allyship for women.

Discuss the struggles you face in these domains as well. Levs cautions that keeping your personal and family obligations secret is bad for you, your coworkers, and ultimately the workplace.[25] In our interview with Levs, he said, "Guys are so wary of talking about this [work-life conflict, the desire for full parental leave, the struggle to be present at home] . . . which hurts men because no one knows what they are dealing with. Men have got to get more involved in working groups related to work-life balance." According to Levs, "It's very helpful when men just strike up a conversation with women [or other men] in the workplace and say something like, 'Hey, I'm having trouble figuring out how to get my kid to school before work. How do you do it?'" When a guy is this transparent about his tensions and struggles to do partnering, fathering, and other personal roles well, he telegraphs to the workplace that work-family tensions are *normal*. Nothing can be so empowering for women wrestling with these tensions, especially in male-centric workplaces where it already feels that their parent identities stand out and make them atypical.

In our interview with Shelley Zalis, president and CEO of the Female Quotient, she described her former boss, Gerry Lukeman, as a role model of this ally action: "His office walls were covered in family pictures. He always told me that the most important priority in business was 'family first.' That was rare to hear a man talk that way about family. Gerry made his family foremost at all times. He always talked about his kids and his kids came to the office. He taught me that I should never put my family in the back seat."

Support Your Partner's Career
without Reservation

Want to support the careers of the amazing women around you in the workplace? It's sadly incongruent for a guy to champion gender equity for his female colleagues if he's not doing the same thing—whole-heartedly—for his wife or partner. Be a legitimate ally by showing advocacy, sponsorship, and full collaboration with your life partner. Recent research on the experiences of heterosexual married women finds that while they are expected to pursue a career and paycheck, many feel they can only pursue their career ambitions to a certain point, in order to ensure stability in their relationships.[26] Despite the reality that many women are breadwinners, that their paycheck is crucial to the family's budget, and that their careers are deeply en-twined with their professional identity and personal well-being, a lot of women don't have male partners and husbands who are all-in fans of their partner's career aspirations, especially if they've got to make some real sacrifices in the rhythm of their own careers.

With dual-career couples now the norm in many professions, cou-ples are finding new ways to navigate having two careers, children, and a lifestyle that works for everyone. Couples are learning to work within the traditional workplace norms while creating pressure for cultural change. Instead of following traditional gender norms for work and family, dual-career couples find it more useful to take a long-term perspective when considering how to integrate two careers and children. Making career decisions based on purely current economic factors such as who has a higher salary, the cost of childcare or bene-fits packages can lead to short-term solutions that can have long-term costs in retirement savings. Adopting a long-term vision for the family is one way to create a strategy that works for both partners. These strategies include a lead-follow relationship in which partners' career needs are balanced with family priorities and life stage.[27] Instead of having one career always in the lead, dual-career couples find it useful to alternate to keep both careers viable over the long haul.[28] Of course, this takes lots of communication, planning, and coordination, which, by the way, often leads to a higher-quality relationship too.

Contrast reluctant or resistant male support for life partners' careers—expressions like, "What? You can't be home in time to make dinner? Great, I guess I'll order pizza." "You need to stay late Thursday? But I was going to grab drinks with a client and can't pick up the kids." "Congrats on the promotion, but with all the extra travel involved, you're not seriously considering it, are you?"—with an example on the opposite end of the ally spectrum. Julie Kratz of Next Pivot Point has described the way her husband, Rustin, went all in as a partner at home so she could launch her consulting career:[29] "Our coaching business and family life would not be possible without Rustin. He maintains the home, takes excellent care of our girls, helps with the business, and is always there when I need that nudge or to vent about travel snafus. He's our family rock." Of course, partnering as a domestic ally need not mean suspending your own career in most cases; it just means leaning in enthusiastically, encouraging your partner to soar at work, and asking how you can help her feel less tension about integrating her work and nonwork identities. Chances are, you're going to need her to help you do the same.

Deliberately Role-Model Allyship for Your Daughters and Sons

To give your sons a huge head start as gender equality allies for women in the workplace and launch your daughters into adult life with a fierce sense of confidence and a willingness to demand that men in their lives—both personal and professional—treat them with full equity, dignity, and respect, show them how full gender partnership looks in the way you treat their mother.

Although highly engaged fathers help both sons and daughters thrive cognitively, emotionally, socially, and, ultimately, economically,

Jessica Bennett reports that strong paternal engagement and encouragement are particularly instrumental in bolstering the self-esteem, autonomy, and aspirations of girls.[30] One study Bennett highlights showed that a girl simply seeing her dad do his share of chores around the house lowered the probability that she would later limit her career aspirations. Several of the women we interviewed spoke about the power of their father's encouragement to pursue any dream without limit. Christine Spadafor, corporate board member, speaker, and consultant, offered this recollection from age five: "My father was a WWII veteran, an engineer, and a man of quiet strength. I was his only daughter. When I was five years old, I recall having a conversation with him about what I might like to be when I grew up. He looked me straight in the eyes and said, 'Little girl, you can do whatever you want and you can be whatever you want.' How empowering was that for a young girl, especially in the 1960s? I believed him. He gave me permission to fly."

But affirmation is only half the battle. To launch your daughters into adulthood expecting equal treatment in their personal and work relationships, you've got to show your domestic savviness as a partner and raving fan of her mom. (See the sidebar "Actions That Demonstrate Partnership for Children.") Spadafor said, "I saw my father serve as a champion of my mother as well. She was an artist and he was all in and her biggest fan. He was so supportive toward her and always treated my mom as an equal partner. His actions demonstrated for me a framework for men as allies and advocates for women."

Never forget that your sons are always watching you. As a father, you have an awesome opportunity to shape the way your sons perceive and value women. Great allies explicitly teach their sons not only to respect women but also to assume and expect that when men and women collaborate and leverage one another's strengths, things work better, at home and at work.

In our interview with Gretchen Carlson, she emphasized the importance of teaching boys how to be allies: "How we educate our boys matters: We have to get to our boys when they're young. We've spent an inordinate amount of time empowering girls recently, but by the

Actions That Demonstrate Partnership for Children

- Make sure children see you doing your fair share of household tasks and childcare, including picking up the slack during those times your partner is spending more time on their career.

- Be open in communicating family and career goals.

- Show your children how to disagree, listen, and share perspectives. Life is naturally messy.

- Let your kids see how and why decisions are made. Demonstrate compromise and balance.

- Loudly celebrate your partner's career accomplishments with the kids.

time they hit early career, a combination of inequity in opportunity for advancement, harassment, and the demands of having children all conspire to push them back and get them off track. Rather than spending more time empowering girls, how about if we get to boys early and teach them to really respect women?"

When you honor and respect your life partner, when you share fully in childcare and housework, and when you are a vocal advocate for your daughters' career aspirations, your sons are getting priceless mentorship in the art of allyship.

Ally Actions

- **Pull your weight at home.** Consistently do at least half of the domestic work at home and share more of the load as needed based on your partner's work schedule and stress level.

- **Take time away from work and leave loudly.** Set boundaries around work by boldly communicating your domestic commitments and publicly stepping away from work to fulfill them.

- **Support your partner's career without reservation.** Collaborate with your partner to create a flexible strategy that maximizes both careers.

- **Deliberately role-model allyship for your daughters and sons.** Practice all-in domestic allyship with your partner to launch your daughters into the world without career inhibitions and teach your sons how to show up in the workplace and in their personal relationships as natural allies for women.

4

Everyday Interactions with Women at Work

Male allies not only understand the business case and the moral imperative for full gender inclusion in the workplace, but practice allyship as an expression of their commitment to dignity and respect. With grace, humility, and some self-effacing humor, they are thoughtful and self-reflective about the way they show up every day for the women they work with and care about.

In this chapter, you'll find ten ally strategies illuminating the way men can regularly show support and partnership for women in the workplace. Some of the essential strategies in this chapter touch on deliberate inclusion, decentering, listening well, and avoiding undue assumptions about women. We'll also cover the encouragement of women to showcase their talents while leveling the playing field so they get the same opportunities as men. We'll also suggest that you engage publicly in women's initiatives and inclusion events. If you deliberately practice these ally actions, if you are patient and open to feedback, we predict it won't be long until some of the women around you start to see you as a genuine and reliable ally for equity.

Include Women

One in five women report being the only woman in the room at work.[1] The probability of flying solo increases radically for senior-level women, those in technical roles, and women in traditionally male-dominated professions, such as finance, law, STEM, and the military. The problem? Women who are surrounded by men in the office are 50 percent more likely to consider leaving; they also experience higher rates of sexual harassment.[2] And she doesn't have to be an "only" to feel subtly or overtly marginalized and excluded in an organization or profession that is traditionally male. According to Joanne Lipman, former editor-in-chief of *USA Today*, women in male-centric environments can experience *belonging uncertainty*. Many women receive subtle—or sometimes, overt—signals that they are not part of the in-crowd. She said, "You are not invited to lunch or drinks with the guys and you don't feel comfortable inviting yourself. When you walk into a meeting, the guys are already in there doing their pre-meeting, talking to each other, laughing, etc., and then they go silent when you walk in." A woman gets the sense women's not really part of the crowd and that no one has her back. Because women's self-concepts are often highly defined by interpersonal relationships, such experiences of exclusion can cause loneliness and attrition from the workplace.[3]

Many of the women we interviewed described how men can serve a crucial role in combating belonging uncertainty in women: *Forbes* columnist and author Kim Elsesser explained that ally behavior can be as simple as being included: "When I worked on Wall Street, there were very few women, zero in some cases. One of the most helpful things that men did for me was just treat me like one of the boys. Just being included was huge." Male allies engage in public friendships with women; make sure female colleagues are included in both crucial work-related meetings and conversations and social gatherings, celebrations, and other opportunities for office bonding.

Men of color, gay men, and other guys who have been marginalized in life and career may be more acutely attuned to the experiences of loneliness and isolation among women in male bastions. Kentucky senatorial candidate in 2020 and former Marine Corps Lieutenant Colonel Amy McGrath said, "The best allies and mentors while I was in the Marine Corps were racial minorities, usually African American men. They understood what it meant to be isolated, so they made themselves more readily available to connect." True enough, but let's remember that white straight men need to get deliberate inclusion right, too.

Understanding that including women is a salient component of allyship, you may be asking, what's an ally to *do*? There are two things to keep in mind. First, *make time for women*, just as you do for the men in your organization. If you are like most people, time is one of your most valuable commodities. When you demonstrate a genuine habit of sharing your time with female colleagues, you'll be communicating care and commitment to their well-being and inclusion in the workplace. Invite conversation, check in often, and have an open-door policy; when she reaches out with a question or issue, get back to her quickly. Women we spoke with appreciated men's true interest and availability. For instance, Laphonza Butler, president of SEIU Local 2015, described her ally: "What I most appreciated about Mike was that he created an environment of trust and he always made time for me. He always encouraged me to stop by and see him despite how busy he was in his demanding position." In a similar vein, Marine Corps Colonel Maria Pallotta said of one of her bosses, "He truly had an open-door policy and never told me he was too busy to talk with me. He was always receptive and willing to let me bounce ideas off him."

Second, *always remember to invite her to meetings, outings, and events*. Do us a favor. Before reading further, watch the short Pixar film *Purl* on YouTube. It will be nine minutes well spent if you want to develop empathy for the experiences of many women in male-dominated workplaces. It is hard to watch Purl struggle to find purchase as the first woman at B.R.O. Capital Inc. A tipping point in her sense of belonging occurs when the "bros" finally invite her to join them in after-work social outings.

This is really not a heavy lift. Be aware of who is in the room and who is not. Look closely at the invite lists for key meetings, off-sites, strategic planning sessions, dinners with key partners, and even unplanned hallway conversations in which crucial information is unveiled or discussed.[4] Are key female colleagues missing? Ask why. Perhaps even more important, male allies take the lead in inviting women to join the team—even if the team is mostly dudes—for lunch or beers after work, all those extra-work social occasions where both bonding and, occasionally, important business gets accomplished. Many women we spoke with reported how meaningful simply being invited to join the bros was. Julie Kratz of Next Pivot Point described an important male ally early in her career: "He made sure I was included in outings that women often get left out of like the company softball team. He made sure I got included in that bro time because that's when relationships are formed and when decisions get made." Kim Elsesser said, "Being included in men's interactions and activities was huge for me. I really appreciated the men who didn't think it was awkward or anxiety-provoking to have coffee or lunch or drinks with me to talk about work." Former Navy Rear Admiral Peg Klein said, "Women want to be part of the team. Allies show in their behavior, once you're on the team, you're on the team. Everyone is included."

We can include women in lots of ways every day, from the big events (e.g., golf outings, box seats at baseball games) to the more mundane (e.g., inclusion in email groups, making room at the table so she's not standing on the sidelines).[5] Invite but don't pressure her to join in (although you might mention to her that social events with the crew are often great networking opportunities). Also, be sure to let her do social events her way. She shouldn't have to change or pretzel herself just to fit in with the guys. Maybe she'd be delighted to join the dudes for craft beer and wings. Maybe she's not a beer fan. She may not drink alcohol or want to drink alcohol with men she works with. She can choose her own libation. Invite, welcome, and honor her approach to fun—let her pick the venue for the next outing. If your office bonding excludes women, something is probably wrong with your office culture.[6] Strip bars and drinking contests? Allies don't participate in these outings themselves, let alone invite valued colleagues.

When you have lunch with a woman or invite her to join you and the other guys in the office on the coffee break or for drinks after work, you're serving as a powerful role model for other men who are watching.[7] Lead by example, and you'll empower other men in the process. Annie Rogaski of Avegant said that one of her allies used inclusion to give women legitimacy in an environment that wasn't so sure about women: "I think he made it normal. We didn't have large numbers, but it felt like we deserved to be there, and the question of our legitimacy was answered by the way he behaved."

Decenter

Men take up more space than women. Not just physically but psychologically as well. For instance, in meetings, we assume we'll sit at the table, that we'll speak first, and when we do, people will listen. Others assume we hold key leadership roles on our teams, and we are implicitly granted credit for our team's achievements. Thanks to male privilege (as we learned in the first two chapters), it is good to be a man in the workplace. But self-awareness of gendered privilege offers us a key allyship opportunity to deliberately step aside and let the light shine directly on others. We are talking about the art of *decentering*. According to Greatheart Consulting CEO Chuck Shelton, decentering requires an understanding that the "center" is largely occupied by men.[8] The normativity of men in leadership roles means we are too often the focus and center of attention in the workplace.

Decentering is the intentional act of stepping out of the central role or the primary focus of attention so that other people and their perspectives can be fully seen and heard. Decentering is a daily choice and key skill for male allies. Evan Smith, CEO of the *Texas Tribune*, encourages men to "learn to deflect the focus of attention . . . decenter yourself and let the women who are doing the great work shine." Sahana Dharmapuri of Our Secure Future observed, "Men as allies are not as effective at creating gender equality by being leaders and being in front. Men need to learn a different role, stepping back into the supporting role for women leaders. Do all those things that need to be done in a supporting role to push those women leaders ahead and make space for them."

An essential point is *not* that women can only step up when men step down.[9] This is not an opportunity to rescue your female colleagues. Decentering is simply an approach to amplifying the excellent work of talented female leaders around you. We guys tend to express prosocial (helpful) behavior through action-oriented behaviors. But decentering requires humility. Loud, public, self-congratulatory decentering is supremely annoying, likely to backfire, and ultimately, not genuine decentering (e.g., "As a champion for women, I'd like to note that Sarah really helped me with this. Sarah, anything you'd like to add?").

The following best practices offer ways to gracefully step back and make space for women in the workplace every day.

Check your spread. Yes, we guys are bigger in stature, but we've also been socialized to take up more physical space around us. At your next meeting, look around the room. Chances are men are sitting with legs spread, leaning back with legs crossed, or leaning into the table with elbows wide. Women are more likely to be contorting themselves into the smallest space possible. Make more room at the table for others. It's hard to decenter when you're taking up maximum space. And making physical space for women applies to situations outside of meetings. Christine Spadafor, corporate board member, shared the experience of one of her own MBA students. A corporate recruiter was on campus. Male students had formed a circle around him, engaging in a conversation. Try as she might, she could not find a way to physically enter the circle and join the discussion. The men were not purposefully excluding her; they just did not notice her. They had formed a wall, and no one noticed she was on the outside trying to get in. Spadafor said, "I encourage allies to be alert to their surroundings, notice women on the outside, and then open the circle to physically include her."

Step out of the spotlight. Stereotyped male communication involves dominating conversations. Be aware of this dynamic in meetings, pitches to clients, formal presentations, and everyday conversations in the workplace. Remember that women around you have equally strong ideas and key contributions but may be socialized to be less dominant in their approach to expressing them.[10] Look for opportunities to step aside, hand her the mic, point out that she is the subject-matter expert on this topic, and recommend that she lead the discussion or presentation.

Amplify her contributions. Be sure to credit ideas to those who come up with them. Women are too often overlooked for their creative contributions because they are more likely to credit their team (a sign of excellent leadership), while men either overtly take credit or allow the gender-biased narrative that, of course, "he" must be behind the idea to go unchallenged. If you are getting the kudos and she deserves it, redirect the credit. (Later in this book, we'll show you how to disrupt meeting dynamics that deprive women of credit for their ideas.)

Use your capital to direct attention to female candidates. When an outside entity asks you to be a guest speaker or panelist, consider encouraging an equally or more qualified woman to accept the invitation. If you turn down a job, think about which women you could recommend for it.[11] When your boss asks you to lead a discussion at a meeting, point out that a woman on your team actually has more expertise on the topic and that she is the most logical person to take the lead in the meeting.

Encourage female colleagues to lead in their own way (not yours). De-centering requires us to remember that a male-centric, agentic, hierarchical leadership style is often less effective than an approach defined by collaboration and democratic decision making. Janet Petro, deputy director of the Kennedy Space Center, reminds men, "Don't assume your leadership style is the most effective. Recognize that her leadership style may be quite different and quite effective." Step back, watch, listen, and learn from her approach to leading others; then amplify her leadership strengths up the chain of command.

Help her create a rich mentoring constellation. Men also need to de-center in their mentorships with women. Mentoring is not about the mentor. Too often, men adopt a guru approach to mentoring women, pretending to be all-knowing, even becoming possessive of female mentees.[12] Decentering here requires us to remember she will be best served when we are active networkers, introducing her to a variety of mentors who might become important contributors to her develop-ment and career success. Remember, you are just one member of her mentoring constellation.

Decentering is a crucial ally strategy. Using your male privilege to make space, step aside, and create opportunity for women's ideas and voices must be a persistent workplace commitment.

Listen Generously

Any idea what women tell men is the number-one attribute of a good male ally? You got it. *Listening*. Julie Kratz told us that "listening is the most important skill of an ally. You don't have to put on your cape, you don't have to rescue anyone, and you don't have to save the day. Just listen." Stephanie Vander Zanden of Schreiber Foods said, "Be a sounding board and a deliberate listener. Let her bounce ideas off you and just listen. Don't fix or solve it for her, just let her process." Sarah Hiza, senior vice president at Lockheed Martin, commented, "Listen with the intent to understand, not respond. Repeat back what she said to show that you've really heard her."

We men have a lousy reputation with women in the listening department. And for good reason. Men are often socialized to fix problems, and fast. But in so doing, we can short-circuit understanding, so our decisions do not sufficiently include others. We are more comfortable telling others than asking and then truly hearing them (aka, *mansplaining*). Too often, when a woman seeks our counsel, we jump on the white horse and gallop into "I got this, I'll fix it" rescue mode when what she is really saying is, "No, I actually need you to sit back and listen to me."[13]

Here is the most important rule we can observe when it comes to improving our brand as outstanding listeners: "You can't listen and talk at the same time." Consider J. T. Metzger of SmartStreet Consultants and his 90 percent rule: "I try to just listen for the first 90 percent of a meeting with a woman. Only then will I provide my thoughts, and I will ask her if she is seeking feedback before doing so."

Once we've closed our mouths, we can begin to practice authentic, spacious, and generous listening. According to Chuck Shelton, listening to women's voices in a way that inspires trust and respect is a fundamental relationship promise male allies can make to women in the workplace: "Generous, world-class listening requires focus, sincerity, empathy, refusal to interrupt, and genuine valuing of both her experience and her willingness to share it with you."[14] Generous listening is well served by high levels of empathy and compassion for women (and any other groups who are not like us).[15] It is also facilitated by the capacity to openly listen to the pain she may have experienced in the workplace. The best listeners for women are *confidants*, creating a trusting relationship for them to express fears, frustrations, and needs without fear of unauthorized disclosure.[16]

The sidebar "The Elements of Generous Listening" offers a list of indicators that you are genuinely listening to a woman in the workplace, adapted from Shelton's list.[17] Each is a hallmark of world-class listening.

The Elements of Generous Listening

As a male ally, I am listening to a woman when I:

- Quiet the chatter in my head, clear away distractions, and focus on what she means to say.

- Work at staying fully present in the moment so she experiences me as attentive.

- Check my understanding and ask questions to clarify what she means.

- Convey appreciation, interest, and empathy for her perspective.

- Value her uniqueness as an individual, honoring her as a woman and seeing other points of identity that she values (e.g., her race or religion).

- Listen because I care that she is a person who has something to share with me.

- Build trust by offering my honest perspective with respect, always making it okay for her to disagree with me.

World-class listening should become a defining feature of the way we show up for women in the workplace. It is much tougher to execute than most of us would like to admit, yet it is a skill set all allies must aspire to master.

Assume Women Are Capable and Competent (Then, Stop Assuming)

"She's a woman so she must need ____." "She probably wouldn't be interested in ____." "She might not feel comfortable taking on

_____." "She'll probably want to step away from work any day to have a baby."

If we're not vigilant, we can make lots of erroneous assumptions about the women we work with. Most of us do this routinely, often without much conscious awareness, and certainly without malicious intent. Even men who truly want to be excellent allies get themselves into trouble by assuming things about women's career interests and aspirations, not to mention their approach to integrating work and family. Robert Cabana, director of the Kennedy Space Center, recalled this example: "I had a female astronaut tell me she wanted to have a family. So, I decided not to assign her to a flight because I assumed this meant she wanted downtime. Then, she came back right after her baby was born and asked me why I hadn't assigned her to a flight. For me, this highlighted the importance of really listening and clarifying what she wants in her career."

Our assumptions about women make fools of us when we assume they are not as confident or competent as men, when we fail to ask them directly about what they want or don't want to do in their careers, when we make decisions about opportunities or assignments for them behind their backs, and when we assume that they will prioritize family over work. So, what's a male ally to do? Assume that she is a capable and competent professional. Then, stop assuming.

Many of the women we spoke with highlighted the critical importance of having key men _radiate_ or _signal_ the clear assumption—both to them and to the entire workplace—that they were capable, talented, and competent. Anne-Marie Slaughter, CEO of New America, commented on her mentor: "He radiated the assumption that you were smart. It's hard to describe, but so important because we pick up these micro-signals, body language, verbal and nonverbal cues. Bob just sent out these cues to everyone that he was going to take this woman seriously and everyone else should too." Rachana Bhide of Bloomberg Radio News also recalled a male boss's assumptions: "Mike always assumed I was capable of doing the job. His policy was 'capable until proven otherwise.' He would verbally and publicly sing my praises with confidence before I was even given a task. He had the gumption to say, 'Oh, yeah, Rachana can do that; she's got that!' It was so good for my own self-esteem to have him assume I was already the manager he expected me to be."

In *Athena Rising*[18], we encouraged men to be mindful of how they view female colleagues. Begin with the assumption that the women around you are "rising Athenas." Capable, competent, fierce, and unique. Because women are more often made to feel like imposters in the male-centric workplace, your affirming lens and overt signals that she can handle whatever comes her way will do wonders for her confidence, while helping ensure that talented women are taken seriously in the workplace.

Validate and Normalize Women's Experiences

In developing our awareness and GQ, we learned about the tensions and obstacles women encounter daily at work. For some, this includes invalidating and dismissive slights that take a toll on a woman's emotional well-being and her sense of belonging, not to mention her feelings of competence. Ipek Serifsoy of Deep Coaching Institute framed it as *death by a thousand cuts*—the constant daily slights, dismissals, and micro-abrasions that undermine women and cause them to feel insecure. They take a toll.[19] She said, "You can see it because they start to become less enthusiastic about work. Little by little, they start checking out. Then, sure enough, when the next opportunity comes along, they opt out. The self-censoring and self-pretzeling women have to go through to survive and adapt in this environment is unimaginable, especially for white men."

This ally strategy involves becoming a trustworthy confidant, validating and normalizing her perceptions and experiences on an emotional and interpersonal level (later in this book, we'll tackle several public interventions and methods for disrupting these gendered slights, dismissals, and micro-aggressions). Amy Orlov of the Forté Foundation shared her own experience with validation when she was director of student affairs at the Wharton School: "I went through ten years in the business school thinking it was only me that was having these experiences (e.g., coming up with an idea and having a man take credit for it, getting interrupted in meetings). I didn't realize these were larger trends. For too long, I thought it was a character defect of mine. I would think, 'Maybe I wasn't assertive enough, or maybe I didn't state my idea as articulately as I could have.'"

If you want to be a better ally for women, watch out for gaslighting. *Gaslighting* is a form of psychological manipulation that sows seeds of doubt in members of a targeted group, making them question their own memory, perception, and sanity. Men have been gaslighting women for years. Too often, when a woman is interrupted, dismissed, made to feel incompetent, or even sexually harassed, and shares her experience with others, men respond with invalidating comments: "I'm sure he didn't mean any harm by that. He flirts with everyone. That's just his way. You might be blowing this out of proportion. You'll have to learn not to be so sensitive." These responses may challenge the legitimacy of her experience, the veracity of her perceptions, or the accuracy and fairness of her interpretations of reality.

Don't participate in gaslighting. Believe a woman and validate her experience. Help her to see that she's not the only one having these experiences. Never underestimate the profound power of communicating to her that she's not alone, that she's certainly not crazy, and that even you have witnessed some of the things she's experienced. Next, we offer several ally actions for validating and normalizing her gendered experiences in the workplace.

Believe her. Your ongoing assumption should be that she is bright, competent, and observant. You have no reason not to believe and honor her perceptions and experience. Feeling believed versus dismissed out of hand will go a long way toward making her feel validated.

Normalize her experience. Sometimes, allyship can be as straightforward as affirming that what she is reporting to you makes perfect sense, that you've heard about other women in your workplace encountering something similar, and that she's certainly not the only one.

Share what you've witnessed. If you see something sexist, biased, or discriminatory happen to her, or other women, pull her aside and tell her what you observed and ask how you can help to counteract the bad behavior. Amy Orlov said, "An ally is someone who asks questions and says something when he sees something. For example, say, 'I just saw ___. Is that what normally happens to you in a meeting?' Or, 'that didn't feel quite right to me. Is that typical?' 'Is that what you usually experience? Are women here constantly experiencing that or was that an isolated incident?'" Of course, your obligation to be an ally doesn't end with validation. Later in the book, we'll ask you to become a watchdog for sexism, bias, and harassment and offer some strategies for shutting it down.

Give her the inside scoop. If you understand the workplace culture or perhaps know about the handful of people who tend to make women feel dismissed or uncomfortable, don't withhold this information. In *Athena Rising*, we remind men that sharing insider knowledge is a key element of excellent mentoring. It is equally important when normalizing a colleague's experiences, and helping her to steer clear of certain toxic personalities.

Validate evidence of prejudice and discrimination. Women are more likely to experience gender bias, prejudicial evaluations, and discrimination at work. The probability of these experiences is amplified when she is a woman of color. An ally validates evidence of prejudice and discrimination and is quite willing to discuss how a colleague might best cope or formally respond to it.[20] Simultaneously, allies call public attention to prejudice and discrimination, disrupt it in real time, and champion policies and systemic changes to reduce it in the future.

Reframe "emotion" as "passion." Women cry more than men. It's a fact. Not only do they have more prolactin—the tear-producing hormone—in their bodies, but they are socialized with more permission to tear up. But in the male-centric workplace, tears mean distress, and "emotional" means "incompetent." Women can become furious with themselves and, then, self-critical when frustration or other experiences cause them to cry. Recent research reveals that when a woman publicly reframes tears as "passion," others are less likely to evaluate her negatively.[21] As allies, we can encourage her to refuse to denigrate herself for tears, making them no big deal, while challenging her to frame tears as a sign of passion about her work, ideas, and commitments. Help her get comfortable drawing this connection publicly if she tears up in a meeting. And when you hear dismissive and biased comments about a woman who cried, use the science to push back on the relevance of tears to excellent thinking, creativity, and performance.

Encourage Women to Let Their Talents Shine

More often than men, women are socialized from an early age to mute their accomplishments, be overly self-critical, avoid self-promotion, and be cautious about upstaging or outperforming men.[22] After all, social norms tell us women should be modest and unassuming, and deny full credit for their work, but always take responsibility for failures. If we men boast about our wins, we're bold and confident. If women do the same, they're perceived as selfish and bossy. Once they enter the workforce, women find that when they do self-promote, taking public credit for wins and achievements, they run the risk of backlash.[23] After all, a bold, self-confident woman who is unafraid to compete with men and publicly outperform them is often labeled with the "b" word. Christine Spadafor framed it this way: "For many women, it's not a lack of confidence that makes them hesitant to speak up, but rather they are not comfortable *showing* confidence." You see the problem here. If our female colleagues are muting their accomplishments for fear of the perception of hubris, they'll never get the credit they deserve.

What should an ally do when even the most accomplished and self-assured woman doubts herself or experiences backlash for performing well? Encourage her. Frequently point out and affirm her talents, strengths, and accomplishments. Elissa Sangster, executive director of the Forté Foundation, encourages us to be very clear about where we see the talented women around us progressing in the organization: "So many women leave companies because they don't see a future, because they haven't heard a steady narrative about where key leaders see them ascending. For women who report to you, this is your responsibility." Encouragement may be most critical when it comes to urging qualified women to seek a promotion. Debunk hierarchy in assigning credit. Too often, calcified hierarchical structures mean that the most-senior person in the chain of command receives credit for big wins or achievements. Instead, drill down several layers to discover the person who actually executed the work or came up with the brilliant innovation. Make sure that person—often a woman—gets the credit and the public shout-out.

Women are also less likely to self-nominate for promotions.[24] Help women see their potential and encourage them to move forward. Avelino Oliveria, business development manager at Schreiber Foods, told us that "you have to point out her great results, and tell her you believe she is the best candidate for the next job opening or leadership opportunity. If you don't spend the time doing this, you may miss out on excellent female leaders."

Many of the women we interviewed shared meaningful examples of how their male allies executed the encouragement and empowerment element of allyship:

- "He saw things in me I didn't see in myself. In a way, he held up a mirror and said, 'Here's what I see in you, Julie. Why can't you see that?' As women, we tend to doubt ourselves. Having someone promote me based on my potential—something men take for granted—was huge."—Julie Kratz, founder of Next Pivot Point

- "As a midshipman at the Naval Academy, I asked a navy captain I admired what he thought about the military opening up combat aviation squadrons to women. He looked me in the eye and said, 'If we're going to do it, we have to have the best women our country has to offer, and you *are* the best.' The enormity of that conversation and the confidence he had in me is something I will always remember."—Amy McGrath, former Marine Corps Lieutenant Colonel and 2020 Kentucky senatorial candidate

- "I was promoted to a department head troop commander role, which doesn't happen in special forces. His insistence on me having that role, using that title for me, writing it into my evaluations is such a big deal."—Andrea Goldstein, navy lieutenant commander

A final component of encouraging and empowering women is to be vigilant for the *imposter syndrome*.[25] Most of us have suffered the imposter syndrome from time to time, especially after starting a new job, accepting a promotion, or entering a workplace in which our minority status is obvious. The syndrome is defined by anxiety-inducing doubts about our competence or qualification. We wonder if we were hired or promoted by mistake. In silent agony, we wait to be revealed as frauds and shown the exit.

Because women encounter frequent gender bias—receiving implicit or overt messaging that they don't fit in, can't hack it, and aren't as qualified—they may be more prone to suffering the self-doubt and insecurity that defines imposter syndrome. Good allies are attuned to this and implement some of the following strategies to help female colleagues counteract imposter feelings.[26]

Normalize imposter feelings. When a woman confesses to imposter feelings, shrug your shoulders, smile warmly, and say, "You and most of the people around you." There are lots of famous women in the imposter club, including Facebook COO Sheryl Sandberg and tennis icon Serena Williams. Remind her that men have the same self-doubts but are often simply more comfortable faking it until they make it. They're no more intelligent or competent than she is.

Empirically challenge any negative self-talk. Stay tuned for self-deprecating comments such as "I totally botched that presentation" or "I have no business being in this job." Patiently stick with the evidence and work to create dissonance between the data and her self-statements: "I've heard from nobody that you 'totally botched' the presentation. Do you mean there are one or two things you'd like to improve next time?" "No business being in this job? So, you're saying the committee of smart people who hired you was wrong?"

Affirm, affirm, and affirm some more. When you detect imposter worries, be quick to counter them with copious doses of affirmation and encouragement. With good humor and grace, look for opportunities to express belief in her, such as when she shares reservations about her competence before a big presentation, or when you nudge her forward for a promotion. Remind her in no uncertain terms about her competence, successes, and milestone achievements.

Deliberately counteract stereotype threat. Remind her that she probably doesn't just *feel* like an imposter, but that women are often *made to feel* like imposters. Regardless of how self-assured, smart, and confident they are, many women in male-dominated workplaces receive both implicit and overt messages that they're out of place, odd ducks, and not true members of the club. Remind her occasionally that performance on key tasks in her job is not affected by gender. Matter-of-factly tell her, "You've got this!"

Share your own imposter stories. Undoubtedly you've had your own imposter moments in the workplace. Tell her about them! Nothing is so uplifting as the epiphany of hearing from a valued colleague that he too has wrestled—and perhaps continues to wrestle—the dragon of imposter anxiety and managed to endure.

Level the Playing Field

Be aware of the unique obstacles and biases women contend with, but don't make the mistake of treating them differently. Women tell us repeatedly that if you treat them differently or have lower expectations of their performance, you'll ultimately sabotage them, making it clear to the guys on the team that women are different, not full members of the crew. Janet Petro of the Kennedy Space Center warned that men should rate women fairly: "It doesn't help a woman if she is seen as a 'quota' or 'token' promotion. If you inflate her performance ratings just to get her promoted, it will damage your credibility and undermine her legitimacy. By the same token, push back on messaging that women must perform at a higher level because they're women."

Several of the women we spoke with confirmed deep appreciation for allies who made them feel fully integrated in the workplace by treating them just like the guys, holding them to the same standards, and viewing them as professionals first. Gretchen Carlson remembered that her boss at one of her first news stations modeled this ally action well: "There was another reporter at the time, a man who was at my level. [My boss] Jim would bring us into his office and say, 'You are both going to be on the news this evening, but whoever brings me the best story will have the lead story.' He treated us as equals in every way. It was a way to make me part of the boys' club and make me feel like we were on a level playing field."

The bottom line is to treat women fairly. Telegraph to everyone watching that they are full members of the team by holding them to the same expectations you have for men.

Be Observant but Don't Give Unsolicited Advice

A male ally is willing to give a female colleague feedback about aspects of her behavior or presentation that could undermine her. As you might imagine, this feedback can be fraught. You don't want to be that sexist jerk mansplaining why she should behave more like a dude. At the same time, if she is doing things that are certain to hold her back, this might be a moment to show some true ally courage.

There are several behavioral habits—more likely to be socialized in women—that can cause them to be discounted, particularly in male-centric workplaces. Sally Helgesen, author and women's leadership expert, shared several with us, including apologizing constantly; using too many words or sharing too much information in male leadership environments with a preference for brevity; leaning toward perfectionism and self-criticism; ending sentences with a rising inflection or question (uptalk); trying to please everyone; holding oneself back in asking for promotions or salary adjustments; volunteering for office housekeeping jobs; and not entering into conversations assertively in fear of the dreaded "bitch" label.

Do you see something in a talented woman's style or presentation that's triggering eye rolls, dismissal of her good ideas, or worse, causing her to be ignored? Is she unwittingly playing into gender stereotypes and biases? Is it something she could address to good effect? A male ally should give her the feedback she needs. But before you tell women how they should change their behavior to fit in, walk through the following items.

First, flip the script. Before giving any woman feedback about her interpersonal or leadership style, flip the situation in your mind and ask, "Would I be saying this to a man? Would a guy exhibiting the same behavior be getting the same pushback?" If not, maybe you should call out the double standards in the workplace and advocate for her, instead of recommending that she change her approach.

Earn her trust before offering feedback. Feedback before trust is a recipe for failure. Establish your know-how as an advocate and ally before offering suggestions for change.

Don't give unsolicited advice; offer her a choice. Nothing may feel more averse than unsolicited advice. Sally Helgesen recalled, "As a young woman, I often enjoyed practicing tennis by hitting a ball against a wall. I couldn't do it without some guy telling me, unsolicited, how I should be hitting the ball differently. I didn't appreciate it." Don't be that guy. Instead, start the conversation in a way that gives a woman choice. Again, Helgesen said, "If she's having conflict with a senior male in the office, try starting with 'I've worked with Jack for years and I've learned some things about how to communicate with him effectively. If you'd ever like my thoughts about strategies, I'd be happy to share them with you.'"

Frame observations as intel about navigating traditionally male spaces. Frame your feedback as cultural intelligence for understanding and adapting effectively to the politics, leadership traditions, and implicit norms of male-centric workplaces. Don't frame observations as feedback about a personal defect.

Consider third-party consultation. If you're noticing a behavior that's sabotaging a female colleague, but feel uncertain about how to broach it with her or aren't sure you've established adequate rapport to do so, consider discussing the situation with a trusted female mentor in the workplace and asking for her advice.

Male allies are attuned to how female colleagues are received in the workplace. Not only do they push back on bias and false narratives about women, but they are also willing to share observations about performance or career-undermining behaviors that might hold a female colleague back.

Practice Transparency

Male allies pull back the curtain hiding information and processes from women. When information related to salary figures, job benefits, effective negotiation strategies, and promotion opportunities are less accessible to women, secrecy perpetuates gender inequities in the workplace. In historically male-dominated organizations, crucial information frequently is passed along over beers after work, on the golf course, or even in the men's room.

Sharing information with female colleagues is essential. For example, Hideko Sera, associate dean of education, University of Redlands, told us that at a previous job, she had been hired at the same time as a male colleague. The two shared nearly identical records of teaching success and scholarly productivity. At one point, they were asked to share a dean position, producing the same positive results in their collaboration around leadership. Upon reentering the regular faculty, the president of the institution asked them to meet with him individually to thank them for a job well done and negotiate their new salaries. Sera recalled, "Sean purposefully scheduled his meeting one day before mine. After he met with the president, he immediately came to my office and wrote down the salary he'd just been offered and handed it to me. He said, 'Hideko, I have a feeling that as a woman, you're going to get shortchanged. Do not accept anything lower than this. We started at the same time; we've done exactly the same work and produced exactly the same results. If you end up making more money, that's fine, but you cannot accept something lower than this.'" Indeed, the following day the president offered her $8,500 less than what he'd offered her colleague. Sera immediately asked him to explain why he was offering her less than her male colleague. The contract was revised, and she got the same salary as her colleague. "If he had not shared his salary with me, I'd never have known."

Information is power. In addition to sharing your salary and the salaries of others at various levels in the organization, you should also share information about the path to leadership, benefits others have negotiated, sweet deals related to extended family leave, and examples of those who have arranged flex schedules and shortened work weeks. There is evidence that women get less coaching on strategies for salary and promotion negotiations.[27] When you have the opportunity, share your own negotiation experiences with women you work with. The more transparent the numbers and precedents are, the better prepared they'll be to negotiate for salary, benefits, and promotion.[28]

Engage in Women's Initiatives and Inclusion Events

This final strategy for showing up for women at work every day will really test your ally moxie. Attend women's conferences, gender inclusion events, and if men are invited, join the women's employee resource group (ERG) in your company. What better way to learn more about the concerns of your female colleagues and how you can become a more effective accomplice for equity than by surrounding yourself with women and . . . listening. (As an added benefit, this exposure will crush any residual gynophobia.)

By leaning in as an ally at events important to your female colleagues, you'll not only demonstrate overt support for women you work with, but also be modeling full engagement with gender equity initiatives for other men. Engage in these events and you'll build better empathy, become better attuned to colleagues' challenges, diversify your network, and spot talent for your organization.[29] If you are a man in any sort of leadership role, your presence and full engagement at women's events are crucial. Attend as many events as your schedule will allow. Sit near the front, stay the whole time, allocate resources to support them, and talk publicly about what you learn each time.

Showing up at inclusion events is the easy part. The tougher challenge and more important question is *how* you show up, which requires your best ally mojo. You'll need a combination of courage (to get yourself in the door) and epic humility (to remain quiet and mindful so that you can truly listen and learn)

Women are sometimes justifiably skeptical when a man attends a women's ERG meeting or event, for a number of reasons. *First*, these gatherings have historically offered women a sense of community and camaraderie, a safe space for sharing experiences and formulating strategies for achieving equality in the workplace. *Second*, sub-tracks and breakout sessions for men at women's events often have labels such as *Manbassador* or *Male Champion*, terrific for drawing guys in, but in truth, rather grandiose to the ears of women who may sigh and ask, "Really, dude? We have to call you a champion just to get you to be fair, respectful, and inclusive?" *Third*, some men who engage in women's initiatives benefit from the *pedestal effect* and are given shout-outs for even minor displays of gender partnership. Stephanie Vander Zanden has witnessed this firsthand: "The women's group at Schreiber has a male and female co-chair. I've seen people call him out and praise him for his leadership, right in front of his female co-lead, but nobody ever singles her out for praise." *Fourth*, overfocusing on men may paradoxically undermine women's autonomy and leadership of their own equity initiatives.[30] After all, we men—especially white men—are socialized to rush in, take the lead, and take control (versus taking the back seat and supporting marginalized groups).[31] *Finally*, there is the problem of the *fake male feminist*. You know this guy. He slings on feminism like a superhero cape when his boss is watching, to impress—or worse, seduce—women, or to avoid being labeled as sexist despite his pattern of sexist behavior. Whatever you do, don't be that guy.

You probably had no idea engaging in women's events and initiatives could be so tough. We've got some rules of the road for you. Follow these and you'll do just fine.

Show up with a genuine learning orientation. Listen, decenter, learn as much as you can about the experiences and concerns of the women around you and don't move on to the following rules until you've mastered this one. Annie Rogaski shared how much she appreciated the example of Frank Bernstein, partner at Squire Patton Boggs LLP, who would attend a women's leadership group: "Frank came to almost every event that was open to men. He came in and just listened. He was clearly there to learn. He didn't come in and take over and say, 'Let me explain things to you.' It struck me how rare it was for a man to come into a women's space and not be the expert but just embrace a position of supporting us."

Respect the space. Large events and local affinity groups have afforded women a powerful platform for sharing experiences, providing support, and strategizing equity initiatives. Tread respectfully into these spaces, and before you utter a word, revisit the previous recommendation.[32]

Ask what you can do. The best male allies at women's events seek true partnership in promoting gender equity.[33] But don't assume what your role should be. Ask the women around you. They've been doing this longer than you have.

Park your steed and put away the armor. The women leading women's initiatives certainly don't need the cavalry. If you act like a "white knight" for the "damsels in distress," they'd be right to toss you out. Autonomy-oriented support that affirms women's competence and leadership—versus efforts at rescuing that reinforce dependency—is the order of the day.

Don't call yourself an ally. You are an ally for a woman when she calls you an ally and never before. Do the work. Listen, learn, and ask how you can be an accomplice to gender equity efforts. Let women decide how to frame your efforts.

Male allies consciously and deliberately show up for women in the workplace. They strive for inclusion, listen generously, and assume that the women around them are more than competent. Allies look for ways to level the playing field by encouraging them, offering feedback, validating their experiences, and practicing transparency. And all-in allies show their support and eagerness to learn by participating in inclusion events and women's initiatives.

Each of the ally strategies we've described bear upon our general attitudes and behaviors around women writ large. In the next chapter—our final chapter on how to show up interpersonally with women at work—we'll delve into a set of strategies for engaging in real workplace friendships with women that are rooted in trust and reciprocity.

Ally Actions

- **Include women.** Combat *belonging uncertainty* among women by inviting them to all work-connected gatherings, generously sharing time, and treating them like one of the guys.

- **Decenter.** Step out of central roles, make physical space for women, and when invited to lead or participate in a high-visibility group (e.g., conference, committee), consider whether a talented female colleague would be a better fit and recommend her.

- **Listen generously.** Listen to women with the intent to understand, demonstrate empathy, and validate her experience—not fix women's problems.

- **Assume women are capable and competent (then, stop assuming).** Scrutinize your automatic—often erroneous—assumptions about women and deliberately signal clear assumptions that your female colleagues are talented and competent.

- **Validate and normalize women's experiences.** Be a trustworthy confidant in hearing about the daily slights, dismissals, and micro-aggressions women so often encounter in male-centric workplaces and show understanding about their feelings.

- **Encourage women to let their talents shine.** Affirm women's capabilities and challenge sexist and biased comments about assertive, competitive, self-confident women as well as hierarchical systems that fail to fully credit them for their innovations and ideas.

- **Level the playing field.** Communicate the same performance expectations for men and women and push back on expectations that women must prove themselves over and over again or achieve a higher standard to earn advancement.

- **Be observant but don't give unsolicited advice.** Avoid sharing unsolicited feedback, and before offering any advice, flip the script and ask yourself if you'd give the same advice to a man.

- **Practice transparency.** Secrecy perpetuates gender inequality, so share information (like salary figures and negotiation strategies) with female colleagues.

- **Engage in women's initiatives and inclusion events.** When you participate in women's inclusion events, listen, demonstrate a learning orientation and gender humility, and ask women how you can most effectively support efforts toward gender inclusion and equity.

5

Trust and Reciprocity in Friendships with Women

Now that you've developed an arsenal of strategies for being an interpersonal ally to women in the workplace, we're going to suggest you become more thoughtful and intentional about developing a core group of trusted friends and reliable confidants among your network of female colleagues. In this chapter, you'll find seven strategies for showing up as a real friend for women at work. We introduce the reciprocal benefits of workplace friendships with women and ways to build a network of such friendships. We'll showcase the value of reciprocity and honest feedback and encourage you to devote time to both discern and then affirm a female colleague's ideal self and career dream. Then, we'll explain how to stay ahead of gossip and make excellent cross-gender friendships part of your ally brand.

Appreciate the Benefits of Friendships with Women

Genuine friendship is profoundly important as an ally action, particularly in male-dominated workplaces. In these contexts, women often report feeling isolated, lonely, and sometimes deliberately excluded. Allies are attuned to this and thoughtful about the power of friendship to buoy a woman's spirits, sense of belonging, and career. Meaningful workplace friendships also improve retention. Ergo, this is good for your organization's bottom line.

But solid friendships with women provide guys with a whole lot of advantages, too.[1] Men with female friends accrue more information about the company and enjoy more social support, broader networks, and more career opportunities. And men with female friends improve listening, empathy, communication skills and overall emotional intelligence.[2] Strong cross-gender friendships help us to develop healthy cross-gender relationship models and relationship reserves that we can implement at work to improve our leadership savvy. We also bring these skills home to enhance our success as partners and parents.

Laura Adams, president and CEO of Rhode Island Quality Institute, explains that men who are friendly allies with women often benefit from reciprocal loyalty. Describing George Vecchione, her board chair, she said, "Women don't just receive allyship. We develop a loyalty, a sense of commitment to the other person. Because of George's allyship, I felt aligned with him, supporting him publicly and privately if anyone took shots at him. He had created an ally in me. I'm not sure that value is seen by most men."

Build a Network That Includes Women

Are you concerned about the diversity of your relationships at work? Do your good friends and colleagues at work all look the same?

Perhaps just like you? If so, that's an ally failure. Look carefully at your workplace relationship network and honestly consider whether it includes women, people of color, and members of other diverse groups. The truth is that we tend to befriend those who look like us. But unless our network of trusted friends includes multiple women, we're shortchanging ourselves, the women around us at work, and our organizations.

Recent research on the gender composition of women's workplace networks confirms that, particularly in male-dominated settings, women benefit substantially from relationship networks that include both women and men.[3] Women who rise to senior leadership levels benefit from social support, gender-relevant information about job cultures, wide access to diverse job-market information, sponsorship, and access to social capital. It often takes a village of men *and* women to accrue all of these functions. Janet Foutty, executive chair of the board at Deloitte, reflected on the importance of male allies in her own network: "There are three groups of men who have been allies in different ways—male leaders who were senior to me, male clients, and male peers. Having that mix of male allies, mentors, sponsors, and close colleagues collectively played a significant supportive role as I advanced in my career."

Male allies support women by deliberately constructing a tribe of female friends. This constellation might include colleagues, mentees, mentors, and confidants. In the same way that women need men's support, sponsorship, and friendship, men need the perspective, insight, and encouragement of diverse female colleagues to make good decisions, become better leaders, and improve the quality and capacity of ally work.

To build your network, look for a female mentor. Try to draw on the wisdom and support of multiple senior women. Research evidence shows that men with a female role model or mentor are more likely to cite the importance of advancing women in the workplace.[4] Not only will a female mentor be a champion, confidant, and resource, but conversations and interaction with her are likely to raise your GQ.

How about seeking out a woman as a coach or consultant? Not all of us can afford this, but if your job comes with some perks or if your HR department offers executive coaching, specifically request a female coach. For Bill Parsons, former director of the Kennedy Space Center, having a woman in his corner as an executive coach was transformative:

> We remain in touch to this day. Her work with me was instrumental in helping me to more effectively work with women later in my career. She would observe me in the workplace, in crucial meetings or events, and then give me feedback. I always found her perspective so different from the way I had been reading things. My typical response would be "Oh, wow! No, I did not realize that!" On a personal front, she was the one who pressed me to get perspective on my extreme work schedule, a schedule that was causing me marital and family problems. Had I had a male coach, I'm not sure I would have been challenged so clearly to focus on work-family balance.

Look around your workplace and identify some of the smart and talented junior women. Some of them might not have received much mentoring. Men who mentor women broaden their networks, improve their relational skills, and benefit from strong reciprocal friendships with their mentees. Women who receive mentoring from more senior males tend to make more money, receive more promotions, and report greater satisfaction with their career progression.[5] This is not because men are better mentors. We often just hold greater rank and political capital, especially in male-dominated industries. Again, the mutual friendships that often result from a mentoring connection can offer enduring personal and career benefits for you and your female friends.

Reach out to some junior women, show genuine respect for their accomplishments and talent, and start offering support, encouragement, and sponsoring. Not sure how to begin? J. T. Metzger of Smart-Street Consultants offered a great strategy: "I have tried to make it less awkward by first offering support outwardly. For instance, 'Hey, I noticed you doing ___, and that was awesome! Have you considered ___? I'm always available to help.' This tends to get some takers, leads to some conversations, and then trust starts to develop."

Be sure to mentor several junior women, not just one. When a man mentors multiple women and men, everyone sees that he is an inclusive leader. When a man mentors only one junior woman and spends an inordinate amount of time with her, he sets himself (and his mentee) up for rumors. Still worried about getting started as a mentor for women? Organizational psychologist Adam Grant recommends starting with small-group mentoring.[6] How about a small mixed-gender group of junior folks? Take them to coffee routinely and find out how you can support them. Not only will your mentoring be more efficient, but your mentees will be building their own cross-gender networks.

Create Safe-Space Friendships with Several Women

Forge some high-quality peer friendships with women at work and you will be on the receiving end of a host of personal and career benefits. Not only will some of these friendships be among the most enduring and treasured of your career, the social capital, self-awareness, and new skills you'll accrue are certain to fuel your job performance. But close cross-gender friendships are also a key element to allyship. Consider the myriad ways women benefit from strong friendships with men at work.[7]

Development of valued, authentic, and expanded identities. These relationships become a safe haven for exploring and constructing strong identities in the workplace. Peer mentorships allow women to bring their full identities to the relationship (e.g., professional, worker, student, wife/mother) for validation and support, even if these identities are not valued by the broader organization.

Psychological growth. Exclusionary, marginalizing, and discriminating workplaces can take a toll on women's well-being. A high-quality friendship can compensate for this by restoring and expanding self-efficacy, confidence, hope, optimism, and resilience.

New knowledge. Close work friends can provide critical access to important or otherwise unavailable sources of knowledge. Also, male friends can help women develop thriving strategies for responding effectively to negative workplace episodes (e.g., discrimination, ignorance). By the same token, female friends can bolster our GQ while helping us formulate our own thriving strategies in the face of resistance to our ally efforts.

So, how does a man go about forging a terrific workplace friendship with a woman? First, abide by the *platinum rule*. Shelley Zalis of Female Quotient told us, "The golden rule (treating her as you'd like to be treated) is not enough. Women need you to use the platinum rule—*do unto others as they'd want done to themselves.* This requires men to have a conscious mindset, to think about what *she* would want in a relationship." So, what qualities do women most often value in close relationships? Here are some of the biggies: mutuality, listening, self-disclosure, empathy, and intimacy (we'll say more about intimacy later).[8] How do these qualities emerge in a friendship? In one word: *trust*.

Trust is making and keeping of promises over time. Of course, listening is a fundamental promise in a relationship.[9] When we truly listen to a female colleague, really hearing what she says, we show we are worthy of trust, which opens the door to genuine reciprocity. Sean Vogel of Lockheed Martin discovered the value of a trusting friendship with a woman: "When I met Sarah, we just clicked. We gave each other candid feedback, advice, and counsel. We affirmed each other's perceptions. We could be transparent about our feelings and perspectives. It was very gratifying that she trusted me and that trust was mutual."

Trust is the secret to creating friendships that offer a truly *safe space*, a confidential zone of authenticity in which mutual disclosure is the norm and you can deliver and receive unvarnished yet caring feedback. The following additional strategies will help you earn trust and form strong friendships with female colleagues.

Show unconditional regard. Convey warm acceptance of her as a human being, value learning about her experience, and appreciate her as a colleague. And, do all of this regardless of how she happens to be currently performing at work.[10]

Don't be competitive. Friends rarely value "one-up-*man*ship," and women often find it particularly offensive. Make your friendship about building her up, not showing off. Several of the women we interviewed talked about the importance of male allies who demonstrated a commitment to their best interests, often expressed in genuine collaboration. Emily Ramshaw, editor-in-chief of *Texas Tribune*, said of her trusted male ally, "He's never proprietary, never selfish about success. Our relationship was never competitive. He always had my best interests at heart. He understood that my success was good for his success." And Laphonza Butler of SEIU Local 2015 observed, "He is incredibly compassionate and finds delight in watching others succeed. He has this trusting demeanor that creates an environment where people can be their best selves."

Create a safe zone for emotional expression. Strong friendships have a high emotional carrying capacity.[11] In other words, the relationship becomes a safe space for the expression of both positive and negative emotions. Reflecting the value of this attribute, Laura Adams recalled, "I never felt like if I shed a tear that I was ruining my career or getting pegged as unable to control my emotions. He allowed a humanness to emerge. He valued my whole person and never held tears against me."

Pass the friend test. Don't ever say anything behind her back that you wouldn't or haven't said to her face. Male allies don't engage in demeaning banter, sexual innuendo, or criticism behind their female colleagues' backs. If your friend hears anything about your behavior when she's not in the room, it should be about how you stuck up for her or shut down undermining comments from others.

Be in her corner for the long haul. Show you're the sort of friend who's all in, even when you're no longer working together. If you haven't seen her for a while, reach out and check in. Suzanne Fogarty, head of Chapin School in New York City, experienced this kind of long-term commitment from a male ally: "Even though I've moved on to a different school, he continues to be an ally and resource for me. When I reach out to him, he gets back to me right away—usually that same day. That kind of attentiveness and care has been so important to me in my new role."

Have her back, but no white-knighting allowed. Many boys are socialized early with the classic rescuing hero/damsel-in-distress *manscript*.[12] If you are one of them, you'll have to be vigilant in guarding against the temptation to swoop in to protect your female work friends, especially in the case of women you feel particularly close to. If you're not sure whether to act, ask yourself if you would do the same for one of your guy friends. Nothing might undermine her autonomy and credibility in the workplace more than a guy who becomes a mixed-martial arts cage fighter with anyone who "messes" with his female colleague.

By now you might be getting alarmed by our use of terms such as *trust* and *intimacy* in reference to your workplace relationships with women. We get it. To make matters decidedly creepy, some men and women even refer to a close friend of the opposite sex at work as their "work spouse." We've heard men refer to female colleagues as their "work wife." That's unacceptable. She's your friend and valued colleague.

The military has traditionally used the concept of *brothers and sisters in arms* to reinforce the bonds of camaraderie in the heat of battle. You can too. Commitment, trust, and intimacy are key elements of strong companion relationships, including the best friendships in the workplace. They are also present in the very best sibling relationships. Consider the experience of Diane Ryan, associate dean, Tufts University. "As a lieutenant in the army, two men were my sounding boards. When I was struggling with something, I could go to them and have a very open and honest conversation and I felt like they had my back. They were like brothers to me. They still are. The military is a family and those men exemplify that."

Deal with your own attraction, should this ever begin to threaten a workplace friendship with a woman. First, keep in mind that the attraction is often one way. A classic stream of research in social psychology on *sexual over-perception bias* reveals that compared to female peers, guys tend to overestimate how romantically interested women around us might be.[13] Second, men often turn to female friends for nurturance and intimacy—something less often available in friendships with men.[14] But we've got to be careful to establish some boundaries and keep her best interests at heart. Remember, she's your colleague, not your girlfriend. Be the kind of person she can count on.

Make It Reciprocal

If you want to enjoy and benefit from strong friendships with women, ditch the formality and hierarchy, which is especially challenging for men who are more senior to the women they work with. Men can too often default—sometimes unconsciously—to the guru archetype of friendship, particularly when they have longer tenure in a company or the friendship begins as a formal mentorship. The guru knows everything, may feel threatened when this is proved false, and is most comfortable in a one-way relationship (e.g., "I'll provide you with wisdom, guidance, and correct answers, but I certainly don't expect to learn anything from you").

Think of ideal friendships with women as a form of peer mentoring. In the earliest study of peer mentoring, organizational psychologist Kathy Kram discovered that the mutuality and lack of hierarchy in genuine peer mentorships make it easier for both parties to communicate authentically, collaborate, and enjoy mutual support.[15] Women in particular often prefer relationships at work without the trappings of hierarchy and power distinctions. Instead, they appreciate supportive partnerships that are mutually growth enhancing and equal, relationships in which partners share social capital (influence, information, knowledge, and organizational resources). In other words, truly *reciprocal* friendships.

In her extensive research on reciprocal relationships in the workplace, Belle Rose Ragins, professor and mentoring relationships researcher, discovered that those relationships with the greatest lifelong impact were truly defined by an appreciation—even a celebration—of mutual listening and learning.[16] In the best relationships, both members learn and grow as a result of the relationship itself. There is a fluid expertise between members. This requires men to keep an open mind, maintain a learning orientation, and recognize that expertise may shift depending on the task or topic. Julie Kratz of Next Pivot Point experienced this quality in her friendship with a fellow MBA student: "The best allyships are fluid. The yin and yang of masculinity and femininity in relationships can really support a nice sense of fluidity, of give and take. We both have things to learn and we're better together. For example, women can be more risk-aversive and tentative, and it can help to have a male perspective, a guy who'll say, 'What's the worst that can happen? Just do it!'"

You may hold more rank and power today, but tomorrow, maybe not so much. Maybe tomorrow, she'll be leveraging her position to pull you up. Mary-Olga Lovett, senior vice president of Greenberg Traurig Law, gave us an example of such reciprocity. As a junior lawyer, Lovett was in a firm that was not a welcoming place for young women. When she had the opportunity to go to another firm and told her good friend and stalwart ally Jim, he went to bat for her: "He said, 'I've been authorized to double your pay.' I told him, 'Jim, I've made my decision. I'm leaving.' He immediately said, 'I'm proud of you! Go kill it!' And twelve years later, I hired *him*." Recently, Jim was honored at an awards ceremony, and in his remarks, he said, "The most important thing for everyone to know is that Ms. Lovett used to work for me, and now I work for her, and that's the way it should be."

Discern Her Ideal Self and Career Dream

As a sculptor, Michelangelo Buonarroti approached his task with the humble conviction that a unique and beautiful piece of art already existed within the stone. The artist's job was merely to release the hidden figure. Michelangelo's approach is a powerful metaphor for how the best reciprocal friends encourage and empower one another's ideal selves to emerge.[17] Channeling Michelangelo, excellent friends gently and patiently chip away the superfluous stone inhibiting the full expression of our best selves. Caring and discerning friends liberate us so we can thrive.

A compelling stream of research in social psychology confirms that in the best relationships, partners sculpt one another to bring each person closer to their ideal self—the person they want to be or didn't realize they could be.[18] Termed the *Michelangelo phenomenon*, a skilled and thoughtful relationship partner becomes committed to first understanding and then reinforcing or drawing out another's ideal form—that unique, promising, but sometimes vulnerable form that might be hidden.

To be a great friend and ally to a woman at work, practice two types of affirmation. First comes *perceptual affirmation*: take time to really see her. Simple as it sounds, it takes some effort and commitment to listen and discern her vision of an ideal career trajectory and an ideal sense of how to be fully herself as a leader and a professional. Once her ideal vision becomes clear, affirm and reinforce that you see it too. Second, practice *behavioral affirmation*. Having gained a window into who she'd like to become, help to open doors and create the opportunities she'll require to get there. Engage with her as though she were already that ideal version of herself. Show her that you see her through that lens. Elicit the behaviors and dispositions that help her to flourish.

There are some practical strategies for discerning her ideal self and career dream. Commit the time. Listen. Demonstrate genuine interest. Ask the kind of curious Socratic questions that tend to draw out the ideal vision. ("In a perfect world, I wonder what you'd be doing ten years from now?" "What's one of your hidden talents and how would it look if you could express it here at work?")[19] Be patient and show empathy and understanding as she shares bits and pieces about her dream job and clues about how showing up fully at work would look. And be unconditionally accepting and generous with affirmation.

Being an excellent ally and friend requires you to be alert to the temptation to clone her in your image or any other masculine archetype in your industry. A recent study by Bloomberg reveals that many of us tend to look for junior colleagues that we can sculpt into mini-me protégés.[20] Accept from the start that her ideal career path may not look at all like yours.

Once you've done the humble sculpting work, listened carefully, and grasped her sense of where or how high she might fly, ask yourself if she might be selling herself short. If so, a great friend and ally won't hesitate to cast a more audacious career vision—not to discount her own vision, but merely as a topic for friendly conversation. Perhaps she doesn't see the full scope of her talent. Perhaps she's been socialized to tamp down her dreams. Maybe nobody has ever asked her if she'd considered flying higher. As an ally, you can discern and affirm her career dream, yet you've also got to be honest with her if you see that her organization or profession might miss out if she didn't at least entertain going further. At times, a female friend may have a cautious mindset, tending toward reserved and risk averse.[21] In those cases, a male ally might reflect back to her skill sets, potential, and talent she may have never appreciated in herself. Then, he might point out some grander possibilities, firmly communicating that any decision about her career is *always* hers to make.

Consider how important these audacious vision conversations were for some of the women we spoke with. Lisen Stromberg, COO/Partner of 3% Conference, said, "A theme for my allies is that they saw something in me I didn't see. They gave me a mirror to see what was possible before I was comfortable enough to own it. These men wanted me to own my own truth. They empowered me to see it without fear or doubt." Myra Nawabi, a multifunctional science and engineering associate manager for Lockheed Martin said that a male ally once told her she belonged on a bigger stage, doing extraordinary things. Although he was nearing the end of his career, he told her that before he retired, he wanted to lay the foundation for her to ascend to significant leadership positions one day. He saw the promise and potential in Nawabi and laid the groundwork to accelerate her career ascendency.

Many of your close female friends will already know their strengths and talents. These women don't need you to consistently reflect them, nor will it be necessary for you to offer a more audacious career dream. Still, accurate discernment and affirmation of her talents and dreams will be a powerful ally strategy.

Don't Shirk Your Honest Feedback Obligation

Previously, we focused on the inestimable value of eliciting unvarnished truth from women who trust and care about you. Now it's your turn. You have to reciprocate and do your part to give your female friends straight talk and caring confrontation. You have to care enough to overcome the anxiety that can accompany difficult conversations. Want those women to have your back and save you from yourself? Then you better step up and give them an equally direct challenge.

In the last chapter, we discussed one of the essential strategies for showing up for women at work generally: being a man willing to provide consultative observations and solicited feedback. But with your network of female work friends, you have to take it to another level. Laura Adams has surrounded herself with a cohort of genuine male allies who lean in for her in this way: "I call it 'carefrontation.' They provide me unfettered, direct feedback and advice. They are on my side no matter what I am going through. I have their unconditional allyship. Our conversations are confidential, so I can talk openly and freely, no judging. We are intentional allies for each other. We are committed to hold each other accountable." Likewise, Mary-Olga Lovett was grateful for the tough love she received from her closest male allies. "They could be incredibly tough on me, never pulling punches. I tell men you have to be every bit as tough on your female associates, and they need to appreciate that this is to make them better, stronger, and to think with more agility. After talking to my peers at other law firms, I realized how good I had it by having respectful, but tough male allies." If you've established trust, then providing *carefrontation* is not only nice to have, but a solemn obligation.

Women get less critical feedback than men in the workplace, which is flat-out unfair.[22] Those authentic—often difficult—conversations about presentation and performance are a gift. To show up as an ally for a genuine friend and colleague, you've got to see honest, straight-up feedback as an obligation. This is part of the recipe for helping a friend get better, to appreciate how she's perceived, and even to inoculate her for the trials certain to come with increased rank and visibility. Emily Ramshaw framed her own male ally's carefrontations this way: "He gives me a lot of straight talk. He's not just about lifting me up; he's also about helping me improve. When I fall short, he's very direct in how I can improve. He's exceedingly loyal and devoted to my professional success. Part of my success is learning from my mistakes."

In her book *Radical Candor*, Kim Scott explores why men find it so hard to be candid with women.[23] Men often are socialized from birth to be gentler with women than with men. We're worried that the unvarnished feedback we'd give a guy will be offensive in some way—or god forbid—make her cry. But candid conversations about her improvement zones are a critical component of equipping her for success.[24] You've got to approach this carefrontation obligation with moral courage and commitment. Don't let her down.

A couple of the women we interviewed appreciated straight talk and direct challenge, commenting:

> He was very supportive at work, but he also challenged my thinking. His challenges let me know he cared and believed in me.
> —Telle Whitney, former CEO, Anita Borg Institute

> As an ally and mentor, he took the time to get to know me over time. He saw the bigger picture of the career decisions I was trying to make. He was a sounding board and provided an honest opinion—that was often hard for me to hear. He spent the time to know me as a person, to hear my frustration of being a female in patent litigation. For the vast majority of my career decisions, I've talked with him—and it's never been an easy conversation. It's always be a soul-searching, hard questions type of engagement where he made me think really hard about everything I was considering.
> —Annie Rogaski, COO, Avegant Corporation

Be careful that you don't give critical feedback for an interpersonal or leadership approach that may ruffle some feathers but that simply caters to biases and double standards around gender (e.g., "She's really aggressive." "She pushes too hard for promotion." "She's excessively devoted to work." "I mean she *does* have children."). Remember that you're not fixing her. As an ally, you may hear about behavior on the part of a work friend that some men find "jarring" or "abrasive."

Of course, you should tell her the truth about what you are hearing, but instead of confronting her to fix her style in order to succeed, push back on these biased comments and confront the men who make them.

Get Out in Front of Rumors

As an all-in ally, you must appreciate how rumors of a workplace romance with a female colleague—particularly if she is junior to you—can tarnish her reputation and even torpedo her credibility.[25] Rumors won't do you any good either. The potential for rumors and false perceptions has always contributed to male unease about fully engaging with female colleagues at work. It is a prime ingredient in what we call the *reluctant male syndrome*—a tendency for men to anxiously avoid meaningful friendships and mentorships with women in the workplace.[26] Some men allow rumors to undermine positive relationships with women at work. Lisen Stromberg recalled: "An important male mentor stopped responding to emails and phone calls. Later, after I left the company, I heard from others that he had been told there were rumors we were having an affair. He may have been embarrassed and didn't know how to handle it. He may also have been trying to protect me. But his response was to just shut down, which left me feeling abandoned and confused. It made me feel less loyal and committed to the company and was one of the reasons I left."

Clearly, this guy's response to a little gossip was dysfunctional, even harmful. Later, we're going to provide you with a playbook for inoculating your friendships with women against gossip. But sometimes people will rumor-monger no matter how careful and transparent you are at engaging across gender. In those instances, you've got to show some courage. Quarantining women and retreating from excellent friendships merely because of a snide comment or sideways glance reinforces the kind of toxic workplace culture none of us want to be part of. Sometimes you've got to stand your ground, show some ally mettle, and confront the cynical gossip mongers at work.

To keep rumors at bay, practice the following strategies faithfully and you will have little to worry about in the gossip department.

Be transparent. Nothing is so titillating to gossip than the appearance of secrecy—perhaps including clandestine meetings—between a man and a woman. Be 100 percent open, transparent, and vocal about when and why you are meeting with female friends and colleagues.[27] Openly put meetings on your schedule and include the meeting topic. Talk about how much you admire and benefit from the women in your network.

Make cross-gender friendship part of your brand. If you have lots of women in your network at work (friends, confidants, mentors, mentees), you take the air right out of that rumor balloon. Have no women in your network, and then suddenly start spending a lot of time with just *one* woman, possibly someone junior? Well, you've just created the perfect storm for gossip. Make it your brand to have a robust tribe of female colleagues.

Don't be a mentor for the wrong reasons. Janet Petro of Kennedy Space Center shared this warning: "The only time I've seen a guy get pushback for mentoring or sponsoring a woman is when he's doing it for the wrong reasons. For example, if she's not qualified, competent, or capable, and he's pushing her forward anyway, people start down the road of 'well, she is young and good looking.'" Unsure about a female colleague's qualifications for advancement? Concerned that your romantic attraction to her could be clouding your assessment? Ask trusted colleagues for their perspective on her readiness for promotion, and then take their observations to heart.

Think about the when and where. Smart allies are aware of the optics surrounding the timing and location of meetings with women, especially those you are mentoring. In *Lean In*, Sheryl Sandberg shares the story of Bob Steel at Goldman Sachs.[28] Recognizing that he was mentoring hardly any of the talented women coming in the door, Steel did some honest reflection and realized all his mentoring conversations occurred over drinks or dinner after work—something only men felt comfortable with. Steel stepped up as an ally to level the playing field and developed his breakfast- or lunch-only policy. Now, he has his assistant book mentoring meetings—with women *or* men—only at breakfast or lunch in a café near the office. With this simple tweak, junior women felt more comfortable meeting with him, and neither party had to be concerned about rumors. Within just a few years, he found that he was mentoring as many women as men.

Never flirt. Some men literally invite gossip by being flirty with friends and colleagues at work. Calling a woman your "work wife," giving her a pet name, giving her hugs (assuming you don't hug everyone you encounter), or acting like a smitten teenager when she walks in a room, all amount to a recipe for self-defeat. If you don't do these things with a guy friend at work, don't do them with a woman.

If you socialize outside work, include your partner. In our interviews with women, many appreciated a great male friend and ally—sometimes a male mentor—who included them in an occasional social outing. This was especially helpful for more junior women struggling with a sense of belonging in the organization. Joanne Lipman of *USA Today* told us about one of her allies: "He said, 'Hey, why don't you join my wife and me for dinner this weekend? Bring a date along if you want to.' It was a nice way to create a bond outside of work and wouldn't appear illicit to an outsider." Of course, this strategy also helps to mitigate any feelings of jealousy on the part of a spouse or partner.

Male allies appreciate the myriad ways strong, trust-based friendships with women benefit women, their organizations, and themselves. In addition to deliberate construction of a constellation of female friends (e.g., colleagues, mentors, mentees), they appreciate the importance of reciprocal relationships with women as an opportunity to build their GQ, receive important feedback, and enhance their relational skills. And they are committed to providing care-based support and feedback in turn. Excellent male allies are patient about discerning the unique ideal self and career dream of their close female friends and then finding ways to affirm and reinforce both. Finally, allies are not naive about the reality of gossip, and they are thoughtful about transparency and public perceptions related to cross-gender friendships.

Ally Actions

- **Appreciate the benefits of friendships with women.** Remember that men with strong collegial friendships with women develop sharper relational skills, broader networks, and enjoy more social support.

- **Build a network of female friends.** Develop a community of female friends at work and intentionally mentor several junior women.

- **Create safe-space friendships with several women.** Build trust in relationships with key female colleagues by practicing listening, unconditional regard, mutual self-disclosure, and caring feedback.

- **Make It reciprocal.** Ditch the formality and hierarchy and invite the reciprocal sharing of social support, social capital, information, resources, and authentic sharing of experiences.

- **Discern her ideal self and career dream.** Affirm her ideal self by reflecting that you see those traits and potential and then creating opportunities for her to express her ideal self in the workplace.

- **Don't shirk your honest feedback obligation.** Honor your obligation to provide *carefrontation,* authentic and sometimes difficult observations about her workplace presentation, job performance, or preparedness for advancement.

- **Get out in front of rumors.** Be stringently transparent about meeting with female colleagues and mentees and talk openly—and appreciatively—about your female work friends.

Part Two

Public Allyship

How to Become a Proactive
Ally for Women

6

Watchdog Skills

As the title for part two indicates, it's time to do some upfront advocacy for individual women and for gender inclusion and equity broadly. Time to put that GQ and ally courage to the test. Thus far, we've asked you to learn about the problem and to get better at forging strong relationships with women in the workplace. Now, you've got to take the next step and put some skin in the game when sexism, bias, and harassment rear their heads. We're going to ask you to use your situational awareness when—not if—you see or hear something that demeans or diminishes women in some way.

Recent research reveals that when you ask a typical dude if he's doing everything he can to support gender equality at work, 77 percent of men agree that they are.[1] That's not bad, you say. Here's the problem; in the same survey, only 41 percent of women agree that men are doing all they can. Part of the disconnect here is that many men adopt a form of *passive responsibility* for gender equity in the workplace.[2] This means that they show an outward appearance of taking responsibility (e.g., empathizing with female colleagues, attending a gender-inclusion event), but that they are ambivalent, reluctant, or flat out missing in action when public action or more risky advocacy is required. On the other hand, *active responsibility* for gender equality is evident in clear public behavior; for instance, letting other men know when they say something inappropriate, pointing it out when a woman is not receiving credit for her idea, openly defending women who are targets of sexual harassment, or advocating for equal pay.[3] Remember the two parts to allyship. The first part—showing as little sexism and as much collegiality in your relationships with women as possible—is the easy part. The tough part involves becoming a courageous watchdog for equity, dignity, respect, and fairness in the workplace—then taking action.

Be a watchdog. Be vigilant and then speak up when you hear or see something untoward. This is not about rescuing. Women need rescuers like fish need bicycles. But it is about standing up for your female colleagues even when they're not in the room. Elissa Sangster of the Forté Foundation reminds us that when a guy addresses gender equality openly and publicly, good things happen: "First, it gives other men an awareness they didn't have before about the experiences of women in the workplace. Second, it gives women confidence that they're not imagining sexism and that they can call out allyship from men."

There's also some good science behind our call for men to step up publicly in confronting sexism and bias. Research shows that in the awkward aftermath of that harassing joke or biased comment, if the target of the sexism (a woman) says something, she is evaluated as less positive and competent as a leader than a man (not the target) who calls it out.[4] When a man—someone without apparent vested interest in gender fairness and equity—confronts bias or sexism, observers are much more likely to be positively influenced.[5] Active confrontations from nonvested persons are especially persuasive in shutting down sexist workplace behavior. A series of studies reveal that when a man suggests in a public meeting or other forum that sexism has taken place, the targets of that sexism (women) report more self-confidence (less self-handicapping, higher personal performance and self-esteem) and are less likely to conform to gender stereotypes than when a woman suggests that sexism has taken place.[6] All of this evidence suggests that men constitute crucial allies against sexism but *only if they are willing to say and do something.*

Crush Bystander Paralysis with the Two-Second Rule

So what should you actually *do* when you hear something offensive or discordant with the rules of respect and dignity in the workplace? In our interview with James Rooney, president and CEO of the Greater Boston Chamber of Commerce, he posed this haunting question to men: "What did you do about it? In the moment, if you see or sense something is wrong, ask yourself, what did you do about it?" Survey evidence reveals that men find it hard to speak up and take action in the context of bias, sexism, or subtle harassment, especially in mixed-gender groups or, worse, groups of men.[7] But many of the women we interviewed said these are litmus test moments for male allies. Kimberley Doyle at Catalyst reflected that it is essential that allies speak up and confront unconscious bias and harmful stereotypes: "I do see men struggling with what to do or say because they're not comfortable, so they let it slide. It is critical that as an ally you speak up. Your actions or inactions speak volumes to those you work with. This is a skill that has to be honed and developed, so men need to be intentional in practicing these behaviors."

Consider the impact of male silence on a woman, when, as the "only" in the room, she has to take overt sexism on alone. Christine Spadafor, a board member and attorney, recalled a profound missed opportunity for public male allyship early in her career. As a senior executive, she found herself—the only woman—in a conference room with an all-male group of investment bankers. As they waited for lunch to be delivered, she was reading the *Wall Street Journal*. A major financial institution had taken a full-page ad listing the names of its newest executives. She said, "I scanned the list and commented out loud that there were only a few women out of fifty people on the list. One of the men said, 'You know why that is, don't you, Christine? Because women don't want to work that hard.'" Seconds ticked by, but none of the other men in the room said a word. "I could not remain silent, so I pushed back while this man continued to assert women don't want to work hard." The other men remained silent. "I finally said, 'Excuse me while I go in the corner and set my hair on fire.' It would have been so simple and the right thing to do for at least one man in the room to say something." These are easy opportunities for courage and allyship from men, in this case, a missed opportunity.

Bystander paralysis is a real thing. A lot of men are allies for gender equality in private, but in public, the dreaded bystander effect keeps too many of us on the sidelines, timid and silent in the face of obvious inequity or sexism.[8] Research on the bystander effect reveals that as the size of a group increases, people feel less personal responsibility to act (*diffusion of responsibility*); we tend to expect someone else to act so we don't have to.[9] Decades of social psychological research on this effect confirm that we men are prone to remain silent in a group—especially a larger group—unless we take personal responsibility for confronting sexism and gender discrimination in the moment that it occurs.[10] Men need to go through the following cognitive steps to notice sexism and ultimately address it:

1. Notice the event or sexist comment

2. Define it as a problem

3. Take responsibility for intervening

4. Decide on a course of action

5. Implement the intervention (aka, say or do something before bystander paralysis sets in)[11]

Sounds like a lot of steps, but with practice, all of this cognitive activity can occur within seconds.

Ready Responses to Sexist Comments or Jokes

- Not cool.

- We don't do that here.

- I don't get it. Can you explain that joke to me?

- That wasn't funny.

- Did you really just say that?

- Actually, that's just a bad stereotype.

While this may seem pretty complicated, consider the *two-second rule*. Within two seconds from the instant that sexist comment or demeaning joke rolls off a dude's tongue, say something. Not sure what? Just say, "Ouch!" The beauty of the *ouch intervention* is that it buys you a few extra seconds to formulate a coherent way to communicate what landed the wrong way with you. So, after you tell everyone in the meeting or within earshot in the workplace that something just happened that wasn't okay, you've now got time to formulate your follow-up elaboration. (The sidebar "Ready Responses to Sexist Comments or Jokes" provides a few good responses, recommended by author, coach, and former executive at Adobe Systems, Karen Catlin.)[12]

If you're still at a loss after delivering your courageous "Ouch," it's always perfectly fine to just be honest and say, "That didn't feel right to me. I found it offensive."

See Something? Say Something

To fully counter the bystander effect in the workplace, men have to have sharp situational awareness and then trust their gut instincts when they sense that something they just saw or heard is demeaning women and therefore offensive to everyone. In our interview with Gretchen Carlson, she predicted that male awareness and willingness to intervene could lead to transformative change in the workplace, drawing on a phrase many Americans are already familiar with: "If you see something, say something. Imagine if that message and sentiment were truly integrated into the experience and behavior of men in the workplace. It would be a tipping point."

Saying "Ouch" and calling out everyday sexism is important. We've all got to do it. But there are times when you've got to do more. In instances of sexual harassment, hostile discrimination, and other egregious forms of sexism or even threatened violence, you need to respond instantly and forcefully with a clear zero-tolerance message for the perpetrator and all the bystanders. These are the real "courageous ally" moments. Although violence is never acceptable in the workplace, you'd better be crystal clear about behavior you won't tolerate.

We'll be sharing several examples of full-on, no-holds-barred male allyship. Channel these allies' examples, and you'll be better prepared. Let's start with an example of racism perpetrated against a woman.

Allies are attuned not only to sexism but also to racism directed at female colleagues. When Hideko Sera at the University of Redlands was an undergrad, she took a summer sociology class. During a discussion on race, a student loudly proclaimed, "You know why Japanese people are short? They're so greedy, they don't want to let go of their heavy money bags, so they're short!" The entire class froze. Sera, who is Japanese American, recalled, "I was so angry. I was sitting in the front row and turned around to confront this student. Before I could say anything, an African American guy, a classmate sitting directly behind me, looked at me and whispered, 'Do not say anything. Do not let them see that they got to you.' He could see she was starting to tear up. He said, 'I got you.'" This guy went after the offending student for the racism, explaining factually how immature the student was and owed Sera an apology.

But this guy wasn't finished. "He then looked at the professor and said, 'You are failing us as an educator. It is your job—not my job and not Hideko's job—to manage comments like that and you are failing us as a professor.'" Later, he shared with Sera that as an African American and the son of a single mother, he very much believed in speaking up. He told her, "I am also a man and there are things I can get away with that you can't."

Or, consider this true tale of both a colossal ally failure and subsequent ally win. Dr. Regan Lyon, a major in the air force and a member of the elite special operations surgical team for the US Air Force Special Forces, is an officer, a trauma surgeon, and a certified badass. We interviewed Lyon while she deployed in Afghanistan. She told us that on a previous deployment, her team faced a mass casualty event with nearly thirty wounded Afghani nationals. After about six hours, a medic approached Lyon, concerned about one patient's vital signs and steady drop in blood pressure. She recalled, "As I walked into the trauma bay, an interpreter, a local man, said he was going to get the patient some water. I told him to wait until I had evaluated the patient. He pushed back and said, 'It's okay. I'll get him some water.' I replied, 'No. I need to see if he needs surgery.' He said, 'I know what I'm doing. I'll get him water.' I turned to the interpreter, looked him squarely in the eye, and responded, 'I said *no!*' The no was stern; the medics all froze. The interpreter became defensive and said, 'You didn't have to yell!'" She tried to briefly explain that the patient couldn't have water until she confirmed whether he needed surgery. The interpreter left the room.

Later, the interpreter stormed into Lyon's supervisor's office (another surgeon and a more senior man) and complained stridently. Although she had already briefed her supervisor on the event, he called her into the meeting anyway. The interpreter yelled, "She shouldn't talk to me like that. I won't stand for it! Women don't talk to men like that. If she talks to me like that again, I'll punch her!" To her astonishment, Lyon's supervisor then said, "Now, you see, even in the US, women doctors have to raise their voices more often in order to gain respect from those they work with." Lyon was floored. "I thought, Excuse me!? Here I thought my supervisor was going to stick up for me, and then I get undermined right in front of him. He asked me to apologize to the interpreter. I refused. So, he said he'd apologize for me later."

Later, as her team finished up the last casualty, two men, another surgeon and the team sergeant asked her what was wrong. She shared the story of the interpreter's threat and how their supervisor had asked her to apologize. "These guys lost it. When the supervisor walked in, my surgeon colleague said, 'I think I can speak for the whole team when I say that [the interpreter] isn't ever invited back here.'" When the supervisor attempted to deflect the discussion to the following day, her colleague continued, "We can discuss it whenever you want to, but he's not welcome back. No one threatens one of our team members, regardless of the circumstances." Her team sergeant blew up. Things got very heated. Both allies became more adamant, and the supervisor had to finally agree to never allow the interpreter back under any circumstances. Lyon said, "Part of me wanted to cry. I had been needing this kind of allyship for the previous three months. To this day, those two men from my surgical combat team are the guys I'll call in the middle of the night if I'm having a combat flashback, or need help with a difficult case. I know they're there for me."

There are many other everyday—perhaps more mundane—moments in the workplace that call for you to say something. The following crop up routinely. Think about a good ally response for each.

Unconscious demotions. A guy, perhaps a visitor to your department, assumes a woman on your team is an assistant. If he's really clueless, he might ask her to fetch him a cup of coffee before the meeting. Massachusetts State Representative Tram Nguyen shared her exchange with a lobbyist who hoped to speak with her. Upon spotting the congresswoman, dressed in a business suit, at the Massachusetts State House he asked, "Are you Rep X's aide?" She replied, "No." He persisted, "Are you Rep Y's aide?" Trying to remain cordial, she responded, "No. I'm Representative Nguyen." Apparently unable to absorb this fact, the hapless, biased dude tried one more time, "Oh, you're Rep. Nguyen's aide." As a testament to Congresswoman Nguyen's Herculean equanimity, she did *not* strangle the man but simply replied, "No, I'm the representative."

Be attuned to these unconscious bias-driven slipups. For instance, when a guy assumes that your science director, vice president for technology, or a senior manager is a male and uses the pronoun "he," it's a simple lift to ask a Socratic question that makes him check his assumptions: "I wonder why you would assume _____ is a man?"

Similarly, be vigilant for assumptions that a woman could not possibly be sitting at the table in a key meeting or gathering. Kathleen Hicks, senior VP, Henry A. Kissinger Chair, and director of international security programs at the Center for Strategic and International Studies, provided this ally intervention example. She was traveling with Edward Warner, then assistant secretary of defense, to a meeting at a marine base in Okinawa. She was only in her mid-twenties, but she was the expert on the trip. When they landed, two cars pulled up. One was to take the assistant secretary with the marine general to the briefing. The other was for her and the men's wives to go shopping. The assistant secretary didn't even blink, but said, "No, that is not how we're going to do this. This is Dr. Kathleen Hicks, our expert, and we'll want her in the briefing room." He wasn't worried about upsetting their plans; he was polite but clear.

In a more subtle context, one female venture capitalist (VC) reported that, in a casual pitch meeting with a male founder and two of her male colleagues, "despite my background and skill set being clearly the most relevant, the founder didn't make eye contact and didn't really listen to the questions I asked before answering." This VC explained that as soon as her male colleague—who reports to her—pointed out that she was the general partner, the men looked to her.[13]

Introduction inequities. These inequities occur all the time in academic settings. A group of professors gather to make a presentation at a professional meeting. The chair introduces all the men with "Dr. _____," while the only woman gets introduced by her first name, "and this is Lisa from the University of _____." Say something here. For example, "I'd like to add that I am a big fan of Dr. _____'s work. She is a luminary in the field." Similarly, Rachel Thomas of LeanIn.Org cautions us not to be silent when a woman's role is diminished by a lackluster introduction: "She's not just the marketing manager . . . She's our *marketing manager*, and she's running point on one of our biggest initiatives this year."

Diversion tactics. Be alert to the unnecessary insertion of gender when a man introduces or refers to a female colleague. We hear this frequently: "She's a woman entrepreneur." "She's a female engineer." "She's a lady programmer." Whether intended or not, such gendered qualifiers often diminish the full weight of her professional competence and capability. A simple ally response here might be, "She's an excellent engineer or she's a successful entrepreneur, in the same way that you're a manager, not a male manager."

Be alert to conversations about women that have the effect of diverting attention from their professional prowess. Joan Fallon, CEO of Curemark, gave us this example: "I was at a business event for venture capital and a man was talking about one of my very accomplished female colleagues in terms of what a great cook and mom she was. Instead of focusing on her professional talents, he was talking about her personally. Men need to focus on women as professional colleagues and talk about them that way."

Baseless comments about what women can't do. We've all heard these examples: "Women can't fight, can't lift, can't do math or programming, can't handle the pressure," and so on. When you hear this kind of nonsense, say something. Maybe ask the speaker to furnish supporting research evidence or cease making such claims. Perhaps ask a Socratic question: "That sounds to me like an outdated stereo-type. I wonder if you actually know the research on gender and math-ematics aptitude."

Former US Army Lieutenant General Robert Caslen of West Point gave us this example of ally action: "While serving as a senior officer in Iraq, I'd hear men claiming that women didn't belong or couldn't hack it in combat. I would say, 'That is crazy! We already have women engineers. Every morning before we go out on patrol, those engineers are out clearing the routes of IEDs, putting themselves in harm's way. Many of the engineering platoons are commanded by women. Women *are* in combat. They're out there putting their life on the line, clearing the way for the infantry.'"

Stereotype threats. The research on stereotype threats is clear.[14] Simply reminding a woman of her gender right before she has to per-form a task—specifically tasks that women are stereotypically consid-ered not proficient at—tends to undermine her performance. Doing so heightens her concern that she is at risk of fulfilling the stereotype about her gender. For instance, in a classic study, merely reminding a woman of her gender right before she takes a math test tends to lower her score compared to women who do not have their gender primed before the test. The takeaway? If you're in a meeting or a presentation and someone refers to a stereotype or a female colleague's gender right before she has to perform a task or make a presentation, push back and call out the stereotype: "Sheila's got this! She's the best we have at _____." And if you see stereotype threat taking a toll on a col-league's performance, have a sidebar conversation with her sometime and talk directly about the stereotype threat research. There is also evidence that simply becoming aware of this phenomenon tends to diminish its impact.

As allies, we're always on duty, attending to the words and behav-iors of men around us so we can quickly disrupt sexism, bias, and harassment in any form. Whether these phenomena are subtle and nuanced or more overt and egregious (as in some of our examples), we need the skills to quickly decipher what we hear and the courage to step in immediately. In the next section, we'll cover how male allies can confidently take full ownership of these interventions.

When You Say Something, Own It

This ally action is brief but exceptionally important. When you say something about sexism, bias, or harassment, own it. Do not attribute your concern or offense to the fact that there's a woman in the room or that women might be offended.

Too often, we see men look around the room after another guy delivers an awkward sexist comment or tells a flagrantly inappropriate joke. In that instant, the uncomfortable male observer is looking at the woman in the room, trying to discern if she was offended, as though he needs confirmation that she is bothered before he's willing to say something. If a woman's eye roll or angry expression confirms what he already knows, he may offer a half-assed ally intervention such as, "Hey, Bob, come on, man, there are women in the room." When you confront sexism, own it personally. In the words of Rachana Bhide of Bloomberg Radio News, make "I statements": "It is very powerful for a male ally to use the 'I' pronoun, implying active ownership of his intervention. When he frames it this way, it becomes internalized, not somebody else's practice or solution but his." Some sample "I statements" include:

- "I didn't find that joke to be funny. I don't like the way it demeans women."

- "I'd really appreciate it if you refer to our female colleagues as women, not girls. Thanks for being mindful of that."

- "Ouch! Charles, you just said that women don't get promoted because they don't work as hard and want to be moms instead. I happen to know that is not true, and I'm happy to share the research evidence with you about the causes of disparities in pay and promotion in our industry."

- "Gentlemen, I just heard the word 'bitch' in reference to a woman in this company. That word and every other disrespectful word for women have no place in our culture. I don't ever want to hear that word again in our workplace. We're better than that."

The common theme in every I statement is that something didn't land the right way with you. Don't blame women for your ally work.

Shut Down Sexist Humor and Gossip

Here is a male ally watchdog bulletin: beware of sexist humor. Bros can be especially adept at cloaking all manner of hostile or benevolent sexism in jokes or banter delivered with a punchline and a knowing grin. Here is the problem: humor is often a Trojan horse for sexism; it can immobilize even the best of allies so that we get confused. Ultimately, our reaction time suffers.

Consider a recent series of studies on sexist jokes in the workplace.[15] Researchers found that when a sexist remark was phrased as a joke, the humor decreased perceptions that the speaker was sexist and ultimately decreased the probability that recipients of the message would confront the perpetrator. Perhaps most alarming, the researchers found that even hostile sexists were less likely to be confronted when humor was employed. Delivering sexist messages via humor actually increased tolerance for sexual harassment in the workplace. The takeaway? Humor can make sexism more dangerous to the culture and more difficult for both women and male allies to confront.

Here's what we're up against: raunchy jokes, lewd body-part references, and humor that demeans women and other minority groups too often chalked up to boys-will-be-boys locker-room talk—often with a sigh and a shoulder shrug. Solution? Men need to make it clear that these "boys" can either grow up or take their juvenescent behavior (and their pink slip) elsewhere. In the words of Marc Pritchard, chief brand officer of Procter & Gamble: "It is important to show zero-tolerance for bad behavior . . . It's not enough to stand by while toxic masculinity is on display and say, 'that's not me.' You need to role model for the next generation."[16]

In our interview with former Navy Rear Admiral Peg Klein at the US Naval War College, she expressed genuine appreciation for male leaders who came down hard on the juvenile behavior: "I had a squadron commander who was vigilant. Whenever a group of guys would start talking or behaving in a way that was demeaning or disrespectful of women, he would shut it down hard. I also had a strike group commander who took it upon himself to publicly go after raunchy call signs for male pilots. He didn't wait for women to point these out. His view was that if you have to take your name tag off before going home to see your children or parents, something's wrong and you know it. These men were proactive in stomping out male buffoonery."

While you're in full watchdog mode, remain alert to some other common sexist comments and behaviors. Be ready to shut these down in your own clear but diplomatic way when they rear their heads in the workplace.

Off-topic comments and inappropriate questions. A typical scenario might look like this: a female colleague has just delivered an excellent presentation and some bro in the audience next to you murmurs, "Smart women are so hot," hoping to elicit a laugh or complicit nod. Or, following a candidate interview, a male committee member wonders aloud if the woman just interviewed might be single. Male allies don't sit still in these moments, waiting for a female colleague to do all the work. Call out the perpetrator and shut it down.

Masculinity contests. Recent research uncovered four masculine norms that are highly correlated with organizational dysfunction.[17] They include: *show no weakness* (never admit doubt or mistakes);

strength and stamina (celebrate endurance by working excessive hours); *put work first* (don't let anything interfere with work, even family); and *dog eat dog* (lack of trust coupled with competition between employees). Not only can male allies point to the evidence showing that such ridiculous bravado actually undermines both the bottom line and the workplace culture, they can also model opposing behavior (e.g., leaving at a reasonable hour, publicly leaving early at times for family events or childcare, acknowledging mistakes, and making collaboration a priority).

Pregnancy bias. Women face a motherhood penalty in hiring and promotions. But they also contend with jokes and banter related to their pregnancies that can marginalize and diminish the value of their contributions at work. Be dialed in to catch any comments about a woman's capability while pregnant ("She's in no shape to travel to give that presentation") or sexist attributions about her psychological functioning while pregnant ("She's got a lot of hormones going on right now. She'd probably be too distracted to take on that new account").

Shoot down gossip: Women—especially strong and assertive women in male-dominated organizations—are often the brunt of innuendo and gossip designed to undermine them personally and professionally. When Diane Ryan of Tufts University was a junior army officer and one of the only women in sight, she recalled, "There were all kinds of stories circulating that I would hear secondhand. For example, I was sleeping with my driver, I was a lesbian, etc. My two male allies would hear this stuff and immediately shut it down. They'd say, 'You don't know what you're talking about' and stop the gossip cold."

Beware the Trojan horse of humor and have your internal sexism sifter on overdrive when a guy begins telling a joke in a meeting or when groups of men are engaged in banter around the office. Be on the lookout for gossip, off-topic comments, and stereotypes about pregnancy. Next, we'll take a look at *how* to confront other men.

Be Strategic in Your Approach to Confronting Other Men

Confronting other men for sexism, harassment, bias, and all manner of inappropriate behavior is utterly essential to your identity as an ally. It is also sometimes really hard. Routine confrontation of other men may be the *hardest* part of allyship. Going against your gender tribe's long-standing bro code to promote an equitable and inclusive workplace is where the cost of allyship quickly gets real. We worry that we're the only guy in the room who objects to something that was just said, when, in fact, research shows many other men recognize and don't appreciate sexism; they simply remain silent until an ally like you breaks the spell.[18] Or, we're concerned that offenders may use their power to undermine us at work. Confrontation demands that we overcome self-doubt, marshal courage, and vanquish anxiety about having our masculinity called into question. And then there's the very real conundrum bearing on whether to call out a bad actor publicly, in the moment, or whether you can achieve a better result by approaching him privately, sometime after the offending behavior has occurred.

Why is it so important that men stand willing and ready to confront other men when—intentionally or not—they demean, offend, or harass? First, research on persuasion reveals that how a message is received is less about how a confrontation is worded and more about the in-group identity of the speaker.[19] So, a confrontation intended to change attitudes and behavior has more impact when it comes from someone perceived to be similar, in this case, another dude who can claim, "That's not who *we* [men] are" and "That's not what *we* [guys] do." Second, when a male speaks up and confronts sexism, people—men and women—are often surprised and more prone to take note and listen.[20] Third, there are typically a lot of good guys around. As Subha Barry of Working Mother Media reminded us, "When a man speaks up and says something, it breaks the spell and enables all the other good men with the *fairness gene* to speak up too." Cindy Gallop, CEO, brand and business innovator, agreed: "The moment a man interjects to put an end to an offensive conversation, it changes the atmosphere. It's jarring. The guys around him are going to look at him differently, most respecting that he was willing to do that. Secretly, the right-thinking men around him are saying to themselves, 'Oh, my God, he's right!'" Fourth, remember all those junior men around you. They're always watching. When a male ally speaks up, he's not only effecting change in the room at that moment, he's inviting and empowering the next generation of men to use him as a courageous exemplar. And that is how we change a culture.

In the moment after a demeaning joke, dismissal of a female colleague's idea or expertise, or sexist diatribe about how all mothers should be at home, allies have a crucial and often instantaneous decision to make: Should I confront *publicly* or *privately*? Which approach will have more impact, both on the offender and the culture? Chris Skaluba, director of the Transatlantic Security Initiative, will sometimes opt for a private confrontation when he believes a guy's sexist behavior was unconscious: "I can go in his office, close the door, shake him by the lapels, and say, 'Hey, wake up. I don't know if you recognize what you said or did, but it's not good and it's not reflecting well on you.'" On the other hand, there are times it's important to confront in public. Quite often, failing to say something following an offensive comment dispirits and further damages the workplace environment.

In making that lightning-quick decision about public versus private confrontation, there are a number of factors to consider (see table 6-1 for several of these variables). Each should cross your mind in that instant before you decide whether a public or private confrontation might be most productive.

Before considering some excellent examples, let's think carefully about the art of confronting. Confrontation is a loaded word. We use the term *confrontation* to connote "bringing sexism and exclusion of women to the attention of men who instigate or perpetuate these attitudes and outcomes in their comments and actions." How to most

TABLE 6-1

Private versus public confrontation considerations

Private	Public
The guy is uninformed (clueless) or perhaps immature but generally well intended.	The guy is a malignant, deliberate, serial misogynist with a history of this behavior.
The guy is from an older generation or a different culture and possibly just out of touch with changing values and expectations.	The guy is young enough and acculturated enough to know better.
He appears open to dialogue and feedback about how his behavior offends and disrupts.	He has previously come across as rigid, defensive, and unapologetic regarding his behavior.
The comment or behavior was biased or sexist but not egregiously so; no one was specifically targeted or appears particularly affected.	The comment or behavior was so egregious or offensive that an immediate response to shut it down cold is a necessity.
You have a positive relationship with a well-intended guy that could lend itself to a productive side conversation.	Your friendship is such that a public confrontation would be well received and not come across as an attack.

effectively confront another man is the million-dollar question. The answer is different in each situation and requires genuine wisdom, emotional intelligence, and some hard-earned ally experience. But one general rule is that most men won't respond well to being humiliated, shamed, or angrily or emotionally confronted. Research confirms that hostile and accusatory confrontation that simply labels a guy "sexist" tends to harden defenses and render the confrontation moot.[21]

While we're at it, let's strike favorite insulting terms like curse words, *jerk*, and *idiot* from our confrontation lexicon. Travis McCready, CEO of Massachusetts Life Sciences Center, offers some excellent wisdom: "I try to presume good intent and see a guy's inevitable failings as an opportunity for him to learn. My approach is, 'Here, let me suggest what you should have said or done there.' That way, every confrontation doesn't take the matter to DEFCON 5 or presume the guy is the enemy."

Here are some specific ally strategies to add to your arsenal; keep them within reach and ready to deploy.

Provide an alternative perspective. Sometimes, you can address something biased or sexist by offering a contrasting point of view. So, when a guy insists that a man should never meet alone with a woman, say, "Actually, I don't agree. I don't experience women as dangerous, and I don't buy into the unsupported claim that women often falsely accuse men of harassment. I also object to the idea of communicating to women I work with that I don't trust—either they or I—to remain entirely professional with the door closed. By the way, if you don't meet alone with women, I sure hope you don't meet alone with men. That's just not fair." Similarly, Lisen Stromberg of 3% Conference adds that allies can simply ask, "I wonder if you've considered that women might experience this differently?"

Use personal experiences or relationships. At times, confrontation through self-disclosure can be particularly effective. Sharing how bias or sexism was harmful to you or, more often, a woman close to you can cause other men to do an informed double take, seeing their own problem behavior through a new lens. Rachana Bhide shared that "I've seen guys say to a group of men, 'My wife experienced this at work and it's really f—d up. I don't want women to experience that here.' This kind of personal story, with connection to women you care about, can be deeply influential for other men."

Shape behavior by balancing confrontation with reinforcement. Famous behavioral psychologist B. F. Skinner was right: it is far easier to shape desired behavior with reinforcement. We have developed a couple of hashtags as a way to keep feedback lighthearted. Let's face it, "bro" is often an endearing term among men; short for *brother*, bro lets the guy on the receiving end of your intervention know you see him as part of your tribe and that your heart is in the right place. First, when a guy goes off the rails with bias, sexism, or harassment, try #BroNo!

You can pull him aside after a meeting and have a #BroNo conversation with him or pull out your phone right there in the meeting and loudly spell out your text to him. It could be fun and make the point. But don't forget to reinforce someone—maybe it will be the same guy later in the very same meeting—who shows some gender awareness, an inclusive mindset, or thoughtful consideration of his female colleagues. At that moment, try #GoBroGo! Allies can move the dial on shaping the behavior of other men with an artful blend of challenge and reinforcement.

Sometimes, humor helps. Sheryl Sandberg shared that "[i]n an earlier job my boss kept calling me by my last name in a demeaning way. He'd shout, 'Sandberg!' Or, Sandberg, get over here!' He would never do that to my male peers. So, a couple of my male ally peers started publicly and loudly calling each other 'good-looking Sandberg' and 'Asian Sandberg' to level the playing field and make the boss aware of what he was doing. It felt really good to have them take my side and show support." Particularly when you've got an existing relationship with a guy and if humor is part of your brand in the workplace, try a short humorous observation as an intervention. So, when that guy implies that women belong at home caring for children, try, "Come on, man! Time to stand upright and stop dragging those knuckles!"

Show an offender some empathy when you call him out. Hilary Jerome Scarsella, a theological studies researcher provided another example of ally confrontation.[22] She was sitting at the airport, working on her laptop, near a guy she had just met at a conference. They were both invited speakers. Another man sat down across from them and started talking—a lot. He found out they were speakers at a conference on theology, trauma, and sexual abuse. He learned they had graduate degrees and thought this was really interesting. Launching into an explanation of his belief that everything happens for a reason, he droned on and on. She listened and asked him questions, letting him know kindly that she disagreed. He worked hard to show her he was right. She told him she understood his perspective but disagreed. He reiterated his points again and then said it was great talking with her but he's going to catch his flight.

Then, her new friend leaned forward as the man was about to walk away and said, "Dude, you missed an opportunity. You had an expert in theology and trauma sitting in front of you. You didn't ask her a single question. You didn't try to learn anything from her. You know she has advanced degrees and is published, but you just tried to show her that you know more about her work than she does. You missed out! Big fail, man." The man got uncomfortable, sat back down, and asked her to teach him for five minutes before he had to board his plane. Her new friend wasn't having it. He said, "No, you have to live with the consequences of your mistake. Time's up." That is how to be an ally.

Hold Hiring and Promotion Committees Accountable

Ever wonder about the seemingly insurmountable gender pay gap in most industries, the inability of many organizations to retain the talented women they recruit, or the difficulty many companies have promoting women to executive and board of director positions? A well-established cause is the bias and gender-discriminating practices at hiring and promotion milestones. Hiring and promotion committees need watchdogs. Not only should male allies volunteer for service on key hiring and awards committees, they should be vigilant for gender-fair practices in application reviews and committee deliberations.

Next time you serve on a hiring or promotion committee, stay attuned for the following gender-biased red-flag phrases and be ready to call them out.[23]

"I'm not sure that candidate is a good fit." Translation: "I can't see a woman fitting in here." "I can't see a woman doing that job." When someone casts doubt on a female candidate using the culture-fit objection, ask for a very specific work-relevant definition. The same might be said for the classic, "I don't see executive presence in that candidate." Push back on these and other vague concepts and demand clear operational definitions so that all candidates are assessed objectively on clear behavioral indicators of required skills or experiences.

"His résumé is really impressive." As a watchdog, ensure that everyone's résumé is graded on the same scale and criteria. Have committee members calibrate their ratings on a couple of practice applications before moving forward with the real reviews. Discuss discrepancies. Establish clear rating scales for all relevant job criteria. Merely raving about someone's résumé without specific ties to objective job criteria is a bit like raving about culture fit. It's just too vague and likely to disadvantage women. At times, it may be quite useful to remove all names and other identifying information from applications so that they effectively become more gender and culture blind.

"Sounds like she's a busy mom." Watchdogs shut down any comment inferring a candidate's family obligations. We know that women identified as mothers are 79 percent less likely to be hired than identical candidates without children.[24] Don't let this motherhood penalty or other speculation about a candidate's personal life disadvantage parents, very often women. Another iteration of the motherhood penalty involves assumptions about what positions she can't—or wouldn't want to take on—at work. For instance, watch for this gem, "She wouldn't want the job given all the travel required." Ouch! This is an obvious assumption and one likely to undermine the hiring or promotion of an identified female parent. Again, be ready: "What I hear you saying is that parents are ineligible for this job? Surely, you're not suggesting that only mothers—not fathers—wouldn't want this job? I'm going to go out on a limb here and guess that she knows this promotion involves travel, and that she has children. If she's the best candidate, shouldn't she make this decision?"

"She's not very likable." Again, what? First, is likability a clearly articulated job requirement? Second, if so, what validated measure are you using to assess all candidates on this dimension? Third, what specifically is not to like? Common gender bias requires women to be "nice," "deferential," and "modest," while those implicit criteria are not required of men. Be ready with your Socratic bias-interrupting question: "I hear you saying that she came across as straightforward, no-nonsense, and efficient in her communication. These sound like things we'd praise in a man. Could there be a double standard at work here?"

"I'd like to see her prove she can handle [responsibility she's already shouldered successfully] before we promote her." Be alert to the prove-it-again bias, more likely to limit promotions for women than men.[25] Research shows that men get a pass for hiring and promotion based on potential. Women, on the other hand, have to prove themselves again and again. If you see a committee ignoring obvious evidence of success in a candidate's job history, perhaps communicating skepticism that she's really experienced or competent enough, be sure to call it out.

You can implement some additional ally strategies for hiring and promotion. First, remain humble about the truth that your own gender biases can sneak into perceptions of job candidates. Check yourself periodically and empower committee members to collegially call out apparent bias when it appears. Second, assign at least one person on the committee to be an appointed bias interrupter. If any of the red flags we've described (or others) appear, the interrupter should say something immediately. Third, be vigilant to committee conversations about female candidates. If you hear something that feels off, ask the committee, "Would we be having this conversation or would you be raising that concern about a man?" Flipping the script on gender can be an excellent strategy for drawing attention to implicit bias. Last, when forming committees for hiring, awards, and promotions, ensure diversity among committee members themselves. Robert

Cabana, of the Kennedy Space Center, commented, "I deliberately have a diverse panel review all candidates and awards. I also specifically ask panel members to ensure diversity is taken into account when pushing people forward as job or award finalists. The same is true for major job assignments. I want a diverse pool of applicants for every position." Insist that any pool of job candidates includes not just one woman, but at least two women. Statistically, research shows that women have almost no chance of being hired if they are the only female candidate for the job. When you double that to two women, they have a 50 percent chance, and if you increase the number to three, they have a 67 percent chance of being hired.[26] Demand a diverse talent pool if you want a diverse workforce.

We offer some clear guidance about crushing gender-based salary discrepancies. Men, especially men in positions of power (e.g., hiring managers, promotion committee chairs) are in an excellent position to understand how and why a gender pay gap manifests in their organizations.[27] On hiring and promotion committees, be vigilant to discrepancies in starting salary offers for men versus women. At annual pay-step discussions, be alert to systematic undervaluing of the contributions of women. Work to create a level playing field for salary negotiations. If women are unaware that aspects of a job offer are negotiable, or if women are socialized not to negotiate salary as assertively as men, then gender pay gaps will manifest from the start of employment.

The male editor of a publishing house reflected on hiring for a senior position. The top candidate was a male. The company made him a salary offer, and he came back with a modest counteroffer, something that seemed reasonable. Then the HR department person jumped in and said, "That is exactly where gender disparity in salaries comes from." The editor was surprised, but then the HR person elaborated, "Men do this and get rewarded for it. Women don't do this and so end up being inadvertently penalized." The editor had never thought about it that way. It was an illuminating observation and changed his approach to hiring.

Be a Voice for Those Not in the Room

Allies don't take a day off from allyship, and they don't switch off the watchdog radar just because there's no woman in the room. When no women, people of color, or other underrepresented groups are present in a meeting or discussion, allies have to be particularly vigilant to the risk for exclusion. Kendrick Brown at the University of Redlands urges men to speak up when no female colleagues happen to be present: "When there is no woman around to see you do it, that is the time when you really become a public ally for women. It might sound like this: 'Look folks, glad we're having this conversation, but we're missing some key people, some key voices, and we're not considering a full range of perspectives as a result.' You've got to put yourself out there when women are not in the room to have a voice."

Allies also think about policies and procedures—both existing and future—in terms of how they might work for their female colleagues. If your startup doesn't yet have a parental leave policy, ask about it. Don't wait for your first pregnant colleague to have to advocate for herself. Or, how about the first person adopting a child? Brown said, "I try to ask out loud whether specific policies and procedures will work for everyone. Not just men, but how about women or people with different identities? This reflects my commitment to a workplace that works for everyone." You've got some serious ally savvy when you're sitting in a facilities committee meeting—comprising exclusively dudes—and you ask, "Do we have adequate close parking for pregnant women?" "Have we asked our female colleagues if we need more or better lactation rooms?" Now that's a watchdog!

Be vigilant to environments or activities that don't feel welcoming to women. Janet Foutty of Deloitte cautioned that men should be more aware that Scotch whiskey tastings, motorcycle trips, golf outings, and sports bars might not encourage office bonding or be company social events that make women feel comfortable, confident, and welcome. To her list, let's add beer pong, strip bars, and mechanical bull-riding—all real-life examples. So, when a group of men is planning something clearly exclusive, you've got to step up: "Have you really thought that through? Do you really think our female colleagues will appreciate that? How about if we survey a few of them to find out?"

Sometimes finding the inclusive office-activity sweet spot requires a learning curve, some patience, and a persistent desire to learn what works for everyone. Kimberley Doyle of Catalyst told us how her boss really made a point of engaging his entire team outside the office. He understood the importance of making a personal connection. He started by implementing after-work happy hours, but a number of parents in the company weren't able to attend given their family obligations. Then, he tried a breakfast event, but again, colleagues had challenges with early-morning family routines. So, he shifted to lunches—taking people to lunch on the company's tab. Who doesn't enjoy a free lunch at work? What really struck her was his desire to ensure that nobody was left out.

Be alert to ensuring fair attribution of credit for work. In group projects, on coauthored papers, or any time a mixed-gender team is involved, women consistently receive less credit for contributions than men. Be a watchdog for fair attribution of credit to female colleagues. Point out their contributions and ask incisive questions about what criteria justify assignment of first authorship or top billing.

Have Your Evidence-based Inclusion Pitch Cued Up

One final watchdog skill for the unabashed and public male ally is to have your data-supported gender-inclusion elevator pitch ready to deploy at all times. We can guarantee that if you're disrupting sexism and bias, shutting down demeaning humor, and calling out exclusion of women, there will be moments when some men are going to push back, saying "Dude, what is your problem anyway?" Or, "Why are you so uptight about the gender thing?" In that instant, take a breath, lower your defenses, nod, and start with, "That's an excellent question. Here is my concern about ____ [e.g., sexist banter, biased language, harassing humor]." Then, calmly give them some of the evidence from chapter 1 regarding current gender disparities in the workplace and the consequences of inequality and gender exclusion for women, men, and your organization's bottom line. A matter-of-fact presentation of data can be far more powerful in opening the mind of a guy who believes the workplace is a gender-blind meritocracy than an angry insult or defensive response.

This is about your brand as an ally. After you've done your homework, studying the issues and hearing stories about gender inequity from your female work friends, you've got to share what you're learning with others in the workplace, including colleagues, team members, and friends.[28] You might consider sharing relevant articles on your social channels or data about the pay gap, retention of women, or climate survey results—both in your industry and in your own company—with male colleagues.[29] The key is to consider how to make allyship a consistent element of your public identity.

Ally Actions

- **Crush bystander paralysis with the two-second rule.** Practice rapid disruption techniques such as the "ouoh" intervention to combat bystander paralysis and workplace sexism using a well-learned arsenal of responses.

- **See something, say something.** Practice watchdog vigilance in sifting the workplace environment for sexist comments and behavior; then be clear and decisive in shutting it down.

- **When you say something, own it.** When you publicly intervene to disrupt inappropriate language or behavior, take full ownership. Do not attribute your concern to the presence of women.

- **Shut down sexist humor and gossip.** Don't be fooled by sexism masquerading as humor; watch for off-topic comments and intrusive questions directed at women and call it out.

- **Be strategic about your approach to confronting other men.** Presume most men have good intent; frame confrontations around sexism as a learning or growth opportunity, while using your experience to decide whether to confront publicly.

- **Hold hiring and promotion committees accountable.** Be alert to red flags for gender bias when evaluating candidates and push for multiple female candidates in every pool of applicants.

- **Be a voice for those not in the room.** Be vigilant to who is not included in key meetings and conversations and speak up for inclusion.

- **Have your evidence-based inclusion pitch cued up.** Know the evidence about why gender inclusion and gender balance in hiring, retention, and promotion are good for men, women, and organizational outcomes.

7

Meetings: Dangerous Places If You're Not a Dude

In meetings, men typically have few concerns. We assume we'll have a spot at the table. We speak up and expect to be heard. We are rarely interrupted, and we expect to receive full credit for our ideas. Historically speaking, meetings have been comfortable *manspaces*. But this is often not the case for our female colleagues. For many women—particularly those in male-dominated organizations—meetings can feel like an episode of *Mad Men*. Women report being talked over (*manterrupted*), dudes hijacking their ideas and dismissing their expertise, getting tasked with office housework, and sometimes tolerating male showboating designed to undermine their credibility or divert attention from their contributions.[1] Many workplaces exude a culture in which women are disinclined to speak up in meetings. Men tend to dominate discussions, on average, speaking for 75 percent or more of allotted meeting time.[2] And when women do speak up, they can be ignored or ridiculed, or a loud male will co-opt their ideas.

A gendered double standard exists even when using humor in workplace meeting presentations.[3] Research reveals that when men add humor to a business meeting presentation, observers view them as having higher levels of status (e.g., respect, prestige) and give them higher performance ratings and leadership potential assessments. However, when women add the same humor to the same presentation, people view them as having lower status, rate their performance lower, and consider them less capable as leaders. This is no laughing matter for our female friends.

When a woman is the "only" in a meeting, each of these risks is exacerbated. Christine Spadafor told us: "Even today with my senior executive status, as the only woman in a room, it is still a challenge for me to be heard. At times, women's voices are not heard by men. Men move the conversation forward without acknowledging her idea, then repeat her exact idea to their own acclaim, interrupt her, or feel the need to mansplain."

In this chapter, we offer six strategies for male allies focused on stepping up as watchdogs and accomplices for women in meetings. These strategies address making meetings deliberately inclusive, safe spaces in which everyone can express opinions; share creative ideas; and feel valued for their unique contributions to the team.

Practice Vigilance and Mitigate Meeting Risks

In September 2018, during a televised White House press conference, the president called on CNN reporter Jim Acosta. When Acosta stood up, he said, "Thank you very much. If you don't mind, after I finish, if one my female colleagues such as ____, ____, or ____ could go after me that would be great." Politics aside, it was a nice example of a man both noticing meeting dynamics (in this case, that female reporters in the room were being systematically excluded), and then using his voice and his privilege to do something about it.

Allies apply situational awareness (SA)—introduced in chapter 2—to workplace meetings. They are familiar with the evidence showing that women are less often heard, more often interrupted, and far more likely to have men either disregard or steal their good ideas. Consequently, allies are vigilant in meetings. They start by reining in their own manspread, creating more space for others. They are alert to who is seated at the table and who is relegated to the periphery of the room, and they consistently invite female colleagues to join them at the table. On occasion, they deliberately mix up seating arrangements so that everyone can experience how it feels to sit in the power seats and along the sidelines. In the same way, they change up the order in which they ask people in meetings to report or respond to questions. They scrutinize meeting interactions with specific attention to who is speaking, who is remaining silent, and who tries to join in only to be interrupted or verbally run over. As they take in meeting dynamics, they are always calculating how to ensure that everyone's voice is included.

As you might have guessed, vigilance in meetings is only step one. Next, you've got to speak up and do something to level the meeting playing field for your female colleagues. When men don't speak up, women notice. Amy Orlov of the Forté Foundation told us, "During my time in business school, when my idea would be taken and I wouldn't be credited for it, there were often men at the table. They just didn't speak up. Allies need to see and say something." Why is it so important for men to call out gender-biased meeting hijinks? In male-dominated workplaces, men naturally listen to men. When women point out an interruption or demotion, they're dismissed as oversensitive complainers. Anne-Marie Slaughter of New America said it best: "Male allies are really aware of unconscious bias. So, when a man interrupts a woman, doesn't give her much time to speak, or takes credit for her work, it's always better if a man says, 'You just interrupted her,' than if another woman does. Every woman in the room is aware of what just happened, but they're also thinking that if they say something, they'll just be seen as prickly."

The remaining five strategies in this chapter provide specific male ally behaviors to deploy in meetings, but these two tangible ally actions will get you started. First, bear witness to what you have observed in meetings yourself. When you see a woman get interrupted and talked over at a meeting, or when a dude restates a woman's idea or suggestion later in the meeting and ends up getting credit for it, do something to disrupt this behavior in real time. But you should also go to her and tell her what you just saw. This powerful ally action validates her experience and lets her know she's not imagining it. This conversation should include some brainstorming about how she—and other women—can mitigate these issues in the next meeting as well as how you plan to intervene moving forward.

Second, offer to have pregame and debrief meetings with women. This may be an especially powerful ally action for junior women or only-women in meetings. If meetings are fraught with gender bias and tend to sideline women, huddle up and have a quick strategy session pre-meeting and then debrief after. What worked, what didn't, what curveballs came across the plate, and how might you approach the next meeting?

Employ "Pull" Strategies to Elicit Women's Voices

Women don't speak up as often as men in meetings, especially when they are a minority.[4] There are lots of reasons why. Some women are socialized from an early age to defer to men, to speak when spoken to, or to hold back until there is a clear break in the conversation. Others have been interrupted, disregarded, or disrespected so often, they've quit trying. And in male-dominated organizations and professions, women can become hyperaware of their "unicorn" status; with few female role models, they can be reluctant to speak up as the inevitable token woman in the room. But a bigger factor is at play here, which has to do with the masculine corporate meeting culture. In meetings, we tend to reward the fastest and loudest (often men) and don't deliberately make space for the voices of women. The outcome of silent or reluctant women, of course, is a profound loss of wisdom, creativity, and brilliance in decision making, visioning, and strategizing.

The male ally solution here? Whenever feasible—especially when you hold positional authority, status, or social capital—use what former Navy SEAL Commander Mike Wisecup termed a *pull approach*: "In meetings, I developed a pull attitude. I would ask very specific and direct questions of those people who weren't normal contributors. I was most aware of this with women, especially those who were more junior. I would make sure to seek their input in some way so that the guys in the room who had the most experience and had that alpha male bravado didn't steal the show just because they were the ones who talked first." Another way to frame the pull approach for your team is to go around the horn. Every former little league player or baseball fan knows the expression "around the horn." After an out, with no runners on base, the infielders toss the ball around to one another to stay loose and engaged. In meetings, institute your own version of an around-the-horn strategy to ensure that—at some point—every voice and viewpoint at the table is heard. Make it a meeting norm and ex-pectation to pause the conversation and go around the table to hear from anyone who has not yet had an opportunity to speak. This, and other norm-disrupting pull strategies, can ensure a more thorough sampling of perspectives in the room.

The following four specific pull strategies for allies ensure that women have both space and direct encouragement to contribute in meetings.

Tell a woman why her voice is essential to mission success. See a smart, creative work friend who tends to keep quiet in key meetings? Tell her in advance of the next meeting what you value about her perspective and why she needs to speak. Nick Childs, chief creative officer of Reprise Digital, uses this strategy: "I have a side conversa-tion with her and explain that her voice and ideas need to be heard. It's important because we hired her for a reason. Diverse perspectives make a difference. We're all better because she is here. Now, I have a role in making sure she is heard."

Encourage her to throw the first punch. In your pregame conversa-tions with women who are not being included and heard in meetings, encourage them to assertively insert themselves in the conversation early. Christine Spadafor explained why this matters: "I am five feet four, I have a small voice, I don't take up a lot of space. So, I show up prepared, I sit in a key place at the table, and I get in the conversation early. If you do not speak up in the first five or ten minutes, no one knows you're there. This ensures my presence is acknowledged, that I will be a contributor, and that I will be heard."

Create space and then actively listen. Resist the temptation to talk first. When the same men don't always wade in, dominating a meeting from the outset, there is more space for other's voices. Instead of talking, look around the room. Make eye contact with some female colleagues, and use your best welcoming nonverbal cues to encourage them to dive in. Then, listen generously, without interrupting or formulating your response. Just listen.

Ask a woman a specific question. Here's a pull strategy that pairs nicely with a public affirmation of a work colleague's experience or expertise. If you see a woman at the table who hasn't yet contributed to the conversation, try asking her a direct question to pull her in: "I know Patrice has done work in this area before. I'd love to hear your thoughts, Patrice." "You always have such interesting perspectives on these questions, Tanya. I'm really curious what your take is." If you come off as pandering, this will flop. Say it because you mean it. Then listen intently, and even take notes.

Interrupt Manterruptions

Women are interrupted midsentence twice as often as men are.[5] What's more, we men often don't even notice it. The tendency for guys to interrupt our female colleagues is not limited to corporate meetings and boardrooms. A recent study of Supreme Court transcripts revealed that male justices interrupt female justices approximately three times as often as they interrupt each other during oral

arguments.[6] The phenomenon of men talking over women is so ubiquitous that it has spawned a new word in the workplace: *manterrupt-
ing*. Joanne Lipman of *USA Today* encouraged allies to "watch for the
interruption. If a woman is getting cut off, you need to have her back.
To be an ally, you need to point it out, then bring attention back to
what she was saying. When you interrupt the interrupter, point out
that someone was speaking, and express interest in hearing the rest
of what she was saying, you publicly recognize the value of the person
who was speaking while calling out someone else's effort to marginalize her."

So how can allies intervene? Implement the following strategies.

Use the universal stop sign. As soon as that dude dives in, cutting off
a female colleague, simply hold up your hand in the universal gesture
indicating *Whoa! Stop!* As you do, calmly but clearly say something
like, "Just a minute, Bob. I was really interested in what Olivia was
saying. Let's have her finish her thought." Not too confrontational, yet
crystal clear. If Bob bulldozes on or gets angry after such a thoughtful interruption, he's probably lacking in the emotional intelligence
department, and others will recognize that.

Use the universal time-out sign. Author Jessica Bennett offers a
brilliant strategy for disrupting male interrupters in meetings.[7] Use
a sports-related signal—the time-out sign—to call attention to interruptions. This move is brilliant because many men love sports,
so stopping an interruption with an easily recognized sports signal
provides allies a way to use dude language to do the job. When that
interrupter strikes, pretend you're an NFL referee, and hold up both
hands in the time-out gesture. To add some levity, whistle and say,
"Dude, that's five yards for unnecessary interrupting! Now, let's have
_____ finish her thought."

Establish a clear no-interruption policy for meetings. If you're
in a leadership role, be proactive and establish a clear policy of no

interruptions for all of your meetings. Then, kindly and consistently enforce it. If you're not the leader, but you see interruptions of women occurring, suggest such a policy. Again, make it fun, if possible. How about using a yellow Post-it Note that a rotating meeting referee can toss when an interruption infraction occurs? Maybe the first offender gets tagged to take notes or bring coffee to the next meeting. You get the idea.

Now, that you're SA is attuned to interruptions and you're prepared to shut them down, let's move on to some male ally antidotes for another common meeting risk for women: men ignoring or dismissing women's clear expertise and experience.

Call Out Her Expertise

Allies look for opportunities to point to a female colleague's expertise and experience in meetings. Too often, either a woman with clear subject-matter expertise is excluded from a key meeting or her expertise is overlooked, minimized, or actively dismissed. In these moments, an ally has to publicly point attention to her subject mastery. The following ally actions are some strategies you can implement immediately.

Insist that she be present at key meetings. Earlier in this book, we highlighted the importance of including women. Here is a more nuanced aspect of inclusion. If a female colleague has crucial experience or expertise relevant to a proposed meeting agenda, recommend that she be invited. Even more important, if her work, her accounts, or her creative idea will be discussed, *demand* that she be invited. Better still, recommend that she take the lead and kick off the meeting. If you're not getting a positive response to these proposals, clearly ask meeting organizers something like this: "I'm confused. Why would we hold a discussion about Lindsay's work, or about a topic on which Lindsay is clearly an established subject-matter expert and not include her?"

Publicly identify her expertise. When women are a minority group in the workplace, they can fly under the radar of key leaders; their voices, previous experiences, and accomplishments and credentials can be easily overlooked. In key meetings, allies can sponsor female colleagues by calling out their expertise. It could be something as simple as, "You know, Maya is really the expert on this topic. I really want to hear what she has to say." Keith Reinhard, chairman emeritus of DDB Worldwide, recommended tying a woman's expertise to the specific mission at hand: "We as men can sponsor a woman and say, 'Wait a minute, you need to hear what she has to say about this because she has a unique and interesting perspective that could really advance our cause.'"

Share a personal testimonial. This is an easy one guys, simply share what you've learned from a female colleague in a meeting as a strategy for calling attention to her unique capabilities. Author Karen Catlin shared this example from a former male supervisor when she worked at Adobe Systems: "We were in a big leadership meeting, and Digby said out loud, 'What I've learned from Karen Catlin is ____' and he went on to amplify something I had said, recasting it in Adobe-speak, using just the right language and emphasis. He gave me public credit. His gesture caused people in that meeting—who might not have known me before that moment—to attach real credibility to me." Sponsorship through compliments is a terrific way to boost a colleague's reputation and credibility. It's also low-hanging fruit: "What I learned from ____ is that ____. It really shifted my thinking about ____ and made me better at ____."

Toss her a lateral pass. Next time you're in a meeting that men have been dominating, look around and identify a female colleague who hasn't yet had the floor. Then, insert yourself into the conversation, and at the end of your comment, figuratively pass the football (microphone) to your female colleague with a transitional comment about why you'd like to hear her thoughts on the topic at hand: "Anyway, that's my two cents . . . but I just realized that Mary has way more experience in this area than I do. What do you think, Mary?"

Redirect questions to the expert. Too often, when a woman with deep and irrefutable expertise is sitting at a meeting table, questions bearing on her area of distinct capability and experience will be directed to men instead of her. Be ready to deftly redirect the conversation back to the expert: "That's a great question. It occurs to me that this is Francesca's specialty. She's got most of us beat when it comes to experience with this. What are your thoughts, Francesca?"

Give Credit Where It's Due

Women experience two salient but interconnected risks when they offer killer ideas in mixed-gender groups. First, the group ignores and marginalizes their ideas and proposals. Second, a male later restates these inspired thoughts so that the group finally hears them and greets them with positive acclaim; he gets the credit for her creative work.

In Greek mythology, Cassandra was granted the gift of prophecy; she could see the future and would tell the truth, warning others about what was to come. The problem? Apollo placed a curse on Cassandra; she could forever see the future, but nobody would ever listen to her. In what is known today as the *Cassandra syndrome*, women in the workplace are far more likely than men to report having their contributions minimized or entirely ignored.[8] Hideko Sera of the University of Redlands recalled that "when I was stepping into academic leadership, one of my colleagues warned me not to fall prey to the Cassandra syndrome. He warned me that people would tune me out when I said something important, only to listen intently when a male said something similar."

Amplification is an ally strategy designed to counteract the risk that women's ideas and creative contributions will be ignored. When you amplify a female colleague in a meeting, you simply reiterate a great idea or observation she shares, increasing its importance and attributing it to her at the same time. The amplification strategy is credited to women working in the Obama administration. Recognizing that men would often downplay or flat-out ignore their ideas in meetings, these women developed the innovative strategy of deliberately drawing attention to and reaffirming each other's comments and recommendations. Guys can join the fun and amplify female colleagues' excellent ideas, too.

There are just two caveats when amplifying a work colleague's contribution. First, be sincere. Don't just parrot everything she says. It will fall flat. Instead, actively listen for the gems, those creative breakthroughs and fresh perspectives that everyone should hear and clearly attribute to her. Second, always remember that you are amplifying her ideas; you are not *legitimizing* them. Her awesome contribution was legitimate before you amplified it.

The second part of this ally strategy is to be aware that after women contribute creative and innovative ideas, not only are the ideas often minimized, but they can also be attributed to a man.[9] This experience is so common for women that terms have arisen to describe the phenomenon in meetings. Two of our favorites include being *hepeated* or having her idea *bropropriated*. So what's an ally to do when he bears witness to this? Some surefire ally actions range from amplifying her idea so that it is not ignored to steering credit for ideas back to their source.

Reinforce her idea before anyone else can steal it. Recognizing that women's ideas are far more likely to be ignored, have your awesome-idea radar on in meetings. Then, when a female colleague contributes something really smart and innovative, start nodding and smiling. Then, chime in—don't interrupt—right away with a verbal shout-out: "I think that's an inspired solution, Maggie. I've never heard anyone recommend that approach before. We should definitely consider that option." Quick, terse amplifications have the effect of validating her comment, unequivocally reinforcing for everyone in the room that it is her idea.

Ask a question. Follow up a great comment with a question designed to continue and deepen the discussion about her idea. The ongoing discussion will help solidify the truth that this was her idea.

Make her idea a discussion or action item. Gloria Feldt, cofounder and president of Take the Lead, suggests making a female colleague's excellent recommendation or contribution an action item for further discussion at a subsequent meeting. This ensures the idea survives and continues to be correctly attributed.

Immediately call out the co-opting with a Socratic question. As soon as a guy restates what a female colleague offered earlier in the meeting—perhaps others are already chiming in with praise for his awesome idea—ask a thoughtful question designed to remind everyone in the room who generated the idea in the first place: "I'm confused. How is that different from what Amber suggested a few minutes ago?"

Deftly attribute the idea back to the woman who generated it. As soon as a man repeats what a woman said, say something affirming to simultaneously reinforce the male speaker while slyly stating, in no uncertain terms, who came up with the idea: "I agree with you, John. Emma's idea was spot on. We should run with it." Author Sally Helgesen pointed out that this strategy avoids unhelpful confrontation, while clearly assigning attribution to the woman who came up with the idea: "Just say something like, 'You're right. That was a really smart idea of Jennifer's,' then build the following discussion around the truth in the room that Jennifer is the originator of the idea."

Continue to promote her idea after the meeting. Use email or social media after the meeting to amplify her idea with shares, retweets, or perhaps some good old-fashioned emojis such as hand-claps, thumbs-up, or bunches of 100's.[10] Consider hitting "reply all" to meeting attendees with a quick note of agreement with her suggestion. And look for an opportunity to tell a key influencer in the organization who might be in a position to fund or implement her idea.

Evenly Distribute Office Housework

We suspect the following scenario might be familiar.

You are in a meeting, and your manager brings up a project that needs to be assigned. It's not particularly challenging work, but it's time consuming, unlikely to drive revenue, and probably won't be recognized or included in your performance evaluation. As your manager describes the project and asks for a volunteer, you and your colleagues become silent and uneasy, everyone hoping that someone else will raise a hand. The wait becomes increasingly uncomfortable. Then, finally, someone speaks up: "Okay, I'll do it."[11]

Recent research evidence shows that this reluctant volunteer is far more likely to be a woman.[12] Women volunteer for tasks that don't lead to promotions more than men do, and they are far more likely to be directly asked to take them on. Women report doing more administrative tasks (such as taking notes in meetings and organizing social events) than men at rates that range from 21 percent to 48 percent.[13] In academe, women faculty are tasked more than male faculty with on-campus service, student advising, and teaching-related activities, while male faculty enjoy more time for research-related activities.[14] Any idea which activity is more likely to lead to academic promotion? You guessed it. Score another one for the guys.

We are talking about office housework. We all avoid housework at work when we can. Examples include social committees, party planning, office administration, cleaning the common kitchen, bringing snacks or coffee to meetings, and training interns. Women find themselves either volunteering or being *voluntold* to take on these activities that shouldn't have any gender tied to them, but do. Not only does the assignment of office housework to women implicitly push them to enact secretary, mom, and caretaker stereotypes, but it also results in serious career consequences for female colleagues. Saddled with low-visibility and low-impact housework, women will inevitably advance more slowly in their careers.

Office housework has sobering consequences for female colleagues and is one more contributing factor to gender disparities in the workplace. Allies need to be ready to respond in any meeting where nonpromotion-enhancing work assignments, collateral duties, or our favorite "special opportunities" come up, and volunteers are solicited. These moments are particularly dicey for women in mixed-gender groups. Research reveals that when both men and women are at a meeting, women receive 44 percent more requests to volunteer than men.[15] Women are also more likely to say yes to such requests when men are in the room. As always, there are some ally actions to take when housework is handed out.

Be attuned to implicit gender assumptions about jobs. Most of us are guilty at some time of assuming that women are just better at ____ (add your favorite office housework chore here), or believing that because she volunteers to take notes or clean the breakroom that she must really love it. Implicit assumptions about the best candidate for a domestic task can be very subtle. The same rule applies to assigning diversity committee members or asking for volunteer mentors for a women's leadership initiative. Push back on assumptions—expressed or implicit—that only women can fulfill these roles.

Say something when housework is directed to a female colleague. All of us will be sitting in a meeting when a thankless, nonpromotion-relevant task gets dropped on the plate of one of the few women in the room; perhaps it will be that work colleague sitting next to you. What a great opportunity! How about volunteering to take it yourself, and when you do, recommend her for a more significant role or project. At the least, you have an opportunity to ask about the rationale for these housework assignments. Author Kim Elsesser recalled: "I was in a technology group at one point. There were only two women in the group. We were doing a charity drive, and the only two women in the group were asked to be the drive fund collectors. My boss noticed it right away, called it out, and explained why it wasn't okay. His action prevented it from happening again."

Find an equitable way to distribute office housework. Take the lead in developing a fair and equitable approach to distributing mundane office chores and annoying ancillary duties that detract from career-enhancing activities. Maybe you design a simple rotational chart: "Frank, sorry, but November is your month to wash dirty mugs in the break room." "Charles, I see you're up to run the prospective intern orientation this spring." Ban asking for volunteers for these assignments.

Encourage female colleagues to say no more often. Sometimes there can be real value in asking a good female colleague if you can point out what you have noticed about her tendency to volunteer too often for office service duties. Some women have been socialized to fill the uncomfortable silence after someone calls for a volunteer. They become so uncomfortable with the silence, the sound of crickets chirping, that women—more than men—finally say, "I'll do it." Consider having a curious, collegial conversation with women who seem to be raising their hands too often for the housework. Tell them what you're noticing, talk about the career progression ramifications, and encourage them to be selective and practice saying no, even if it feels uncomfortable.

We trust you'll never see a meeting as "just a meeting" ever again. Using your SA, you'll quickly perceive potential threats and opportunities for the women you work with and then thoughtfully spring into action. These strategies will also improve the quality and effectiveness of your team's daily business, but with the added benefit of making everyone feel valued. In the next chapter, we'll consider how to intentionally advocate for women in advancing their careers in the same way we do for our male colleagues.

Ally Actions

- **Practice vigilance and mitigate meeting risks.** Apply your SA to workplace meetings; disrupt meeting dynamics by saying something when women are marginalized and offer to hold pre-game and debrief meetings to mitigate bias and sexism.

- **Employ "pull" strategies to elicit women's voices.** Create space for women to contribute fully, ensure everyone's voice is heard in meetings, and convey to female colleagues that you value their perspective and hope they'll contribute their ideas.

- **Interrupt manterruptions.** Calmly and consistently call out interruptions in meetings; consider establishing a no-interruption policy for meetings and propose humorous but effective strategies to enforce it.

- **Call out her expertise.** Learn about a female colleague's experience and expertise and look for opportunities to bring it up in public venues.

- **Give credit where it's due.** Be alert to hepeating or bro-propriation of women's ideas by men in meetings or other venues; when it occurs, make a comment that clearly attributes the credit for the original idea to the woman who generated it.

- **Evenly distribute office housework.** Be attuned to gender assumptions about jobs; say something when office housework is directed at a female colleague.

8

Sponsoring Women Loudly

Doing real ally work for women requires more than showing up as an excellent colleague. It goes beyond noticing and confronting bias, sexism, harassment, and inequality. It requires you to become an all-in advocate for talented women who should be noticed, pushed forward for opportunities, and promoted to serious leadership positions. Recent evidence suggests that many women are undersponsored and, therefore, fail to advance in their organizations.[1] Particularly in male-dominated industries, women benefit mightily from the sponsorship of men who are well positioned and well networked.[2]

Sponsorship entails advocating for a woman—especially at key moments in her career—by creating visibility, supporting her promotions, and ensuring she gets the training and development opportunities she needs to soar. In an Ernst & Young study of top male sponsors for women, the authors summarized the key ingredients of sponsorship this way: "Male champions stood up for female protégés in performance reviews and promotion rounds; ensured they were considered for career opportunities; increased their visibility within the organization; helped expand their networks by introducing them to important stakeholders; challenged biased opinions and stereotypes about them; coached them before significant career moves or assessment processes; and took personal responsibility for removing barriers."[3]

Sponsorship requires a full-on commitment to publicly and persistently advocate for a woman's next opportunity for advancement or promotion. In many cases, sponsorship will be a natural and compelling extension of the excellent mentorship you learned about in chapter 4.[4] In other cases, deliberate sponsorship of a woman may occur outside of any ongoing developmental relationship. Increasingly, companies are requiring leaders above a certain level to sponsor at least one high-potential employee. Ernst & Young requires executives to sponsor at least two high-potentials. Here's the problem, on the whole, men are not doing so well at sponsoring women publicly. A recent study from the Center for Talent Innovation reveals that less than a third of identified sponsors are loudly advocating and promoting the person they sponsor.[5] Just as important, men continue to sponsor other men disproportionately, in the best cases, treating women with kindness and offering encouragement, but ultimately failing them as a vocal sponsor. Our Naval Academy colleague US Marine Corps Colonel Maria Pallotta reminds aspiring allies that "it's not enough to be kind to women; you have to be out there publicly and vociferously supporting them."

Before launching into the key strategies of sponsorship, we'd like to challenge you: do an honest, soul-searching audit and ask yourself if you are boldly sponsoring some high-potential employees. If not, get busy. If you are, ask yourself another question: "Does everyone I sponsor look like me?" If so, be intentional about diversifying those you pull up and push forward. Become creative and deliberate about finding junior women to sponsor. For example, Stanford sociology professor and Director of the Stanford VMware Women's Leadership Innovation Lab, Shelley Correll, worked with a National Science

Foundation grant program for women in engineering and was struck by the clusters of women who had the same dissertation advisers— mostly men: "At Cornell in our School of Engineering, women on our faculty had been mentored by a few men from schools around the country. It was really clear that there were a few men who, over the long haul, had been able to figure out how to mentor and sponsor women in a way that worked and attracted more talented women."

Whatever you do, do not sponsor only those who ask you to. Women and people of color may feel unable to reach out to a senior male, especially a white male. If you're serious about allyship, then notice high-potential women and sponsor them. Psychologist Adam Grant has a simple formula: every time you open a door for men, you need to give equal access to women.[6]

The following five strategies address the art and science of out- standing sponsorship for women. Practice them often. Remember, pushing female rock stars forward is great for everyone, especially your organization. Reflecting on the men who sponsored her, Joanne Lipman of *USA Today* told us, "This was not about charity for the little woman; this was about smart business thinking. These men kept me promoting because it made the organization better."

Be Her Raving Fan

Here's the challenge: if you're going to demonstrate allyship through sponsorship, you've got to get comfortable with out-loud, all-in, fan behavior. Talented women don't get enough of it. Cindy Gallop, a brand and business innovator said: "I was at a tech conference several years ago, and a man said, 'Honestly, my business partner is amaz- ing. The minute I began to partner with her, I began to see all these possibilities I hadn't seen myself.' He raved about her! I've never for- gotten the incident because it is so f-cking rare. That's how powerful it is when men genuinely, authentically, sincerely, praise women and demonstrate respect for their abilities and skills."

Sheryl Sandberg's mentor, Larry Summers, exemplified the art of sponsoring a mentee: "Larry was my professor in college. He volunteered to be my thesis adviser. He sat me down and said, 'Not many women go into economics; you should!' He gave me my first job out of college, making me his chief-of-staff when he was secretary of the US Treasury. At every stage, he mentored me. Then, when I got to the World Bank, he went out of his way to introduce me to key people and would always promote me: 'This is Sheryl Sandberg. She was my research assistant. She was number one in economics at Harvard.' It went on and on!" Although initially embarrassing, Summers's opinion of her was a huge confidence boost. In retrospect, Sandberg understood he was sponsoring her.

Becoming a vocal fan for talented women is an essential ally action for equity. The following four actions are for publicly sponsoring women.

Give her a ringing endorsement. Many of the women we interviewed shared poignant examples of male sponsors offering very public claims about their competence, excellence, and readiness for an assignment. Marjorie Clifton, principal of Clifton Consulting, reported that a male business partner was often a public advocate in meetings: "He's the first man I've ever seen who was strong enough to sit in a meeting and say, 'Marjorie knows this business better than anybody, so listen to her.' It was so uplifting for me. He saw me for my capabilities." Janet Petro of the Kennedy Space Center recalled that her sponsor, Robert Lightfoot, would always go out of his way to introduce her and recognize her in meetings in a way that immediately elevated her stature: "He would say, 'JP is really good!' They knew Robert. He was trustworthy. So, his powerful introductions gave me instant credibility and advantage."

Increase her visibility by bringing her to key meetings. Give her credibility by association simply by creating opportunities for exposure to key leaders and decision makers. Bring her to key meetings and have her speak for you or your team. Romy Newman, president and CEO of Fairygodboss, recalled how Michael Rooney, senior vice president of the *Wall Street Journal,* advocated for her: "He empowered me more than anyone in my career just by including me in the room. He would bring me to every executive meeting. That provided so much exposure to management. I presented regularly to the CEO because of him. Instead of Michael presenting my ideas, he would have me come and do the presentation." Likewise, Susan Feland, Stanford Graduate School of Business, had a male sponsor who deliberately included her in meetings: "He knew I would get the visibility, and the credibility by association being there with him. He could have easily presented material by himself, but he invited me to present to ensure I got the credit."

Put her name forward for visible assignments. Sponsor a highly talented woman by nominating her and pushing her forward for key tasks that will allow her to shine and showcase her talents so that everyone can see her succeed. Mary-Olga Lovett of Greenberg Traurig Law shared how this sort of sponsorship requires some risk tolerance:

> As a first-year lawyer, I had one male boss who would split closing arguments with me, and these weren't small cases. I was permitted to make those arguments and cross-examine witnesses in my first trial with this much more senior partner. When someone else in the firm asked him, "What do you think you're doing letting her make arguments?" or an opponent in court tried to take advantage of my inexperience, this man took it in stride and said, "No, I don't need to take over. I've chosen the right person for the job. She can do it!" That's real allyship!

Nominate her for promotions (don't wait for her to nominate herself). For various reasons, women can be reluctant to put their names into consideration for promotions or stretch assignments. This reticence can easily be exacerbated in male-dominated industries and organizations. Allies can serve as an antidote to reluctance by sponsoring women loudly for promotions. Telle Whitney of the Anita Borg Institute offered an excellent illustration of this ally action from Alan Eustace, senior vice president at Google: "At Google, you had to put yourself forward for promotions. Eustace observed that women were not doing this at the same rate as men. So, when Eustace had opportunities in meetings, he would essentially nominate women by asking them out loud to put their names forward right then and there. This had a significant impact."

Nominate her even if it means your organization might lose her. Sometimes the stretch assignment means she leaves your organization. When this move is in her career interests, don't be selfish. If you're her sponsor, you believe in her, you have her best interests at heart, and you prove this by supporting *her* career dream. At times, her best next opportunity might be elsewhere. Suzanne Fogarty of Chapin School shared how her boss, Bob Vitalo, alerted her to the head of school position opening at Lincoln School, told her that she'd be an incredible head of school, and encouraged her to apply. She explained, "He acknowledged that he didn't want to lose me, but that this position would be good for me, my career, and I was ready." Are you worried that sponsoring women well will lead to a mass exodus of your most talented female colleagues? You needn't worry. Excellent mentoring and sponsorship heighten loyalty to the organization in which it occurs.

Talk about Her (Positively) behind Her Back

Great male allies and sponsors for women talk about them behind their backs, when they're not in the room. It's one thing to push a woman forward for an opportunity or promotion when she's right there. It's another to be her raving fan when you're in a meeting with other leaders or having a conversation in a group composed—primarily or exclusively—of other men. This is *consistent and uncondi-tional sponsorship.* Go to bat for her. Leverage your position and power to make things happen in her career when she's not around to thank you for it. After all, you're not sponsoring her for praise; you're doing this because she's talented, because it'll be excellent for the organiza-tion to retain and promote her, and because it's what allies do.

In our interviews with successful women across a range of indus-tries, the theme of discovering—often much later—that male allies had been sponsoring them behind closed doors recurred with sur-prising frequency. Lisen Stromberg of 3% Conference said, "I had so many male sponsors, and at the time, I didn't understand that's what they were doing. It was happening when I wasn't in the room. Confident male allies are out there when we don't even know they're advocating for us." And Susan Feland shared, "As a junior air force of-ficer, I was sent to France to serve as our liaison officer to the French air force. I previously worked with a senior French air force officer in the US. Before I even arrived in France, he communicated to the offi-cers there that I was excellent and knew my stuff. So, when I arrived, I had credibility. This was especially important in France where the military is still very male-dominated."

Another ally strategy relates to sponsoring women out loud when they're not around. Be an all-in sponsor in recommendations. Recom-mendations for high-talent women can take many forms: formal letters, social media endorsements, verbal reference checks, and back-channel casual conversations. Research evidence suggests that recommenda-tions for women—versus men—include more doubt-raising phrases.[7] Women receive more doubt-raising qualifiers in recommendations they never hear. In table 8-1, compare the recommendation phrases signaling only faint praise (these undermine anyone but get used more when describing women) versus all-in bold sponsorship phrases.

You should banish flimsy and faint sponsorship phrases from your recommendation playbook. The lesson for allies? No hedging allowed. Chances are you wouldn't offer only faint praise to her face, so don't write or say them behind her back.

TABLE 8-1

Faint versus bold praise in sponsorship recommendations

Faint praise	Bold praise
She might be a good fit.	She's perfect for this role.
She'll be okay.	She'll knock it out of the park.
She needs only minimal guidance.	She's a motivated self-starter.
She shows the potential to . . .	She's proven she can succeed at . . .
As a busy mom, she still manages to . . .	She's an exceptionally competent . . .
I recommend her for . . .	She has my strongest recommendation.

Provide Cover and Share Your Social Capital

You've most likely got some relational resources and assets you can leverage to sponsor a woman at work. Unlike human capital that resides in individuals, *social capital* resides within relationships and includes such resources as influence, information, knowledge, support, advice, and goodwill.[8] Excellent sponsorship includes the sharing of social capital. Each time you introduce a talented woman to a member of your network, include her in an email thread among leaders, or invite her to a conference or key meeting and ensure people hear her name and how terrific she is, you are depositing some of your social capital in her credibility account.[9] The following ally actions are geared to leveraging your own reputation and capital in the service of promoting the visibility of a rising star.

Send her forward with your coat of arms. Think of sponsorship as equipping a junior person with a shield bearing your coat of arms.[10] In a symbolic way, your accrued power and reputation go before her to melt barriers, open doors, and provide access to influential people who might not ordinarily give her a second look. Consider how this facet of sponsorship might look when you sponsor a woman in a new leadership role. When Bill Parsons of the Kennedy Space Center brought Janet Petro on board from outside the center as his deputy director, Petro appreciated his unequivocal cover: "Right off the bat, he told the senior leadership team, 'You go to Janet for decisions. She speaks for me on all matters. I trust her decisions so whatever she says goes.'" In our interview with Parsons, he confirmed that his sharing of capital was deliberate: "There were not many women in leadership at the time and Janet was the first female deputy director. I knew it was important to make it clear that Janet was essentially running the center day to day. People needed to understand that I saw her that way, that what she said was the bottom line."

Add her to your network before she asks. Most male allies reading this have an active network of colleagues, both in your current organization and, more broadly, in the industry or profession. Consider how easy and powerful it would be to intentionally link a high-potential woman with one or two well-chosen members of your network, people who might be in a position to open a career door, include her in a career-enhancing project, or offer her a next promotion or new job. Diane Ryan of Tufts University told us how meaningful it was when a male sponsor did this for her before she asked, perhaps before she even recognized how important such networking might be: "When men have anticipated that a certain introduction and connection to people they know could be key to my advancement, and they've gone ahead and made that introduction for me without waiting for me to ask, it has made a big difference for me." Susan Feland acknowledged that sponsoring a woman through your own network requires you to stick your neck out and explain why she is really good and should get consideration. She raved about an army officer who sponsored her in this way: "I was transitioning from the military to civilian industry in Silicon Valley. He networked me in, making at least twenty introductions for me to everyone he knew in Silicon Valley. He used his credibility, tapped me into his network, and instantly created a network for me."

Use your social capital to open doors. Annie Rogaski of Avegant Corp. recalled that as a junior lawyer, she accompanied a senior male partner to a pitch meeting in which lawyers would try to show clients why they would be a good fit for a specific corporate case:

> I thought we were there to pitch the firm and I was there to support him. Instead, sitting right next to me, he starts talking about me, how I'm really experienced with this type of case, and how long he's worked with me and admired my work. He went on about how I'd be the perfect lawyer for their case and that they should hire me. As a young, female lawyer, that final "ask" was something I hadn't seen modeled. He wasn't asking for himself, he was asking for me. He put his credibility and social capital on the line for me with a client that already trusted him. They ended up hiring me.

Prevent her from getting mommy-tracked. When in a position to influence promotions and new positions, use your social capital to promote a female rising star who—owing to parental responsibilities or family leave—does not follow the typical promotion track. Use your credibility to bring her to the attention of decision makers. Joanne Lipman of *USA Today* recalled that early in her career as an editor at the *Wall Street Journal*, with two young children at home, she was offered a promotion that would have required a geographic relocation. She said no. For most women with little kids at home who refuse a promotion, that would be it. A lot of those women get mommy-tracked. By the time they're ready to rev up and return to work, they've been written off. That didn't happen to her because for five full years, her boss, Paul Steiger, kept asking her if she was interested in various opportunities. She would say no. Lipman recalled, "Finally, he came to me and said, 'Would you like to start a brand-new section of the paper that doesn't exist and you get to create it?' I said, Yes! Hell, yes! Since that time, I've reflected how fortunate I was that he kept advocating for me. Otherwise, my career may not have unfolded."

Take a Risk: Nominate Her for
Stretch Opportunities

Male allies who master the art of sponsoring women take this mantra to heart: *no risk, no reward*. Pushing a talented woman forward for a role that neither she nor the organization thinks she's ready for requires an ally to do a few things. First, you've got to see her talent and unexpressed potential and believe in it (and her). Second, you've got to have the courage to do the right thing and take a risk in sponsoring her loudly for a promotion that may cause both she and others to raise their eyebrows. Third, when you sponsor her for the new assignment, provide her with the support to succeed. Without your support, the incredible opportunity becomes the glass cliff—a type of benign sabotage in which a woman is set up to fail. These big leaps and opportunities to deploy untested skills are particularly important—yet all too rare—for women.

According to Janet Foutty at Deloitte, sponsoring a high-potential woman for a stretch opportunity because it is both the right thing to do and good for business is a "magical combination" when it comes to sponsorship motivation. Reflecting on her own sponsor, a managing partner, she recalled, "He took significant risks in pushing me forward. He believed in me personally—which gave me a ton of confidence—and he affirmed a personal belief that I belonged in leadership roles. Like many women, I tended to focus on outcomes in my current role instead of competing for leadership roles. His taking a risk and sponsoring me was a signal to me that it was time for me to take on bigger things."

Stretch opportunities—those difficult, high-visibility assignments and roles filled with learning challenges and quantum leaps in professional growth—turn out to be especially critical to the career advancement of women.[11] Deliberate sponsorship of women for stretch opportunities can help to keep them on track with their male counterparts in pay and promotions. (See the sidebar "Why Women Miss Out on Stretch Opportunities.")

Why Women Miss Out on Stretch Opportunities

Male allies take risks and sponsor women for stretch roles that allow them to shine, get recognized, and ultimately, get rewarded by the organization. So, why do so many women miss out on this brand of sponsorship? Organizational research suggests that there are several obstacles in play:[12]

- **Socialized reticence.** Girls, more often than boys, are socialized to hold back and express self-doubt about readiness or qualification for a new challenge. In adulthood, this can translate into lower confidence. So, while a dude with far less experience and talent is waving both hands in the air for a promotion, she has not even considered it. And there is evidence that many women won't seek a promotion until they believe they are 100 percent qualified (something few people ever are).

- **Previous rejections.** New evidence shows that a previous experience with perceived rejection when putting in for a promotion or opportunity can cause women to suffer belonging uncertainty and questions about their potential and readiness.[13]

Sponsorship for stretch opportunities inspired deep gratitude in many of the women we interviewed. Rachel Thomas of LeanIn.Org recalled that the chairman of a social gaming company took notice of her when she came in to consult on a project: "He thought I was smart, fast on my feet, and he offered me the job of vice president of marketing, really taking a risk on me for a job I wasn't qualified for on paper. I met only a few of the criteria and wouldn't have even considered applying for the position. He took the risk and I was quite successful."

Stephanie Vander Zanden of Schreiber Foods described the experience as a "tap on the shoulder" moment in her career:

- **Risky investment bias.** Too often, organizational decision makers—unconsciously or not—see women as a risky investment. While men get opportunities based upon potential, women have to prove themselves before getting the nod (of course, they can't very well prove themselves if nobody gives them the nod). This explains why women, more than men, get promoted to jobs with familiar responsibilities.

- **Assumptions about interest level.** Male managers too often assume that a woman is not interested in stretch assignments unless she explicitly signals her interest.[14] Assumptions about what a woman would or would not be interested in can undermine allyship through sponsorship.

- **Assumptions that performance alone will lead to promotion.** Women often enter the workforce expecting that their hard work and excellent results will speak for themselves, leading to timely advancement. Assuming this to be true, some women may not seek or welcome sponsorship from allies, thereby missing out on the social capital necessary to overcome workplace gender bias.

Male allies tap you on the shoulder for roles you wouldn't have otherwise gone for. When I had only been in sales for six years, only twenty-nine years old and probably viewed as a "girl" by a lot of people in the company, my boss at the time put me forward for a three-year international assignment, managing director for sales in Mexico. This was such a huge stretch opportunity for me, from individual sales to director level. He saw potential in me, threw his support behind me, and put my mind at ease, expressing real confidence in my ability to do the job. I still don't know what he said behind closed doors, but he must have been convincing others about my potential when I wasn't aware of it.

Are you geared up for some out-loud sponsorship of talented women? Are you ready to put those women forward for some stretch opportunities? Six ally actions are designed to make those recommendations successful.

No risk, no reward. Nominating someone for a stretch assignment takes some courage and risk tolerance. Sahana Dharmapuri of Our Secure Future acknowledged that sponsorship by nature involves incurring some personal risk: "When a man is putting a woman forward and vouching for her in front of his peers, he is putting his trust in the person he is championing. This is personal." And it involves more personal risk to promote her for an opportunity that you see as commensurate with her talent but that others might see as a bridge too far. Bob Vitalo, head of Berkeley Carroll School, told us he didn't allow risk to get in the way of sponsoring talented women: "I just refuse to be concerned about making a mistake. It benefits women, it benefits me, and it benefits my institution." In another act of risk in the service of sponsorship, in 2015, Arizona Cardinals head coach Bruce Arians officially hired Jen Welter to become the NFL's first female coach. In an interview shortly after, Welter said, "Bruce is known for saying 'no risk, no biscuit,' and that statement definitely applied to his decision to hire me. His courage in hiring me, a woman, has now opened the door for many other coaches to follow."

Back her on the basis of potential, not just performance. Women too often find themselves in a double bind. They are required to prove they can handle a job before anyone will give them the job.[15] Evan Smith of the *Texas Tribune* and other male allies we spoke with challenged men to push back on this bind. Smith said, "I am not a proponent of people needing to prove they have done the work before they can move into a new position. Lack of experience is not a disqualification. We have to recognize talent and then provide women with the opportunity to grow into a job while ensuring they are successful by providing resources and support." Julie Kratz of Next Pivot Point recalled the sponsorship of J. T. Metzger when she decided to change careers and enter the consulting world: "He really took a chance on me. He backed me as a consultant on the basis of my potential, not my performance, because I was new to the space. He put me in a position to lead a team, hired a leadership coach for me, and put me in a facilitator role, even though I'd never done that. He backed me for all these 'firsts' so I could get the experience."

Don't wait until she feels ready. Sponsorship is an opportunity to throw down a challenge while building confidence. Too many men let down rising Athenas by failing to push, dare, and challenge them.[16] Challenging a rising star to embody and recognize her own talent sometimes demands a willingness to sponsor her for stretch assignments long before she sees herself as meriting them. Consider how Emily Ramshaw of the *Texas Tribune* was challenged by the paper's cofounder, Evan Smith: "He launched me into leadership opportunities before I believed I was ready and provided the mentorship I needed to be successful in those roles. He put me in situations that really required me to stretch my skills. I was a reporter and he made me an editor. I was uncomfortable being on TV, so he threw me into those situations and taught me to shine there. He knew before I did that I could accomplish these things and he set me up to succeed."

Provide support to go with the stretch opportunity. Once you identify that high flyer and nominate her for that stretch opportunity, your job is far from finished. The best sponsors are all-in to mentor, advise, and offer moral support as a means of ensuring her success. To push her forward for a big challenge without your support amounts to benign sabotage. Consider how important sponsorship and support was for Kirsty Graham, senior vice president at Pfizer: "The key to his allyship and championing for me was ensuring I was successful in the opportunity. He was prepared to sit down and discuss what to expect, what I needed to know, and even to walk me through 'dry runs' of important things I might face."

Trust her and don't micromanage. When you nominate her for that stretch opportunity, you have to be able to trust her, without micro-management. Stand by for advice and encouragement, but let her "do her," possibly learning from mistakes as she goes. Former Marine Corps Lieutenant Colonel Kate Germano commended her Marine Corps sponsor for his approach: "He was really good at giving us stretch roles that required us to get out of our comfort zone. He would say, 'I think you'd be really good at this, even if it isn't within your current purview, but I want to see you take it wherever you want.' He would give you the creative freedom to make that role what it needed to be from your perspective." Janet Petro concurs; she cautioned allies to avoid *token sponsorship*: "Don't undermine her by not giving her full support, appropriate resources, and genuine decision-making authority. If you're only offering superficial support, you're not really sponsoring her."

Sponsor her for "men's" jobs. To show some serious ally moxie, look for opportunities to sponsor a talented woman into a "first" for women in your profession or organization. Then, be prepared to weather the pushback. Brigid Schulte, director of Better Life Lab at New America told us that her sponsor, a newspaper bureau chief, exemplified this ally action: "I was a regional correspondent, and Rich pushed me forward to be on the Pentagon beat, which was a very male beat. He saw something in me and pulled me up into a position I hadn't sought out. He took a lot of heat for doing that. People said I only got the job because I wore a skirt and the paper was worried about diversity numbers. Rich really believed in me. He stood by me and ignored all the crap people were saying."

Another example from Keith Reinhard of DDB Worldwide nicely encapsulates many of the ally actions we've covered here.

In the 1980s, DDB had a very important beer account, and according to Reinhard, "those ads were one big boy's club. Beer was about guys, jokes, outings, and lots of time at the bar." There was a young woman in his agency at the time who Reinhard believed would be perfect as a creative lead, writer, and creative director for one of the beer brands. But he knew that the moment he said "she" in pitching her, he'd get, 'What? We're going to have a woman writing beer ads?' Keith decided to do it anyway. "I told the client we had a writer who'd done amazing work with the likes of McDonald's, General Mills, Xerox, etc., and I thought this talented writer should take a crack at his brand." Without revealing her gender, he had her create a reel of her ideas for the brand and showed it to the client. "He was very impressed. Then, I said, I have one more thing to tell you. The writer's name is Susan. Of course, he was shocked, but he came along, and she was hugely successful with the brand and she turned out to be one of their favorites."

Support Women in Leadership Roles

So far, we've discussed how to sponsor women for opportunities and promotions. But what about women who have already ascended to key leadership roles? How can an ally be a champion and advocate for senior women? A key element of allyship is demonstrating loyal and transparent support for women in leadership, perhaps your own boss.

To be consistent as an ally for gender equity, you've got to support women in charge.[17] Nothing torpedoes women who ascend to leadership more quickly than gender biases surrounding competent leadership.[18] Women who lead more democratically and collaboratively—a distinctly effective leadership style—are often dismissed as not strong or tough enough in traditional workplaces. Women who lead more like men—at least according to gender stereotypes—and are more agentic and hierarchical are called your favorite "b" word (bossy). If you participate in bad-mouthing women leaders (or remain silent while others do) merely because they are women, you've scored a big fat ally failure.

We can show up for women who've risen to positions of significant leadership in several ways. First, telegraph your personal support for female leaders—especially to other men. Cindy Gallop recommended that men "look around at women leading in your workplace and think about what you really admire about them and their approach. Identify them as role models. Then, intentionally and frequently tell other men what you admire about those women in a way that signals that others should take a look at her from your positive perspective. Be transparent about having senior women as role models."

Second, be stalwart and reliable in making time for women when they seek consultation and support. Several of the powerful women leaders we interviewed talked about their genuine appreciation for allies who were always there, always available, honest, and loyal as followers. Gloria Feldt of Take the Lead said of one ally, "He offered to meet with me and spent a significant amount of his time helping me to think about large complex problems and organizations. His advice and counsel shaped the course of my leadership and my life." Janet Foutty reflected that "male allies helped me understand the dynamics and politics in play that might be working against me. They were attuned to whether my thoughts and ideas were being acknowledged and I was getting credit for them."

Another strategy is to be thoughtful if you disagree with a woman in public. Even better, register your concern or disagreement in private communication, but follow her lead in front of others, especially men. This brand of loyal followership is particularly salient in the military where women are few. In this context, men directly below the female leader must be her staunchest allies in order to shut down gendered objections to her command. Diane Ryan at Tufts, a former army colonel, described her experience in command of a company of soldiers in the vaunted 82nd Airborne Division. She affectionately thought of the 82nd as the "he-man women-haters club" at that time. Only 2 percent of the division were women. It was a total culture shock for her. Her first sergeant, a very tough, seasoned guy who had never before worked for a woman, made it his firm commitment to help her succeed. He knew they always needed to be on the same page and that the men should see him delivering her orders without blinking. She recounted, "He came in my office, closed the door, and said, 'Ma'am, we've got to see eye-to-eye out there.' We actually developed a little eye-to-eye symbol between us. We decided right there and then that we would never disagree in public. If we disagreed, we'd do it behind closed doors. I believe his loyalty was key in establishing my leadership credibility."

Ally Actions

- **Be her raving fan.** Increase her visibility and publicly and vocally advocate for her next advancement or promotion opportunity.

- **Talk about her (positively) behind her back.** Even when she's not in the room, look for opportunities to tout her talent, achievements, and readiness whenever upcoming vacancies, new roles, or promotions are discussed.

- **Provide cover and share your social capital.** Introduce her to key players in your own professional network that might be important for her advancement and make it clear she has your full trust and support.

- **Take a risk: Nominate her for stretch opportunities.** Back her for stretch opportunities on the basis of her talents and potential, without expecting her to prove she can do the job in advance.

- **Support women in leadership roles.** Telegraph your support of female leaders and help ensure her success by serving as an honest consultant, sounding board, and loyal follower.

Part Three

Systemic Allyship

Becoming an Advocate for
Organizational Change

9

Organizational Change Starts with You and Your Leadership

Until now, our focus has been on everyday guys in the workplace as change agents. We now argue that if you occupy a leadership role, showing up as a transparent and consistent ally for women and other marginalized people is fundamental to your leadership brand. No matter your role, it's time to turn your attention to what you can do to fix the broken system we've all ignored or blindly accepted for far too long. Many salient ally actions such as pursuing self-awareness, understanding others, demonstrating empathy, creating an inclusive work environment, advocating for others, and helping employees achieve their potential are all essential, both to running a successful business and to creating a workplace defined by respect, fairness, and equality. You really can't be an effective leader without also being an all-in ally.

How the message of allyship is communicated and by whom matters. There is a groundswell of pressure for leaders to broadly advocate for gender equity initiatives and role-model ally behaviors. This top-down approach is important because people look to leaders to understand what they should or should not do, and more fundamental, who they should be as employees, colleagues, and human beings at work. Without support from the top, fixing the broken system is even harder.

Leaders who are public allies increase curiosity within and across gender conversations about equity and inclusion, and create the freedom to safely sanction non-inclusive behavior. As a leader, you can redefine what it means to be a man in an organization in such a way that gender equity through partnership becomes regarded as a defining feature of who we are and what we do in men's everyday lived experiences.

Leading as an ally has to come from the heart. Your messages about equity and allies have to be personal and authentic. If your followers don't see you owning, modeling, and fully engaging in programs and initiatives to drive equity in the workplace, chances are they'll tune out. Too many leaders merely delegate or outsource allyship messaging (e.g., diversity and inclusion experts, HR administrators), but alone, this compartmentalized training often fails to produce the intended behavioral change or, even worse, backfires. In many cases, unconscious bias training, diversity training, and sexual harassment training—delivered in isolation or without full and vocal leader support—produce unintended consequences.[1] Moreover, this training too often focuses on changing individual attitudes, beliefs, and behavior—without considering how systemic factors (culture, policy, practice) affect individual behavior.[2]

Robert Coughlin, CEO of the Massachusetts Biotechnology Council, offers an example of deliberate leader accountability for achieving gender equality. Coughlin views his role as that of *systemic change agent*, by which he means that he is responsible for changing the way decisions are made. Looking at his own organization, Coughlin said that "MassBio is a leading organization and I happen to be the leader, so it's my responsibility to not accept the status quo and to make the change. It's our responsibility as allies, and if we have the ability to leverage our influence and power—let's use it for good and get it done."

Leaders need courage to hold themselves and their organizations accountable. So, before we jump into ten specific ally strategies for leaders, consider this authentic example of learning from missteps on the road to leading as an ally.

Ambassador Donald Steinberg recalled how, in the late 1990s, the Angola peace process fell apart and he recognized that gender inequity was integral to the failed process. At a press conference at the conclusion of the peace negotiations, a journalist asked him what special provisions for women were in the agreement. He proudly said that the peace agreement was gender-neutral; it did not discriminate against women. When he was in the field about a month later, he told us that he thought about that comment and realized how stupid it was because the peace agreement didn't include anything about gender. It wasn't gender-neutral, but actually did discriminate against women. There were no women on the peace commission that would implement the process. Even worse, there were agreements in the ceasefire that provided amnesty for crimes against women in the past—thirteen different amnesties including anything the signatories might do over the next six months. There were no provisions addressing sexual violence, girls' education, or reproductive health care. Most importantly, the peace commission was implementing the agreement through male-led organizations. The commission quickly tried to change course, involved women in the negotiations and implementation process, included gender advisers, and provided psychosocial support for women, but it didn't work. The peace process fell apart, and another civil war broke out that lasted three more years and cost another two hundred thousand lives.

For Steinberg, this was his wake-up call, when he realized that unless women were involved in peace and security issues, had a leadership role, and were planners, implementers, and beneficiaries, the plan simply wouldn't work. Through this experience, Steinberg learned the importance of gender equity and partnership—albeit at a very high level. The increased awareness gave him the understanding and clarity to communicate the importance of gender equity to global development organizations, governments, and ultimately the United Nations.

If gender equity is crucial to an organization's future—and it is—then leaders must demonstrate how these strategies to fix the system are valuable in everyday workplace interactions connected to business outcomes. Gender strategy consultant Jeffery Tobias Halter recommends asking yourself and your team these three questions to check your gender diversity efforts' progress:

- Can you articulate the day-to-day actions you are taking to improve the retention and advancement of women?

- What metrics do you have in place to track progress?

- How are you holding your direct reports accountable, specifically men and middle management?

If these questions are challenging to answer, you know where to start focusing more emphasis.

Design Clarity, Transparency, and Accountability into Your Workplace

In her 2016 book *What Works: Gender Equality by Design*, Harvard University behavioral economist Iris Bohnet finds three factors that are pivotal in designing organizations to effectively reduce gender bias and discrimination: *clarity, transparency,* and *accountability.*[3] First, leaders must be clear about the purpose of gender equity initiatives and be comfortable communicating these purposes and expectations to stakeholders, employees, and customers. It's not enough to talk about gender equity; leaders have to *show* they are committed.

In 2013, a video message from Australian Chief of Army Lieutenant General David Morrison to Australian army personnel went viral across the globe. In responding to investigation results finding that the denigration and harassment of women were rampant in the military, he provided a clear message that organizational leaders still use as an example to emphasize the importance of unambiguous communication about social norms and organizational identity—who we are and who we are not. In a YouTube video, he explained his expectations for military service members and how those expectations were connected to their legacy and national interest. He then directly and emphatically stated, "If you're not up to it, find something else to do with your life. There is no place for you amongst this band of brothers and sisters. Those who think that it is okay to behave in a way that demeans or exploits their colleagues have no place in this army. If that does not suit you, then get out."[4] We're confident that there was no doubt in anyone's mind what the general expected.

Bohnet's second factor, full transparency, is about communicating exactly what each equity initiative is designed to achieve and how it is being accomplished. Diana van Maasdijk, CEO of Equileap, said, "One of the biggest obstacles to accelerating workplace equity is the lack of transparency from many companies regarding initiatives such as efforts to close the gender pay gap, to provide paid parental leave to both parents, or to recruit without discrimination."

Do you want to recruit and hire more talent, develop trust with your board, and increase your customer base? Show them *what* you're doing, *how* you're doing it, and the *progress* you're making. Organizational disclosure is a powerful tool and promotes trust. For example, ninety-nine investors representing more than $1.61 trillion in assets recently requested that companies increase public access to workplace equity policies and practices across demographic diversity. The investors believe that these disclosures can have a significant impact on investing decisions and enable a comparative analysis of company culture and risk. According to Andrew Behar, CEO of As You Sow, "Leaders willing to publicly disclose their policies and practices on gender, race, and sexual orientation will be the companies that succeed by attracting and retaining the best and the brightest employees, and reducing risk to shareholders." Leaders know that full transparency about their gender equality initiatives is essential to effectively measuring their progress.

Bohnet's third factor is leader and organizational accountability. Measure what's important, and these measurements will drive leader and organizational behavior. If you know you are being held accountable for a gender diversity goal, you direct resources to achieve that goal and account for your progress. And if hiring and retaining more talented women is a business objective, be aware that women respond more favorably than men to credible evidence of diversity gains.[5]

Accountability for gender equity and inclusion is not just paying lip service or telling women how to fix themselves. We're talking full-on ownership. Research suggests that establishing who is responsible and fostering a sense of responsibility and a method for holding leaders accountable predict increased organizational diversity, inclusion, and equity.[6] Male leaders with a low sense of responsibility blame gender inequities on women because of their "choices."[7] Logically, their solution is for women to change their attitudes, behaviors, and decisions. That's the wrong approach. The good news is that male leaders with a high sense of responsibility recognize that men are part of the problem and the solution for gender equity, and are more likely to lead change.[8]

If holding yourself and your organization accountable is one hallmark of an ally in leadership, a second hallmark involves using your position and power to hold other organizations and companies accountable. For instance, as a high-profile exemplar, you wouldn't participate in a nondiverse conference panel of all white men, and you shouldn't agree to serve as a board member on a nondiverse board. Robert Coughlin told us that in his role as CEO, he is asked to be on many company boards. When he chooses to decline, he will recommend for the board seat three or four women who have better résumés than he does. He said that, from his perspective, "an ally is really just a friend—men and women being colleagues and teammates. I get invited to sit on boards because I'm friends with the people who are making the decision, so why can't women be friends with us, too? It seems so simple, but it's really about networking—introducing people to be friends. That's where allies can make a difference."

Allies expect and demand accountability for themselves from others—even as leaders. You have to ask people to hold you accountable and give you feedback when you aren't being consistent and courageous.

Be Clear about Your Expectations and Then Set the Example

People across your organization need to hear you clearly and plainly communicate the importance of full gender inclusion and diversity and how this imperative aligns with your purpose and intention as a leader. Then, they need to see your priorities in your day-to-day interactions. How you lead, help others grow, welcome expression of the whole person in mentees, and build community will establish trust with colleagues and certify your commitment as an ally.[9]

In our conversation with former Army Lieutenant General Robert Caslen, he recounted the importance of clarity in communicating the purpose for his efforts in creating gender parity: "I could see we were way behind at West Point with regard to the proportion of women. I pushed hard to increase the number of women appointed. I took a lot of heat from alumni for doing this, but it's clearly essential to making the army a more competitive and capable force moving forward. West Point is a hundred times better today than it was when it was an all-male school." Mission effectiveness is always at the forefront of leaders' minds, and keeping gender parity inextricably connected to the most important outcome is both strategic and a best practice for leaders setting the example from the top.

Being consistent in your day-to-day ally actions requires real courage. Allies are challenged every day to prove themselves and their good intent. These are times when you will need to reach deep inside and connect with your motivations, values, and beliefs to stay the course. Bob Vitalo of the Berkeley Carroll School shared how he approached these situations: "I've had criticism over being heavy-handed, but the world's not going to change unless you change it. If I can help our school increase women and women of color in responsible positions, then I'm going to seize that opportunity. Some people are turned off by this. When I see organizations where the population they serve is half female and their leadership is 90 percent male, I think something dramatic needs to happen. I've taken those demonstrative steps." Allies need to demonstrate resolve, conviction, and consistency in their decision making and actions.

How do we know what's important to our leaders and organization? Leaders value what they spend time and energy talking about and doing. It must be important if the boss is talking about it and doing it, right? As a leader, you can shift followers' perceptions and priorities simply by where you focus attention when interacting with your employees. If you want allyship and gender equity to be priorities in your organization, then you have to set an example in words and deeds. The following are just ways, based on research by Deloitte Insights, for how male leaders can set an example:[10]

- Start all meetings with a thoughtful personal story.

- Put your own imperfection on display.

- Have one-on-one conversations with people that go beyond workplace formalities.

- Check in on people who seem like they need it the least.

- Publicly take vacation and parental leave.

Purposefully Use Your Influence

What leaders say and do demonstrates what's important and valued. Role-modeling and setting an example start at the top. Use your positional power and influence to call attention to gender disparities, and look for systemic ways to include women fully at all levels of leadership. Sometimes that means being the eight-hundred-pound gorilla, the guy insistent on doing what's right and fair despite the inevitable resistance from some quarters. Staying true to your purpose, practicing transparency, and mustering some moral courage can help overcome this resistance.

Many of the senior leaders we interviewed for this book were notable exemplars of visible and vocal allyship from the C-suite. For example, Laura Adams of the Rhode Island Quality Institute told us that her board chair, George Vecchione, boldly supported her initiatives in creating a health information exchange. Vecchione took a real hit within his own organization when he used information from Adams's health exchange to reduce unneeded or redundant medical tests and procedures. The problem? It reduced his hospital's revenue. He was attacked because this didn't appear to make business sense, but he knew it made *moral* sense. Adams said, "By supporting my exchange, he opened doors and gave me credibility. He's the 'eight-hundred-pound gorilla in town' with the power and influence in the industry, so when he decided to support me, it made it almost impossible for other people not to do the same."

Senior leaders also need to walk the talk by showing up at events, conferences, and any initiative promoting gender inclusion and equality—this encourages other men to engage in allyship. In attending these events, male leaders demonstrate support, develop empathy, diversify their networks, and identify high-potential female talent. Of course, the benefits extend to women through diversifying their networks with male allies, connecting with career sponsors, and fostering gender partnership. Publicly supporting these groups and events is a best practice. Be that leader who not only attends but stays the entire time, engages fully, takes notes, and asks great questions.

Joanne Lipman of *USA Today* told us that there's a difference between mouthing the words and truly showing up. When she spoke at a publishing company to a mostly female audience, "the head of the company, a male, canceled his appointments to show up for this talk.

He was engaged, asked lots of questions, and you could see the difference it made in the room in terms of how people were feeling about the organization to know that their CEO cared enough to be present and be part of the conversation."

Similarly, Rachel Thomas of LeanIn.Org told us that she usually talks to companies about what they can do to right the imbalance in gender equity in the workplace, and usually looks out in the audience and sees mostly women. All the heads are nodding, because she's preaching to the choir. However, sometimes a very senior man will sponsor one of the events and explicitly tell the men who report to him that he expects them to attend. For example, she said that Jon McNeill, COO of Lyft, sponsored an event last year. He was loud and proud about sponsoring it, why he was sponsoring it, and why it mattered to the business, and he was explicit with the men in the organization that he expected them to show up."

In another case, when Brian Olsavsky, CFO at Amazon sponsored a LeanIn.Org event, Rachel Thomas commented that "I heard from several of the senior men who attended that they had received very direct emails from Brian making it crystal clear he expected them to be there. As a result, when I looked out in the audience, it was one of the very few times I can recall seeing at least half the audience was male. Brian was sitting up front, he sponsored the event, and he communicated his expectations for the other men in the company to show up and engage fully." Leaders like Olsavsky exude a sense of ownership, not only for the problem, but the solution. They know that solutions must include men.

Be Intentional in Attracting Diverse Talent

Intentionally attracting diverse talent will help you make your organization more attractive to women and diverse people generally. Your organization is what people see, so be deliberate in choosing social media, art in the workplace, brochures, and advertisements. These media are the face of the company; they tell customers and potential employees who you are and who is welcome. This might seem trivial, but it makes a significant difference in how people feel valued and welcomed.

Navy Reserve Lieutenant Commander Andrea Goldstein was assigned to a special forces reconnaissance team that included women. She related her experience working with leaders who embodied full gender partnership: "They worked to change the messaging of our command so that it was a more attractive place for women to work. This included how we talked about ourselves, the pictures we put in our briefings, and who we brought with us when recruiting. They actively talked about this around the command." If Navy SEAL leaders are on board with intentionally messaging to diverse talent, you should pay attention, too. Here are some specific examples for how to do this.

First, examine your company's digital and print media for diverse, respectful, and healthy depictions of women and men. Replace anything that reeks of outdated gender stereotypes. Then ask yourself this: considering the diverse talent you want to hire and retain, and the diverse customer base you want to work with, what images would make those people feel valued and included? Honestly look at your organization from the outside. Can you see that its culture and its people make it a good place for you to work and do business, now and in the future? If the answer is yes, then congratulations! If the answer is no, keep reading. We'll provide examples of what this looks like in other organizations.

Second, take account of the images displayed throughout your work spaces for gender inclusion—you have to see it to be it. How many of your conference rooms, hallways, lobbies, and lecture halls are filled with pictures of only white men? It's time to rethink the dude wall and what it's telling people about your organization.[11] Iris Bohnet confided that, many years ago, several leaders at the Harvard

Kennedy School noticed that there were no women in the portraits that lined the walls. This sent an implicit message to students and staff about what was possible and important. While not intentional, it signaled that women were not leaders. However, when it was brought to leaders' attention, they led the charge to add portraits of Ida B. Wells, US civil rights activist and suffragist; and Ellen Johnson Sirleaf, the president of Liberia, winner of the Nobel Peace Prize, and a graduate of the Kennedy School.[12]

Third, review educational and training content for inclusion of diverse experiences. This subtle messaging in organizations extends beyond what we see in portraits to the stories we tell. Susan Feland, Stanford Graduate School of Business professor and president of AcademyWomen, explained how Charles O'Reilly, Stanford Graduate School of Business professor modeled allyship and went out of his way to ensure the school was developing instructional video and case study material that included the unique experiences of women in business. Feland said that "using that content in our executive leadership development efforts and curriculum has a big influence on driving awareness of the challenges women face and how men can be part of the solution. It was particularly powerful to encourage men to think about creative policies and strategies for improving the experiences of women."

Fourth, employ a truly representative diverse workforce. For all minority groups, feeling included and seeing a future for yourself in an organization is affected by those you see around you. James Rooney of the Greater Boston Chamber of Commerce related that his organization has increased the number of women on its board by 53 percent in the last two years. His staff is 83 percent women. Of its seven vice presidents, six are women and one is a person of color. He said, "We feel good about how we have embraced promoting women and breaking down barriers in our organization. I think that's important if I am going to credibly and publicly advocate public policy positions like women's pay equity—that we walk the talk."

Connect Women's Initiatives to Leader Responsibilities

Advocate for full funding of women's initiatives, inclusion events, and employee resource groups. Tie these initiatives to leadership development. This makes it less stigmatizing and more likely that leaders will feel responsible. In their busy everyday lives, you have to help leaders prioritize gender equity. When leaders have a reasonable expectation that others will hold them accountable, that they'll have to explain their resourcing decisions in light of the organization's transparent commitment to inclusion, they make more equitable decisions.[13]

First, integrate gender and inclusion initiatives with leader development training and mentorship programs, and hold leaders accountable for achieving those goals as a business outcome. Organizational field research demonstrates that unconscious bias and diversity training delivered in isolation—not connected to leader responsibility and business outcomes—is not effective.[14] When programs for women involve male leaders, men's sense of responsibility and social interaction increases—leading to more gender equity. Consider how you can best embed accountability, authority, and expertise within each business unit and make that leader responsible for reaching diversity and inclusion goals.

Second, fully fund women's initiatives, leader development, and employee resource groups. Travis McCready of the Massachusetts Life Sciences Center holds himself and his leaders accountable for reaching their diversity and inclusion goals through a women's venture capital initiative—spending their money to prove their commitment. As a black male CEO, he is fatigued with reports and posturing about diversity that rely on the bad habit of "analysis paralysis." As a leader in the health sciences industry, he is pivoting the council's resources and strategy to *executing*. He said, "We launched a multimillion-dollar initiative investing in women entrepreneurs in the life sciences with unrestricted capital, and we built a diverse executive coaching team that provides counsel, mentoring, and capacity building to our young cohort of women entrepreneurs with the specific intent of bending the curve on the amount of venture capital that goes to women entrepreneurs."

Put Policies and Practices in Place
to Stop Sexual Harassment

No matter at what level you lead in your organization, one distinct ally role and responsibility is to establish or support clear reporting, non-retaliation, and grievance policies for victims of sexual harassment. Too often, male leaders are unfamiliar with these policies, despite being responsible for implementation. If you don't feel high enough in the food chain for policy work, use your ally voice and influence to make the case to your boss. Better yet, help your boss make the case to his or her boss. Do your homework first. Be familiar with the policy. Listen to your female colleagues' assessments of whether the existing policy works and then work alongside them to advocate for change. Here are several specific strategies for getting this ally action right.

First, be bold in in your messaging about sexual harassment. Gretchen Carlson supports legislation to abolish arbitration clauses for sexual harassment (in effect, forcing victims to keep their experience a secret) that has some companies such as Uber and Microsoft becoming early adopters. She advised that male leaders need to say, "This will not be tolerated in the company that I run. And, if you come to me as either a victim or a bystander and report, I will honor that." This changes the dynamic from an assault on the victim (isolating her, hiding her, protecting the predator) to "The buck stops with me; we're not tolerating this. We're going to encourage and support people who stand up and say something."

Second, provide personal support when female colleagues report sexual harassment. Allies start by believing and affirming their female colleagues and then asking how they can help. Too often, legitimate complaints are shrugged off or minimized, ultimately letting the perpetrator off the hook or blaming the victim by suggesting they're being too sensitive or misinterpreting what they experienced. Andrea Goldstein shared a personal experience highlighting this ally action. When she was assigned to a navy special reconnaissance team, she endured a boss who was an abusive bully. He also sexually harassed her. A male leader told her he was ready to go to the chain of command to bring this to their attention for her and corroborate her report when she was ready. She said, "Lance was the first person I called when I was ready to report, and he backed me up saying that 'This was unacceptable behavior; I have your back.' He went in and alerted the executive officer (second in command) that I was coming to report this behavior and that he could confirm everything I say."

Third, find creative and adaptive solutions that work for everyone in the organization, taking into account organizational culture. Tiffany O'Donnell, CEO at Women Lead Change, told us how Rockwell-Collins (now United Technologies) instituted an ombudsman program for victims of sexual harassment. The ombudsman is typically a senior person in the company who is outside the direct line of reporting for the victim and can provide an independent and impartial investigation, including guidance for the victim. While HR is an advocate in preventing and educating about harassment, when an incident occurs, HR is ultimately responsible to the organization—not the victim. An ombudsman is a designated advocate for victims.

When developing a policy that supports victims and immediate reporting, protects the organization, and eliminates sexual harassment, doing what's best for the victim is a proxy for what's best for the organization. As an ally, you have to insist that this remain the purpose of any policy or process—and then demonstrate through action that is how it really works in practice. Otherwise, people will see it as another legal compliance policy for the company. Transparency and accountability are your friends; use them.

Create Flexible Work Options That Allow Everyone to Thrive

This strategy focuses on designing a workplace that allows everyone to thrive to maximize the value of your business. Because women are still more likely to carry the majority of caregiving responsibilities in their families, flexible workplace structures are game changers. The ability to work from home, adjust hours as needed, care for a sick child, or simply take time off—all while feeling like they are still being seen for their hard work and stellar performance—is incredibly valuable to women and their career progression. Show that you value flexibility and creativity in how people get their work done. It's all about time, schedule, and location.

First, acknowledge and support employees' lives outside the workplace. Ignoring employees' personal lives actually sabotages productivity and is a recipe for failure. Start with the basics—people cannot work eighty- to hundred-hour weeks and enjoy a life outside of the office, practice self-care, or be efficient. Sure, there are periods of time when you need people to work longer hours or travel for extended periods of time, but that should be balanced with deliberate time away.

Creating a culture of working long hours isn't going to allow people to thrive in the long run. Brigid Schulte of New America said, "When you praise someone for working weekends and late nights, you're sending the message that is what is expected." Don't forget to hold yourself accountable too. Remember that junior employees are looking to you as a work-life balance exemplar; they will follow your lead. You're not doing anyone a favor by working a hundred hours a week—you might as well tell your followers outright they should too.

Several organizations are already creating best practices in this area. For example, to combat the devotion-to-work norm of the "always on, always available" workplace, organizations are finding innovative ways to help employees balance their family roles with the demands of paid work.[15] One firm discovered that when it held its employees accountable for taking scheduled time off to engage in activities unrelated to their paid work, work performance actually increased. Less time at work leads to more collaboration and efficiency, while allowing people to be more equal partners at home. Less time at work also results in increases in job satisfaction, retention, and the quality of client service and products.[16] Crazy as this may sound, it's not new. Research evidence dating back more than a hundred years shows why the forty-hour workweek and other labor laws and policies from FDR's New Deal era are good for families, employees, and are just plain good business—better decisions, fewer mistakes, more efficiency, and higher productivity.[17]

Second, change how you value time in and outside the office. Across industries, companies valuing creativity over availability have been experimenting with ways to value time off the clock. 3M started its "15% time" in 1948 to encourage innovation; this program is most famous for creating the Post-it Note.[18] Today, companies like Google and Hewlett-Packard have adopted similar creative workdays and integrated them into their culture to show they value flexibility in how work is done. The advertising industry has recently joined the push for valuing creativity outside normal work hours with the #ClockOutConcept.[19] Have your employees clock out once in a while to show how you value their creative work contributions outside the workplace and then have them talk about the contributions using the hashtag.

Third, develop flexible work schedules and telework options to allow people to maximize their job effectiveness. Would you rather have a mediocre employee who is less efficient and effective working full-time on-site, or the talented and exceptional employee who is on a flexible work schedule that includes telework? By finding work sched ule solutions that allow talented employees to continue working in your company, you retain that talent, save hiring and retraining costs, and encourage employees to grow into higher levels of management when their life situation changes.

Carefully Assess Your Parental Leave Policies

Once you've given your people the flexibility to get work done, all the while emphasizing time away from the office, establish formal company policies that support men and women, especially considering those who are in caregiving roles. Important policies include paid family leave and support for parents and other employees to facilitate their unique combination of work and family.

First, implement exit and reentry opportunities for women returning from maternity leave or those who have been away for years. Support women returning to positions of equal pay and status, without inhibiting their opportunity for advancement.[20] For women and employees transitioning in their caregiving roles, job sharing is another valuable option in retaining talent while people transition and adapt to new roles as parents or caregivers.

Second, establish formal company policies for paid family leave or conduct a formal review to ensure that they are having the desired effect and being utilized. Evan Smith of the *Texas Tribune* told us, "One of the most important workplace challenges today for both men and women is family leave policies. I did a complete overhaul of our family leave policy to provide four months of paid maternity, paternity, family and sick leave. This puts men and women on an equal footing in the workplace."

Sheryl Sandberg, emphasized considering all types of employees in your workforce and how various life events affect thriving at work. Facebook had four months of maternity and paternity leave—relatively robust by industry standards—before Sandberg's arrival, thanks to Mark Zuckerberg. Sandberg told us, "Since then, we've added bereavement leave, and we've moved to ensure a living wage for contractors because lower-wage jobs often affect women disproportionately."

You might discover that groups of employees aren't using the leave. Find out why. Are middle managers discouraging usage or is there a workplace culture that discourages family leave? Use presumptive language, setting the expectation that people will use the leave: "See you in sixteen weeks." "What dates are you scheduling your sixteen weeks?" Such presumptive phrasing sends a different signal compared to "How much time do you need?" Don't pressure a junior employee who is a new parent and may be concerned about how time away will reflect on his or her performance and loyalty. Put their mind at ease and normalize the transition.

Third, ensure using paid family leave doesn't impact career advancement. Patrice Milos, cofounder and CEO of Medley Genomics, said that when she worked for Pfizer, her boss transparently told her that he was pushing her forward for promotion. After the closed-room discussion about her promotion, he said that he was challenged because someone mentioned that she took three months "off" for maternity leave. He told her that he absolutely believed it didn't matter and that all her accomplishments were worthy of promotion. She said, "Later when I was on a promotion committee myself, his example allowed me to raise questions about whether we were promoting men and women equally." Allyship and advocacy done well has far-reaching effects, empowering others to become allies.

Often allyship opportunities present themselves when you least expect them, requiring us to adapt and be creative in supporting new parents. Author Karen Catlin shared her story of pregnancy with her first child. When she could no longer hide the pregnancy, she realized that she had to tell her boss. She had a meeting scheduled with her manager, who said, "Karen, I have this great idea. I want to promote you to director, and you're going to be running a key team for the company." She responded, "That sounds great, and by the way I'm pregnant. I want to take four months maternity leave, and when I come back, I want to work part-time." She said that she still remembers his enthusiastic response: "Cool!" She did end up getting that promotion while pregnant and then taking leave, working part-time, and still enjoying the new role. Catlin was fortunate to have a boss who was prepared for this situation and had the tools to allow him to do what was best for everyone. As an ally, review your company's policies and if you can't say "cool" when an employee presents you with a situation like this, look for ways to create policies that allow managers to do what is best for their employees (in most cases, this will also be best for the company).

Fourth, meet with pregnant employees before their maternity leave to create a plan for what work will be through the pregnancy, during parental leave, and after the leave ends—a "job plan."[21] Like a birth plan, the job plan maps out a vision and set of expectations that keeps employees connected to the organization and shows that they are valued. But make it clear that the job plan is flexible and that you expect modifications based on how the transition progresses. Your goal is to demonstrate commitment and care as you collaborate with your employee in building a long-term future with the organization. For example, you may need to consider extending return dates to part-, flex-, or full-time work depending on how the baby is sleeping or other factors conducive to parents returning to the planned work schedule. Beyond welcoming women back following generous parental leave, consider avenues for women who decide to take a career pause when children are young. Consider a formal "returnship" program to leverage women back into the workforce and refuse to allow midcareer gaps to torpedo a woman's opportunities. (See the sidebar "Mothers' Rooms.")

Fifth, with the average annual cost of day care in the United States at over $16,000 in 2018, accounting for more than half the median income of single mothers, leaders need to support options for affordable access to childcare.[22] Options might include on-site services, referrals, or cooperative programs with other organizations in your area. The bottom line is that affordable and accessible childcare which includes infants at the age when parental leave ends is not just something nice to have—it's essential to supporting a thriving workforce.

While so many of these policies are focused on women who have children, it's important to also create policies and practices that include single women who provide a disproportionate amount of caregiving for family members and friends.[23] Too many leaders seem to

Mothers' Rooms

Employers covered by the Fair Labor Standards Act are federally required to comply with the federal Break Time for Nursing Mothers law to provide basic accommodations for breastfeeding mothers at work. This covers most employers, but if it does not apply to your company, set up a mothers' room for breastfeeding mothers so that they can pump. Even if you don't have any pregnant employees now, don't wait; start scoping out spaces. See if there are any mothers who can consult with you on best ways to organize, decorate, and outfit the space. Don't have a room that you can convert? There are lots of commercial options for portable lactation rooms. You've probably seen these in the airport or in a convention center recently. Outsource your mothers' room if necessary.

---

believe that having no spouse and no kids means no work-life balance. Single and childless employees are a growing population, with women outpacing men.[24] They must be included in the work-life conversation and need allyship.[25] Incorporate inclusive language and perspectives into your advocacy and support to include single and childless workers. Call out people who apply stereotypes to single, childless women as lonely and isolated. This is a myth! Single women have more extensive relationship ties and are involved in more hours of community service (volunteering) than their married counterparts.[26] Don't assume they can work late, cover every conference or work emergency, work every weekend, or be in the office to accept the early breakfast delivery for the 8 a.m. meeting.

Don't allow single women to feel that their lives and the unpaid work they do outside the workplace are invisible, especially to their married bosses and coworkers. Be sensitive and aware when singles have to justify taking time off, vacation time, or time to care for extended family and friends. Recognize that while their married counterparts are covered by the federal Family and Medical Leave Act to care for their spouses, the significant other in their life is not covered. Taking time off for singles to provide this type of care comes with financial risk since they can't rely on the married couple safety net.

Create External Accountability for Your Organization

Develop formal policies that establish requirements for doing business with your organization. Committed to being a leader in allyship? It's time to put your money where your mouth is!

First, your company shouldn't sponsor or participate in conferences without equal representation of women or do business with companies that don't have at least 30 percent of board members or C-suite leaders who are women. And if your company has not yet reached these goals, set accountable, time-focused goals for yourself. This may seem really challenging in the early stages of creating equity in your organization, but you have to start somewhere. Several companies are leading by example—and it's working.

Robert Coughlin of the Massachusetts Biotechnology Council decided to formalize its policy for doing business exclusively with organizations that meet minimum requirements for gender diversity and equity. Coughlin explained: "If you want to change how things are, you have to change how you do things—and nobody was changing how we do things. I'm never going to sit on another 'manel' [all-male panel], and I challenge every other man to do the same thing." MassBio now has a policy of not having any events with all-male panels, its employees will not sit on all-male panels, and it won't partner with any events that have all-male panels. Coughlin stressed, "We didn't do it to get good press. We didn't even do it because it was the right thing to do. It was a good business decision. Diversity is good for business; you have better outcomes." In our follow-up with Coughlin, he said that he is encouraged that the other companies MassBio works with are following his lead and creating their own policies, changing the way they do business.

Require that women are represented when your team travels for business with other entities. Sheryl Sandberg told us that Vittorio Colao, CEO of Vodafone, requires meetings and events with his company to have at least 30 percent women. She said, "When he brings his team to Facebook, he always brings at least 30 percent women on any trip like that. He reaches into the organization if he needs to in order to get to that."

Extend diversity and representation requirements to your suppliers and customers. Romy Newman of Fairygodboss finds that you can put pressure on suppliers to change the way they do business. She commented, "Companies like Microsoft are not working with suppliers who don't provide paid leave to their female employees. HP and Verizon are not working with advertising agencies that don't show up with diverse teams. Nothing speaks louder than money." Companies are creating equity in lots of different ways; be intentional and transparent. Remember—no guts, no gender equity!

Establish a policy with your employees that they never have to do business with anyone who makes them feel uncomfortable. This should go without saying, but we feel compelled to put it in writing. Show them you have their back. Eva Helén, CEO of EQ Inspirations, said that when she worked in the tech industry, she felt it was important for her male boss to support her. During a trip at a sales conference, a man from a company they were working with walked next to her but leaned over her, peering down at her while saying something inappropriate. She explained to her boss how uncomfortable she felt. She said, "My boss told me, you never need to do business with anyone who makes you feel uncomfortable. As an ally, he was telling me that I am more important than the potential business partner, that there are other people we can do business with that don't make us feel uncomfortable."

Get Pay Equity Right

Vocally and persistently address pay equity. Employees expect a work culture that aligns with their personal values. Increasingly, employees expect freedom to prioritize work and life, experience a sense of purpose and belonging, and be treated fairly and equitably. Nowhere is fairness more clearly expressed than in pay equity. Employees connect pay equity to the company culture and leaders' values. If a company and its leadership hold fairness and equity as core values for their employees and customers, pay equity is one way to prove it. Leaders who value pay equity are both transparent and tenacious in tracking progress. A lack of transparency in pay equity creates a loyalty problem and can result in employee disengagement, dissatisfaction, and reduced productivity. And it can affect the company's reputation and ability to recruit talent.[27] (See the sidebar "Best Practices to Increase Transparency and Pay Equity in Your Organization.")

Best Practices to Increase Transparency and Pay Equity in Your Organization

- Stop asking for salary history.
- Establish transparent hiring and salary criteria from the outset when interviewing.
- If salary is negotiable, state "salary negotiable" in job ads so that everyone knows they can negotiate.
- Develop salary bands.
- Conduct annual pay audits and pay equity reviews.
- Develop unconscious bias training around pay equity.

James Rooney of the Greater Boston Chamber of Commerce marshaled support for the passage of the Massachusetts Equal Pay Act. Because he represents all companies in Boston, he needed to lead the change to state law on pay equity. He explained to us how this legislation had been filed every year for twenty years, and businesses and chambers of commerce generally opposed this kind of legislation. When he became CEO, he reviewed the legislation and found a way to build support for it. Rooney said, "I began reaching out to some of the major businesses and employers to understand the specific issues that were problematic in their mind, because almost universally, everybody agrees with the concept of gender pay equity." Rooney spent a lot of time with legislators and the attorney general's office in developing more definition and clarity in the language so that the business community would support the legislation. He confided, "It took listening, understanding, being empathetic on both sides of the argument, discerning the core issue or root of the problem." His public ownership of pay equity for an entire state, his commitment to creating change, and his transparent investment of his own social capital are hallmarks of allies in leadership.

Ally Actions

- **Design clarity, transparency, and accountability into your workplace.** Be clear about the purpose of gender equity initiatives and transparent in communicating what they are designed to achieve, while establishing accountability for yourself and others.

- **Be clear about your expectations and then set the example.** Plainly communicate how gender inclusion and diversity relate to your purpose, intent, and values as a leader, and keep them connected to your business outcomes.

- **Purposefully use your influence.** Use your positional power to overcome resistance to organizational change and demonstrate your support and expectations for others to support gender and inclusion events.

- **Be Intentional in attracting diverse talent.** Examine your company's digital and print media for diverse, respectful, and healthy depictions of women and men and review educational and training content for inclusion of diverse experiences.

- **Connect women's initiatives to leader responsibilities.** Integrate gender and inclusion initiatives with leader development training and mentorship programs, and hold leaders accountable for achieving these goals as a business outcome.

- **Put policies and practices in place to stop sexual harassment.** Be clear in your messaging that you do not tolerate sexual harassment and encourage and support victims and bystanders.

- **Create flexible work options that allow everyone to thrive.** Acknowledge and support employees' lives outside the workplace by placing realistic boundaries on time at work.

- **Carefully assess your parental leave policies.** Establish formal company policies for paid family leave and conduct a formal review to ensure that they are having the desired effect and being used.

- **Create external accountability for your organization.** Do not sponsor or participate in conferences without equal representation of women or do business with companies that don't have at least 30 percent of board members or C-suite leadership who are women.

- **Get pay equity right.** Set transparent hiring and salary criteria and conduct annual pay audits in your company.

10

Developing a Culture of Allyship

Before you head out to fearlessly test your allyship savvy in the workplace, we offer this final chapter on the critical task of building ally communities. Ultimately, allyship is about people being allies for each other. We must be intentional and deliberate in growing our communities of allies through purposeful networking. Create a constellation of dudes who get it and can be resources, supporters, and advocates in gender equity work—*with women*. Communities of male allies can be formal or grassroots. In either case, a community of allies serves two functions.

First, it frees the influence, creativity, and passion of an untapped resource for equity in organizations. Getting men off the sidelines and into the gender diversity and inclusion conversation is a real game changer. By making men stakeholders in gender partnership, they're not outsiders wondering, "What is my role?" Second, ally communities provide a forum where men get involved, educate each other, become comfortable asking difficult questions, clarify their own thinking, and learn how they can best contribute through meaningful and intentional action.[1] Marjorie Clifton of Clifton Consulting affirmed that "we have to create a safe space at work where men can figure out gender equality, understand it better, talk about it, and ask questions. There's this perception that men can't participate in this conversation unless they're perfect—there's not a forgiving place where you can 'step in it' and correct course. We have to give everyone a margin of grace and a space for men and women to share their stories and perspectives."

This chapter contains four strategies on how to advance an allyship culture at work in order to build and leverage a broader community, cultivate connection and collaboration, and transform culture.

Launch a Male Allies Community

Who should you include when initially building an ally community? Start with the cadre of dudes who get it, show interest, and have the heart for the work. Then expand through your networks—invitations and nominations are a good starting point. Appreciating the range of reasons why men attend and participate in ally initiatives goes a long way toward building an inclusive community. Thriving ally communities educate, inspire, and support men. You will not attract or build anything through compulsory and "CYA" programming. You are building connections in a community of people who care and are committed to changing the status quo, while shifting the culture. Start small and dream big. The following seven actions will help.

Cast a wide net. Allyship initiatives can be powerful because they have a broad reach. They create a knowledge base for managers as well as individual contributors. Include all aspects of your organization, every business unit, and don't forget satellite or remote parts. To promote connection within other employee resource groups, reach out to their leadership with an invitation to connect.

Leverage your legends. Legends comprise that small group of male leaders who are widely known for championing diversity in your organization.[2] Reinforce and develop your legends as male influencers and role models. Their influence on other men is incredibly powerful; through their behavior, legends strengthen a courageous sense of aspiration and purpose in the allyship of junior men.

Identify those allies who have expressed an interest in developing themselves.[3] Meet them where they are, understand their motivation, and carefully develop and sharpen their commitment. Give them opportunities to share their experiences and understand the meaning of their allyship. Sharing personal ally stories ("why I care about gender equality") helps other allies to reflect on their own experiences and feelings about the importance of gender partnership. Sharing and storytelling build connections between members and weave a sense of belonging into the community. This is especially important as you need to draw on resources, commit to action, and overcome resistance.

Encourage tempered radicals and rebel leaders. Tempered radicals and rebel talent are those cultural insiders with an outsider perspective—people who understand gender equity.[4] Look for men who demonstrate rebel leader expertise. Their passion, curiosity, and creativity enable organizational change. Challenging the status quo, traditional gender roles, and expanding perspectives comes naturally and authentically to them. These leaders are particularly helpful in overcoming resistance and barriers to change; they're not afraid to confront when needed. Encourage these guys and let them lead.

Solicit nominations. Ask managers to nominate members of their team who might be strong male ally candidates. Engage the women's networks in your company to identify men who they perceive as established or aspiring gender diversity advocates.[5]

Enhance the nomination and invitation process. Notify nominated and invited men with an affirming emphasis on how others view them as strong advocates for gender diversity. Never underestimate the power of affirmation and recognition. Affirming notifications and invitations also reinforce the message that gender equity is an organizational priority. To foster greater interest, have the executive sponsor advocating for the ally initiative send an email to each nominee's direct manager.[6]

Launch an open invitation for self-selection. Sending an open ally-community invitation allows interested men to self-select. Finding men outside the usual suspects helps to broaden the appeal of a male ally group. You may be surprised who expresses interest. Men who previously seemed apathetic about gender diversity may come forward and become passionate advocates.[7]

Strategically Grow Your Allies' Community

Practice what you've learned. The two components of allyship must remain front and center when building a male allies community. First, promote gender fairness and equity through supportive and collaborative relationships *with* women. Allies work *alongside* women, not *for* women, not *instead* of women, and certainly not to *rescue* women. Return to this foundation of allyship often in building an ally community. Without women alongside as allies, gender partnership is simply not possible. Ambassador Donald Steinberg created a community of male allies in the global development sector called Mobilizing Men as Partners for Women, Peace and Security. This international community employs the mantra: "Nothing about us without us."[8] This means, in essence, to work alongside women to ensure equal access and inclusion of women in all aspects of the workplace, and never presume to speak for women, only amplify their voices. This community has an official charter and principles in which the mantra is repeated to keep its purpose clear and fresh. It perpetuates a mindset of learning from women. You can also leverage this mindset to collaborate with the legions of women who have been leading gender equity work for decades in your own organization.

Second, drive systemic change through public acts of sponsorship and advocacy. There is nothing like committing publicly to show transparency and have others hold you accountable for your actions. Create a set of pledge principles for allies to sign, which increases commitment and ownership. Then leverage that public commitment to recruit and reinforce additional advocates for gender equity. (See the sidebar "Sample Pledge Principles.")

With these two allyship tenets guiding your efforts to launch an ally community, integrate the following best practices into your community.[9]

Partner closely with a women's initiative in your organization. Whether in an employee resource group, women's leadership initiative, or an informal grassroots group of women for gender equity, work in close partnership to align action and advocacy. Offer to create a male and female cochair structure for both your male ally community and the women's resource group. Ask a senior woman to be your executive sponsor if your community is an official part of the company.

Start small; don't try to boil the ocean. Work within your sphere of influence looking for small wins. In resource-constrained environments, grassroots efforts are how to work these days. You may not have time to plan and develop a formal program, but you can work at your local level. Work laterally with the men and women near you first.

Keep it action oriented and focused on outcomes. The power of a community is in combined resources and synergistic efforts to drive real change. Don't let it devolve into mere cheap talk and social gatherings. Male allies are looking to understand what they can do.

Avoid costly bureaucratic structure. Focus on advocacy. Stay agile. Unnecessary ally community structure and hierarchy divert attention from the real work of allyship. They also waste money and energy that could be spent to create change.

Sample Pledge Principles

1. The rationale and motivation for our work comes from a commitment to both human rights and gender equality.[a] We are intent on changing gender power dynamics through engagement and allyship.

2. We will focus on advocacy objectives that are time bound, measurable, and outcome oriented.

3. Our advocacy is rooted in the evidence from current research evidence on gender inequality in society, the workplace generally, and our organization specifically. Our ally work is based on the concept, "Nothing about us without us."

4. We will promote healthier and more just gender identities (e.g., promoting healthy and inclusive expressions of masculinity).

5. We will take actions to address sexual harassment and abuse reflected in the global #MeToo movement, especially as they relate to gender power dynamics. While we seek to cast a broad net, individuals with past records of abuses will not participate.

6. Our participants will represent the male diversity evident in our organization (e.g., race, ethnicity, age, sexual orientation, gender identity, religious affiliation).

7. We recognize that the same principles that apply to marginalized women also apply to other marginalized communities in the workplace. We deliberately apply ally strategies to these groups when possible.

a. "Mobilizing Men as Partners for Women, Peace and Security," Our Secure Future charter, March 20, 2019, https://oursecurefuture.org/sites/default/files/3.20.19%20 Charter.pdf

Base the community's advocacy on evidence and facts. Keep women's actual experiences and voices at the forefront and ensure that your group's actions are rooted in ground truth. Challenge unsupported narratives, myths, stereotypes, and biased perceptions, such as the idea that meeting alone with a woman is dangerous or that women are just waiting to falsely accuse men of harassment.

Facilitate contact with senior leaders as program sponsors to strengthen community efforts and ties. As the community grows, diversify networks to broaden the scope and influence of your advocacy.

Promote healthy gender identities. Recognize how traditional forms of masculinity lead to biased behavior and stereotypes. Foster healthy norms of masculinity that don't artificially constrain men and women in the workplace or at home. Deloitte's research on men provides insight into how men feel stuck in the traditional workplace and how rigid gender rules inhibit gender partnership.[10] Men have overwhelming pressure to avoid asking for help from their male or female colleagues. Men are also less likely to have friendships and personal relationships based on trust with men or women that can be outlets for pressure and fear. To avoid signs of weakness, men learn to cover and become hypercompetitive and stoic, and don't disclose stress and anxiety. Many of these behaviors can be detrimental to the careers of women and other underrepresented minorities.[11]

Promote actions and advocacy to address sexual harassment. By recognizing men's role in stopping sexual harassment, drive systemic change in language and behavior through bystander intervention and education.

Include participants from a wide variety of backgrounds. Reaching broader groups of men and being taken seriously in social justice work mean you have to be fully inclusive in your own ally community. Does your community include men of color, gay men, and men from different generations? Ask often how you can reach across cultural boundaries to pull diverse men into the ally fold. If your organization has employee resource groups, start by reaching out to connect with each of these groups and invite them to collaborate.

Focus on dos, not don'ts. Instead of telling men not to steal women's ideas, show them how to amplify and ensure they give credit. In a space that is heavily focused on what not to do, male ally groups do just the opposite. They equip men with both the rationale and the tools to act. They also show men that there is more than one way to be a male ally.

Develop an expectation of accountability. Allyship requires getting comfortable with being uncomfortable. This includes an expectation that each of us will be held accountable for our language and behavior. Because allies both make mistakes and sincerely want to get better, they expect to be confronted. Real allies both invite and thoughtfully implement feedback.

Implement bystander intervention as part of ally education. The research is clear that ally development must include the development of skills for bystanders to intervene. Diffusion of responsibility is part of the human condition, and you must thoughtfully address the challenges to overcoming bystander paralysis in male allies. Bystander intervention helps allies to notice an event, define it as a problem, take responsibility for intervening, decide on a course of action, and implement the intervention.

Clarify Desired Outcomes

Ally networks and communities provide a space to discuss and share things they are learning about women and allyship with other men and women. Having a community where men feel they're included leads them to be more engaged. Attorney Frank Bernstein of Squire

Patton Boggs LLP explained that gender partnership also makes us better business partners by encouraging humility and eliminating blind spots. Bernstein said, "A man's got to know his limitations, and recognizing what we know and don't know is key in all aspects of life. People who aren't like me bring different perspectives and something important to contribute." Effective ally communities leverage learning and inclusion to achieve five desired outcomes.[12]

Making gender real and relevant. Men in these communities often describe their involvement, especially after hearing women's workplace experiences, as "opening my eyes" and "breaking me out of a bubble." What was once theoretical became concrete. When these accounts come from women they know, it creates that personal connection that motivates action.

Deepening understanding. Through connection and listening, men come to appreciate the nuance and complexity of gender equity in the workplace. Previously random incidents start to coalesce into predictable patterns of behavior. Men's mindsets shift to see that progress requires not only changing behavioral norms but also changing organizational systems and structures. Through the opportunity to partner with their female peers, men appreciate the need for women and men to work together to drive change. For example, PNC Bank's male allyship program includes a learning exercise where each man reaches out to three female colleagues and asks questions about their experience as a woman at the bank.

Understanding the critical role of listening. Men develop an awareness of the need to talk less and listen more. They come to value listening at work and at home, too. They ask their partners how they can be better allies for them, listen carefully, and take the feedback to heart.

Becoming more self-reflective. Men participating in male ally groups are prompted to consider how their—past and current—behavior affected women at work and their spouses and partners at home. Ultimately, many men have the epiphany that they have been part of the problem and now need to be part of the solution.

Clarifying men's role in supporting gender diversity. In the workplace, men achieve clarity about what does and does not help to support women at work. One of the many benefits of male ally involvement is that instead of feeling lost and confused, men come to feel empowered and want to use all they've learned to support change.

Connect allies through networks outside your organization, including allies at conferences or other forums. Women's leadership conferences increasingly are welcoming men as allies to learn and connect. Some of these forums are encouraging men's learning, awareness, and ally development through specific tracks and programs. Because your allies' community is closely partnered with women's resource groups, there is a terrific opportunity to learn together at these conferences. Allies benefit by participating in ongoing, supportive education and networking opportunities at forums, learning best practices, and connecting with like-minded gender advocates; such participation is essential to developing ally skills.

Cultivate Connection and Collaboration

Now that you've identified the core group of guys who get it and have started laying the foundation for creating an ally identity, it's time to focus on interpersonal relationships, networking, and team building. You need to maintain a positive and aspirational approach to developing collaborative relationships with your female work colleagues. Focusing on increased interactions results in more positive exposure to women and, ultimately, greater validation of ally efforts by female colleagues. Here are a few best practices, with emphasis on benefits, positive outcomes, success stories, and interconnectedness.

First, create opportunities to interact with women in your organization through networking, mentoring, and professional develop-

ment events. As we've already suggested, if your organization has a women's employee resource group, start by coordinating events with them. This serves three purposes: it provides positive interaction with women in leadership, increases male allies' motivation and commitment, and solidifies a relationship with a group of women who have an overlapping purpose—classic allyship. Subha Barry of Working Mother Media stressed that allyship and increased cross-gender professional interaction needs to start early. She suggested starting with entry-level personnel: "Build mentoring networks where men and women are working together within the organizational culture from the beginning." More frequent and positive interactions help people to reduce group differences, dispel myths and stereotypes, and build connection.[13] Cultivating connection and collaboration is about developing men as allies and having women accept men as allies. The social connection that male allies enjoy through positive interactions with women produces feelings of acceptance, support, and belonging as an ally.[14] Positive reinforcement of the ally identity leads to personal commitment and motivation in allyship that fosters gender equity. Rachana Bhide of Bloomberg Radio News said that women and men need to reinforce the capabilities of men as allies because many men don't realize how much positive reinforcement they need. Without reinforcement, getting them on board is difficult and slow. She suggested that "if you tell men they've been identified as showing many of the skills and attitudes of excellent mentors and allies for women and invite them to a workshop on that basis, I can't imagine they're going to cross their arms and be defensive. We need to create that positive framing."

Second, communicate support for social change as part of your interactions with women. Male allies thoughtfully consider how their presence and actions influence the motivations, identities, and resolve of their female friends.[15] Having an awareness of their privilege, allies offer autonomy-oriented support that empowers women; it doesn't make women dependent on men's support.[16] And don't fall into the trap of co-opting the messages of women's groups and making this about men as allies. Janet Foutty of Deloitte said that "it's one thing for me as a female leader to set expectations for my team, but incredibly important that the men on my team are as loud and clear as I am on gender partnership. These have been important allies because they've had to lean in to reinforce and amplify messages based on the trust issue in work relationships between men and women."

Third, periodically reflect on the purpose, progress, and development of your allies' initiative. Early in the creation process and at regular intervals after, check in with women leading gender initiatives to ensure that your efforts are aligned, ask for feedback and guidance, and reinforce the need to hold men accountable to their female colleagues.[17] Be ready to shift your approach as the cultural narrative changes. Do small things on your team right now to give women more opportunities and voice. Don't spend endless time looking for the latest research or best programs. Just get started. Use your own friendships and collaborations with female colleagues as a prime opportunity to intentionally role-model allyship for other men.

If your community-building efforts even smell like CYA training or mandatory participation, you will fail. As Gretchen Carlson explained, "Don't do it the way we used to train for sexual harassment prevention—this is not effective. Don't make it a compliance issue." A culture of allyship is based on authentic connection and supportive and collaborative relationships based on action, not "check the box" training programs of the traditional twentieth-century workplace.

Ally Actions

- **Launch a male allies community.** Identify those allies who have expressed an interest in developing themselves and encourage cultural insiders with an outsider perspective as men who understand gender equity. Include all parts of your organization, every business unit, satellite or remote locations, and other employee resource groups.

- **Strategically grow your allies' community.** Base the community's advocacy on evidence and facts and keep it action oriented and focused on outcomes working within your sphere of influence to create small wins.

- **Clarify desired outcomes.** Make gender real and relevant by deepening understanding and appreciating the nuance and complexity of gender equity in the workplace, while clarifying men's role in supporting gender diversity.

- **Cultivate connection and collaboration.** Create opportunities to interact with women in your organization through networking, mentoring, and professional development events.

Conclusion

The Future in a World of Allies

Although this may be the end of the book, it's just the beginning of your allyship journey. Time to move expeditiously and implement the toolbox of ally strategies we've outlined. Allyship is a team sport, so recruit other key men and women to join you in partnership to transform workplace culture, one ally at a time.

The future depends on the involvement of all men. In a world that includes male allies, we can more rapidly eliminate the gender inequities that historically exclude and marginalize women, which threatens our safety, prosperity, and happiness. The stakes are high. When men are involved in creating gender parity, the outcomes in political, economic, and social systems can be life altering.

Imagine a global culture of male allyship in which women are equally represented in decision making at every level of government—less armed conflict and violence, longer-lasting peace agreements, lower levels of corruption, and higher trust in government.[1] Imagine allyship-fueled gender parity in the workplace where women have an equal voice in the economic decisions, leading to elimination of the gender wage gap, reductions in poverty, and an estimated $28 trillion added to global GDP.[2] Allies know that gender-balanced decision making also leads to better quality of life through more focus on social welfare resulting in lower rates of disease, lower levels of child mortality, and higher life expectancy.[3] This is a snapshot of a world in which 50 percent of the population (women) are equally included and not marginalized. Of course, getting there demands that the other 50 percent (men) engage in ally behavior. We simply cannot afford not to act. We need you to purposefully and deliberately commit to being an all-in ally today!

Most of our focus has been on workplace behavior and organizational processes. But we'd be remiss if we didn't remind you that gender partnership starts at home. Pressure to change the way we work outside the home will necessarily include the way we work inside the home. Nowhere is this truer than for people in the bottom quintiles of income—those who make up the majority of the paid workforce in our society. Regardless of your hierarchical position at work, we all need to practice allyship at home to show the need for change in the way we work.

The twentieth-century workplace is the past. The current workplace demands a new set of attributes, skill sets, and knowledge for its workers, managers, and CEOs to lead, develop, and advance the diverse workforce we recruit today. Advocating for those who don't look like you, have similar experiences, or share the same cultural background or family background is the new norm. We wrote this book through the lens of gender allyship, but we intend these strategies to develop the skills necessary to make you a more inclusive leader for everyone. As you master allyship for women, we are confident these same skills will translate for others you work with.

There is a growing discourse about male allyship in the media, HR offices, and among diversity and inclusion leaders, but the reality is that there are few well-developed allyship programs of record. Don't let this dissuade you. In this guide, we've provided all the tools you need to start an allyship program. We have confidence that you will find a community of men ready for the conversation about leaning in to gender equity, equality, and fairness. All you require now is the courage to act.

Notes

Chapter 1

1. A. Hegewisch and H. Hartmann, "The Gender Wage Gap: 2018 Earnings Differences by Race and Ethnicity," Institute for Women's Policy Research, March 7, 2019, https://iwpr.org/publications/gender-wage-gap-2018/.

2. Ibid.

3. Jonathan Woetzel, A. Madgavkar, K. Ellingrud, E. Labaye, S. Devillard, E. Kutcher, and M. Krishnan, "The Power of Parity: How Advancing Women's Equality Can Add $12 Trillion to Global Growth," McKinsey Global Institute, September 2015, https://www.mckinsey.com/~/media/McKinsey/Featured%20Insights/Employment%20 and%20Growth/How%20advancing%20womens%20equality%20can%20add%2012%20 trillion%20to%20global%20growth/MGI%20Power%20of%20parity_Full%20report _September%202015.ashx.

4. K. Bennhold, "Another Side of #MeToo: Male Managers Fearful of Mentoring Women," *New York Times*, January 27, 2019, https://www.nytimes.com/2019/01/27/world/ europe/metoo-backlash-gender-equality-davos-men.html.

5. B. Kingma and W. van Marken Lichtenbelt, "Energy Consumption in Buildings and Female Thermal Demand," *Nature Climate Change* 5, no. 12 (2015): 1054–1058.

6. J. Fortin and K. Zraick, "First All-Female Spacewalk Canceled Because NASA Doesn't Have Two Suits That Fit," *New York Times*, March 25, 2019, https://www .nytimes.com/2019/03/25/science/female-spacewalk-canceled.html.

7. C. J. Kahane, "Injury Vulnerability and Effectiveness of Occupant Protection Technologies for Older Occupants and Women" (No. DOT HS 811 766), 2013 Washington, DC: National Highway Traffic Safety Administration; C. N. B. Merz et al., Knowledge, Attitudes, and Beliefs Regarding Cardiovascular Disease in Women: The Women's Heart Alliance," *Journal of the American College of Cardiology* 70, no. 2 (2017): 123–132.

8. Alexis Krivkovich, Kelsey Robinson, Irina Starikova, Rachel Valentino, and Lareina Yee, "Women in the Workplace 2017," McKinsey & Company, 2017, https:// www.mckinsey.com/~/media/McKinsey/Featured%20Insights/Gender%20Equality/ Women%20in%20the%20Workplace%202017/Women-in-the-Workplace-2017-v2 .ashx

9. Krivkovich et al., "Women in the Workplace 2017."

10. C. Fairchild, "Where Women in Finance See a Gender Gap, Men Don't," CNBC, June 26, 2018, https://www.cnbc.com/2018/06/25/where-women-in-finance-see -a-gender-gap-men-dont.html.

11. Ibid.

12. A. Kehn and J. C. Ruthig, "Perceptions of Gender Discrimination across Six Decades: The Moderating Roles of Gender and Age," *Sex Roles* 69, no. 5–6 (2013): 289–296; H. R. Radke, M. J. Hornsey, and F. K. Barlow, "Changing versus Protecting the Status Quo: Why Men and Women Engage in Different Types of Action on Behalf of Women," *Sex Roles* 79, no. 9–10 (2018): 505–518; J. C. Ruthig et al., "When Women's Gains Equal Men's Losses: Predicting a Zero-sum Perspective of Gender Status," *Sex Roles* 76, no. 1–2 (2017): 17–26.

13. A. H. Eagly, *Sex Differences in Social Behavior: A Social-Role Interpretation* (Hillsdale, NJ: Erlbaum, 1987); D. A. Prentice and E. Carranza, "What Women and Men Should Be, Shouldn't Be, Are Allowed to Be, and Don't Have to Be: The Contents of Prescriptive Gender Stereotypes," *Psychology of Women Quarterly* 26 (2002): 269–281; C. L. Ridgeway and S. J. Correll, "Unpacking the Gender System: A Theoretical Perspective on Gender Beliefs and Social Relations," *Gender & Society* 18, no. 4 (2004), 510–531.

14. S. Benard and S. J. Correll, "Normative Discrimination and the Motherhood Penalty," *Gender & Society* 24, no. 5 (2010): 616–646.

15. M. Reyes, "How to Deal with the Stigma of Taking Paternity Leave," *New York Post*, February 25, 2018, https://nypost.com/2018/02/25/how-to-deal-with-the-stigma-of-taking-paternity-leave/.

16. P. Glick and S. T. Fiske, "Ambivalent Sexism," in *Advances in Experimental Social Psychology*, vol. 33 (Cambridge, MA>> Academic Press. 2001), 115–188.

17. Ibid.

18. D. Meyerson and M. Tompkins, "Tempered Radicals as Institutional Change Agents: The Case of Advancing Gender Equity at the University of Michigan," *Harvard Journal of Law & Gender* 30 (2007): 303–322.

19. S. Dharmapuri and J. Shoemaker, "Feeling Guilty about #MeToo? Three Ways Men Can Do Something about It," *Ms. Blog Magazine*, April 13, 2018, https://msmagazine.com/2018/04/13/feeling-guilty-metoo-three-ways-men-can-something/.

20. E. N. Sherf, S. Tangirala, and K. C. Weber, "It Is Not My Place! Psychological Standing and Men's Voice and Participation in Gender-Parity Initiatives," *Organization Science* 28, no. 2 (2017): 193–210.

21. I. Hideg, J. L. Michela, and D. L. Ferris, "Overcoming Negative Reactions of Nonbeneficiaries to Employment Equity: The Effect of Participation in Policy Formulation," *Journal of Applied Psychology* 96, no. 2 (2011): 363; R. K. Ratner and D. T. Miller, "The Norm of Self-Interest and Its Effects on Social Action," *Journal of Personality and Social Psychology* 81, no. 1 (2001): 5–16; Sherf et al., "It Is Not My Place!"

22. D. R. Hekman et al., "Does Diversity-Valuing Behavior Result in Diminished Performance Ratings for Non-white and Female Leaders?," *Academy of Management Journal* 60, no. 2 (2017): 771–797.

23. M. Krentz et al., "Five Ways Men Can Improve Gender Diversity at Work," Boston Consulting Group, October 10, 2017, https://www.bcg.com/en-us/publications/2017/people-organization-behavior-culture-five-ways-men-improve-gender-diversity-work.aspx.

24. M. Flood and B. Pease, "Undoing Men's Privilege and Advancing Gender Equality in Public Sector Institutions," *Policy and Society* 24, no. 4 (2005): 119–138; Krentz et al., "Five Ways Men Can Improve Gender Diversity at Work."

25. S. DeTurk, "Allies in Action: The Communicative Experiences of People Who Challenge Social Injustice on Behalf of Others," *Communication Quarterly* 59, no. 5 (2011): 569–590.

26. L. A. Rudman, K. Mescher, and C. A. Moss-Racusin, "Reactions to Gender Egalitarian Men: Perceived Feminization Due to Stigma-by-Association," *Group Processes & Intergroup Relations* 16, no. 5 (2013): 572–599.

27. K. Catlin, *Better Allies: Everyday Actions to Create Inclusive, Engaging Workplaces* (San Mateo, California Karen Catlin Publishing, 2019).

Chapter 2

1. American Psychological Association, *APA Guidelines for the Psychological Practice with Boys and Men* (Washington, DC: APA, 2018).

2. C. Ashcraft et al., *Male Advocates and Allies: Promoting Gender Diversity in Technology Workplaces* (Boulder, CO: National Center for Women in IT, 2013).

3. B. J. Drury and C. R. Kaiser, "Allies Against Sexism: The Role of Men in Confronting Sexism," *Journal of Social Issues* 70, no. 4 (2014): 637–652; Promundo-US, *So, You Want to Be a Male Ally for Gender Equality? (And You Should): Results from a National Survey, and a Few Things You Should Know* (Washington, DC: Promundo, 2019).

4. Promundo-US, *So, You Want to Be a Male Ally for Gender Equality?*

5. Ibid.

6. C. L. Anicha, A. Burnett, and C. Bilen-Green, "Men Faculty Gender-Equity Advocates: A Qualitative Analysis of Theory and Praxis," *Journal of Men's Studies* 23, no. 1 (2015): 21–43; J. Prime and C. A. Moss-Racusin, *Engaging Men in Gender Initiatives: What Change Agents Need to Know* (New York: Catalyst, 2009).

7. The Free Dictionary-Medical Dictionary, "Gynophobia," thefreedictionary.com. https://medical-dictionary.thefreedictionary.com/gynophobia.

8. LeanIn.Org and SurveyMonkey survey, February 22–March 1, 2019, https://leanin.org/women-in-the-workplace.

9. LeanIn.Org and SurveyMonkey survey, March 6–10, 2019, https://leanin.org/women-in-the-workplace.

10. J. S. Abramowitz, B. J. Deacon, and S. P. H. Whiteside, *Exposure Therapy for Anxiety: Principles and Practice*, 2nd ed. (New York: Guilford, 2019).

11. Ashcraft et al., *Male Advocates and Allies*.

12. K. Catlin, *Better Allies: Everyday Actions to Create Inclusive, Engaging Workplaces* (San Mateo, CA, Better Allies Press, 2019).

13. S. Dharmapuri and J. Shoemaker, "Feeling Guilty about #MeToo? Three Ways Men Can Do Something about It," *Ms Magazine*, April 2018, https://msmagazine.com/2018/04/13/feeling-guilty-metoo-three-ways-men-can-something/.

14. J. C. Williams and R. Dempsey, *What Works for Women at Work: Four Patterns Working Women Need to Know* (New York: NYU Press, 2018).

15. A. K. Sesko and M. Biernat, "Prototypes of Race and Gender: The Invisibility of Black Women," *Journal of Experimental Social Psychology* 46, no. 2 (2010): 356–360.

16. Williams and Dempsey, *What Works for Women at Work*.

17. American Bar Association, "You Can't Change What You Can't See: Interrupting Racial and Gender Bias in the Legal Profession," 2018, https://www.americanbar.org/groups/women/initiatives_awards/bias-interrupters.html.

18. E. Goffman, *Stigma: Notes on the Management of Spoiled Identity* (Englewood Cliffs, NJ: Prentice Hall, 1963); K. Yoshino, *Covering: The Hidden Assault on Our Civil Rights* (New York: Random House Trade Paperbacks, 2007).

19. A. K. Newheiser and M. Barreto, "Hidden Costs of Hiding Stigma: Ironic Interpersonal Consequences of Concealing a Stigmatized Identity in Social Interactions," *Journal of Experimental Social Psychology* 52 (2014): 58–70.

20. L. Smart and D. M. Wegner, "The Hidden Costs of Hidden Stigma," in *Social Psychology of Stigma*, eds. T. F. Heatherton, R. E. Kleck, M. R. Hebl, and J. G. Hull (New York, NY: Guilford Press, 2000), 220–242.

21. M. Flood and B. Pease, "Undoing Men's Privilege and Advancing Gender Equality in Public Sector Institutions," *Policy and Society* 24, no. 4 (2005), 119–138; J. M. Ostrove and K. T. Brown, "Are Allies Who We Think They Are?: A Comparative Analysis," *Journal of Applied Social Psychology* 48, no. 4 (2017): 195–204.

22. P. McIntosh, "White Privilege: Unpacking the Invisible Knapsack," *Race, Class, and Gender in the United States: An Integrated Study* 4 (1988): 165–169.

23. M. Z. Johnson, "160+ Examples of Male Privilege in All Areas of Life," *Everyday Feminism*, February 25, 2016, https://everydayfeminism.com/2016/02/160-examples-of-male-privilege/.

24. Flood and Pease, "Undoing Men's Privilege and Advancing Gender Equality."

25. S. Davidai and T. Gilovich, "The Headwinds/Tailwinds Asymmetry: An Availability Bias in Assessments of Barriers and Blessings," *Journal of Personality and Social Psychology* 111, no. 6 (2016): 835–851.

26. S. DeTurk, "Allies in Action: The communicative Experiences of People Who Challenge Social Injustice on Behalf of Others," *Communication Quarterly* 59, no. 5 (2011): 569–590.

27. J. Bennett, *Feminist Fight Club: A Survival Manual for a Sexist Workplace* (New York: Harper Collins, 2016).

28. J. Bennett, *Feminist Fight Club: A Survival Manual for a Sexist Workplace* (New York: Harper Collins, 2016), p. 276.

Chapter 3

1. US Bureau of Labor Statistics, "Table 4. Families with Own Children: Employment Status of Parents by Age of Youngest Child and Family Type, 2017-2018 Annual Averages," US Bureau of Labor Statistics, April 18, 2019, http://www.bls.gov/news.release/famee.t04.htm.

2. C. Lyonette and R. Crompton, "Sharing the Load? Partners' Relative Earnings and the Division of Domestic Labour," *Work, Employment and Society* 29, no. 1 (2015): 23–40.

3. S. J. Glynn, "Breadwinning Mothers Are Increasingly the U.S. Norm," Center for American Progress, 2016, https://www.americanprogress.org/issues/women/reports/2016/12/19/295203/breadwinning-mothers-are-increasingly-the-u-s-norm/.

4. W. Wang, K. Parker, and P. Taylor, "Chapter 3: Married Mothers Who Out-Earn Their Husbands," Pew Research Center, May 29, 2013, https://www.pewsocialtrends.org/2013/05/29/chapter-3-married-mothers-who-out-earn-their-husbands/.

5. US Bureau of Labor Statistics, "A-19. Employed Persons by Occupation, Sex, and Age," US Bureau of Labor Statistics, July 5, 2019, https://www.bls.gov/web/empsit/cpseea19.htm; Catalyst, "Quick Take: Buying Power," Catalyst, November 27, 2018, https://www.catalyst.org/research/buying-power/#footnote4_q9ulgsb; R. Siegel, "Women Outnumber Men in the American Workforce for Only the Second Time," *Washington Post*, January 10, 2020, https://www.washingtonpost.com/business/2020/01/10/january-2020-jobs-report/.

6. S. Ballakrishnen, P. Fielding-Singh, and D. Magliozzi, "Intentional Invisibility: Professional Women and the Navigation of Workplace Constraints," *Sociological Perspectives* 62 (2019): 23–41.

7. Promundo-US, *So, You Want to Be a Male Ally for Gender Equality? (And You Should): Results from a National Survey, and a Few Things You Should Know* (Washington, DC: Promundo, 2019), https://promundoglobal.org/resources/male-allyship/#.

8. C. Lawrence, E. D. Arthrell, J. B. Calamai and A. Morris, *The Design of Everyday Men: A New Lens for Gender Equality Progress*, Deloitte, 2019, https://www2.deloitte.com/content/dam/insights/us/articles/ca1671_design-of-everyday-men/DI_The-design-of-everyday-men.pdf.

9. A. C. Crouter et al., "Implications of Overwork and Overload for the Quality of Men's Family Relationships," *Journal of Marriage and Family* 63, no. 2 (2001): 404–416.

10. V. Bolden-Barrett, "EY Says Its Female Turnover Dropped, Thanks in Part to Equal Leave for Dads," 2019, https://www.hrdive.com/news/ey-says-its-female-turnover-dropped-thanks-in-part-to-equal-leave-for-dad/555902/

11. N. Chesley, "Stay-at-Home Fathers and Breadwinning Mothers: Gender, Couple Dynamics, and Social Change," *Gender & Society* 25, no. 5 (2011): 642–664.

12. Promundo-US, *So, You Want to Be a Male Ally for Gender Equality?*

13. J. Dew and W. B. Wilcox, "If Momma Ain't Happy: Explaining Declines in Marital Satisfaction among New Mothers," *Journal of Marriage and Family* 73, no. 1 (2011): 1–12.

14. L. ten Brummelhuis and J. H. Greenhaus, "Research: When Juggling Work and Family, Women Offer More Emotional Support Than Men," *Harvard Business Review*, March 21, 2019.

15. A. Daminger, "The Cognitive Dimension of Household Labor," *American Sociological Review*, 2019, https://doi.org/10.1177/0003122419859007.

16. S. Behson, *The Working Dad's Survival Guide: How to Succeed at Work and at Home* (Carlsbad, CA: Motivational Press, 2015).

17. J. Bennett, *Feminist Fight Club: A Survival Manual for the Sexist Workplace* (New York: Harper Collins, 2016).

18. D. L. Carlson, S. Hanson, and A. Fitzroy, "The Division of Child Care, Sexual Intimacy, and Relationship Quality in Couples," *Gender & Society* 30, no. 3 (2016): 442–466; M. D. Johnson, N. L. Galambos, and J. R. Anderson, "Skip the Dishes? Not So Fast! Sex and Housework Revisited," *Journal of Family Psychology* 30, no. 2 (2016): 203.

19. S. Ballakrishnen, P. Fielding-Singh and D. Magliozzi, "Intentional Invisibility: Professional Women and the Navigation of Workplace Constraints," *Sociological Perspectives* 62, no. 1 (2019): 23–41.

20. R. Bhide, "Six Things Great Male Allies Do: Lessons from a Project on Male Allyship," LinkedIn, December 2017, https://www.linkedin.com/pulse/6-things-great-male-allies-do-lessons-from-project-allyship-bhide/.

21. Lawrence et al., *The Design of Everyday Men.*

22. J. Levs, "To Make the Case for Parental Leave, Dads Will Have to Work Together," *Harvard Business Review*, March 2019.

23. J. Sudakow, "4 Ways Working Dads Can Make More Time for Family," *Harvard Business Review*, April 9, 2019.

24. K. Catlin, "Better Allies: Everyday Actions to Create Inclusive, Engaging Workplaces," Karen Catlin Consulting, 2019.

25. Levs, "To Make the Case for Parental Leave."

26. S. Ballakrishnen, et al., "Intentional Invisibility."

27. D. G. Smith and M. W. Segal, "On the Fast Track: Dual Military Couples Navigating Institutional Structures," in *Visions of the 21st Century Family: Transforming Structures and Identities* (Bingley, UK: Emerald Group Publishing Limited, 2013), 213–253.

28. A. Wittenberg-Cox, "Being a Two-Career Couple Requires a Long-Term Plan," *Harvard Business Review*, February 26, 2018.

29. Bhide, "Six Things Great Male Allies Do."

30. Bennett, *Feminist Fight Club*.

Chapter 4

1. E. Hinchliffe, "Female Employees Who Are the Only Woman at Work Are 50% More Likely to Consider Quitting," *Fortune*, October 2018, http://fortune .com/2018/10/23/women-only-one-lean-in-survey/.

2. K. Parker, "Women in Majority-Male Workplaces Report Higher Rates of Gender Discrimination," Pew Research Center, March 7, 2018, https://www.pewre search.org/fact-tank/2018/03/07/women-in-majority-male-workplaces-report-higher -rates-of-gender-discrimination/.

3. B. Liang et al., "Mentoring College-age Women: A Relational Approach," *American Journal of Community Psychology* 30 (2002): 271–288.

4. K. Catlin, *Better Allies: Everyday Actions to Create Inclusive, Engaging Workplaces* (San Mateo, CA: Better Allies Press, 2019).

5. S. Granger, "Want to Be an Ally to Women at Work? Here Are Five Things Men in Tech Have Been Doing," Slate.com, January 2018, https://slate.com/human-interest/ 2018/01/want-to-be-an-ally-to-women-at-work-five-things-men-in-tech-have-been -doing.html.

6. Ibid.

7. K. Elsesser, *Sex and the Office: Women, Men, and the Sex Partition That's Dividing the Workplace* (Lanham, MD: Taylor, 2015).

8. C. Shelton, "How Men Can Decenter So Women Can Step Up," LinkedIn, March 2016, https://www.linkedin.com/pulse/how-men-can-decenter-so-women-step -up-chuck-shelton/.

9. Ibid.

10. M. Krentz, O. Wierzba, K. Abouzahr, J. Garcia-Alonso and F. B. Taplett, "Five Ways Men Can Improve Gender Diversity at Work," BCG, October 2017, https:// www.bcg.com/publications/2017/people-organization-behavior-culture-five-ways -men-improve-gender-diversity-work.aspx.

11. J. Bennett, *Feminist Fight Club: A Survival Manual for a Sexist Workplace* (New York: Harper Collins, 2016).

12. K. A. Rockquemore, "A New Model of Mentoring," *Inside Higher Education*, July 2013, https://www.insidehighered.com/advice/2013/07/22/essay-calling-senior-faculty -embrace-new-style-mentoring.

13. The Female Quotient, "Men of Action," *Female Quotient*, https://www.thefemale quotient.com/wp-content/uploads/2019/01/MGTE-3.pdf.

14. C. Shelton, "What Happens When Men Listen to Women to Build Trust?," LinkedIn, March 2018, https://www.greatheartconsulting.com/blog-1/what-happens -when-men-listen-to-women-to-build-trust-part-1.

15. K. A. Gonzalez, E. D. B. Riggle, and S. S. Rostosky, "Cultivating Positive Feelings and Attitudes: A Path to Prejudice Reduction and Ally Behavior," *Translational Issues in Psychological Science* 1 (2015): 372–381.

16. Catlin, *Better Allies*.

17. Shelton, "What Happens When Men Listen to Women to Build Trust?"

18. W. B. Johnson and D. Smith, *Athena Rising: How and Why Men Should Mentor Women* (Boston: Harvard Business Review Press, 2019).

19. Liang et al., "Mentoring College-age Women."

20. G. M. Russell and S. G. Horne, "Finding Equilibrium: Mentoring, Sexual Orientation, and Gender-Identity," *Professional Psychology: Research and Practice* 40 (2009): 194–200.

21. E. B. Wolf et al., "Managing Perceptions of Distress at Work: Reframing Emotion as Passion," *Organizational Behavior and Human Decision Processes* 137 (2016): 1–12.

22. C. L. Exley and J. B. Kessler, *The Gender Gap in Self-promotion* (No. w26345), National Bureau of Economic Research, 2019.

23. J. L. Smith and M. Huntoon, "Women's Bragging Rights: Overcoming Modesty Norms to Facilitate Women's Self-promotion," *Psychology of Women Quarterly* 38 (2014): 447–459.

24. S. Cheng et al., "Calling on Male Allies to Promote Gender Equity in IO Psychology," *Industrial and Organizational Psychology* 11 (2018): 389–398.

25. R. P. Clance and S. Imes, "The Imposter Phenomenon in High Achieving Women: Dynamics and Therapeutic Intervention," *Psychotherapy Theory, Research and Practice* 15 (1978): 1–8.

26. W. B. Johnson and D. G. Smith, "Mentoring Someone with Imposter Syndrome," *Harvard Business Review*, February 2019.

27. Cheng et al., "Calling on Male Allies."

28. Ernst & Young, "Women Fast Forward: The Time for Gender Parity Is Now," 2016, https://www.ey.com/Publication/vwLUAssets/ey-women-fast-forward-thought -leadership/%24FILE/ey-women-fast-forward-thought-leadership.pdf.

29. Catlin, *Better Allies.*

30. L. Droogendyk et al., "Acting in Solidarity: Cross-group Contact between Disadvantaged Group Members and Advantaged Group Allies," *Social Issues* 72 (2016): 315–334.

31. L. D. Patton and S. Bondi, "Nice White Men or Social Justice Allies? Using Critical Race Theory to Examine How White Male Faculty and Administrators Engage in Ally Work," *Race, Ethnicity, and Education* 18 (2015): 488–514.

32. N. Berlatsky, "A Short History of Male Feminism," *Atlantic*, June 2014, https:// www.theatlantic.com/politics/archive/2014/06/a-short-history-of-male-feminism/372673/.

33. J. A. De Vries, "Champions for Gender Equality: Female and Male Executives as Leaders of Gender Change," *Equality, Diversity, and Inclusion: An International Journal* 34 (2015): 21–36.

Chapter 5

1. K. Elsesser, *Sex and the Office: Women, Men, and the Sex Partition That's Dividing the Workplace* (Lanham, MD: Taylor, 2015).

2. B. R. Ragins, "Relational Mentoring: A Positive Approach to Mentoring at Work," in *The Oxford Handbook of Positive Organizational Scholarship*, eds. K. S. Cameron and G. M. Spreitzer (New York: Oxford University Press, 2012), 519–536.

3. Y. Yang, N. V. Chawla, and B. Uzzi, "A Network's Gender Composition and Communication Pattern Predict Women's Leadership Success" (Proceedings of the National Academy of Sciences, 201721438, 2019).

4. R. S. Bhide, "Engaging Men in Diversity: The Science of Effective Inclusion" (master's thesis, Columbia University, 2016).

5. A. M. Valerio and K. Sawyer, "The Men Who Mentor Women," *Harvard Business Review*, December 2016.

6. A. Grant, "Men Are Afraid to Mentor Women: Here's What You Can Do about It," LinkedIn, February 2018, https://www.linkedin.com/pulse/men-afraid-mentor-women-heres-what-we-can-do-adam-grant/.

7. B. R. Ragins, "Diversity and Workplace Mentoring Relationships: A Review and Positive Social Capital Approach," in *The Blackwell Handbook of Mentoring: A Multiple Perspectives Approach*, eds. T. D. Allen and L. T. Eby (Malden, MA: Blackwell, 2007), 281–300.

8. B. Liang et al., "Mentoring College-age Women: A Relational Approach," *American Journal of Community Psychology* 30 (2002): 271–288.

9. C. Shelton, "What Happens When Men Listen to Women to Build Trust?," *Greatheart Consulting* (blog), March 2018, https://www.greatheartconsulting.com/blog-1/what-happens-when-men-listen-to-women-to-build-trust-part-1.

10. D. G. Smith and W. B. Johnson, "Male Mentors Shouldn't Hesitate to Challenge Their Female Mentees," *Harvard Business Review*, March 2017.

11. Ragins, "Diversity and Workplace Mentoring Relationships."

12. W. B. Johnson and D. G. Smith, *Athena Rising: How and Why Men Should Mentor Women* (Boston, MA: Harvard Business Review Press, 2019).

13. M. G. Haselton, "The Sexual Overperception Bias: Evidence of a Systematic Bias in Men from a Survey of Naturally Occurring Events," *Journal of Research in Personality* 37 (2003): 34–47.

14. L. B. Rubin, *Just Friends: The Role of Friendships in Our Lives* (New York: Harper, 1986).

15. K. E. Kram and L. A. Isabella, "Mentoring Alternatives: The Role of Peer Relationships in Career Development," *Academy of Management Journal* 28 (1985): 110–132.

16. Ragins, "Relational Mentoring."

17. S. M. Drigotas et al., "Close Partner as Sculptor of the Ideal Self: Behavioral affirmation and the Michelangelo Phenomenon," *Journal of Personality and Social Psychology* 77 (1999): 293–323.

18. C. E. Rusbult et al., "The Part of Me That You Bring Out": Ideal Similarity and the Michelangelo Phenomenon," *Journal of Personality and Social Psychology* 96 (2009): 61–82.

19. R. Bhide, "Six Things Great Male Allies Do: Lessons from a Project on Male Allyship," LinkedIn, December 2017, https://www.linkedin.com/pulse/6-things-great-male-allies-do-lessons-from-project-allyship-bhide/.

20. J. Green, "Managers Pick Mini-me Protégés of the Same Race, Gender," *Bloomberg*, January 2019, https://www.bloomberg.com/news/articles/2019-01-08/managers-pick-mini-me-proteges-of-same-gender-race-in-new-study.

21. E. Polman, "Why It's Easier to Make Decisions for Someone Else," *Harvard Business Review*, November 2018.

22. E. Luxton, "Why Managers Give Women Less Feedback," World Economic Forum, October 2016, https://www.weforum.org/agenda/2016/10/managers-give-women-less-feedback/.

23. K. Scott, *Radical Candor: Be a Kickass Boss without Losing Your Humanity* (New York: St. Martin's Press, 2017).

24. Smith and Johnson, "Male Mentors Shouldn't Hesitate to Challenge Their Female Mentees."

25. Elsesser, *Sex and the Office*.

26. Johnson and Smith, *Athena Rising*.

27. Elsesser, *Sex and the Office*.

28. S. Sandberg, *Lean In: Women, Work, and the Will to Lead* (New York: Knopf, 2013).

Chapter 6

1. Promundo-US, *So, You Want to be a Male Ally for Gender Equality? (And You Should): Results from a National Survey, and Few Things You Didn't Know* (Washington, DC: Promundo, 2019), https://promundoglobal.org/wp-content/uploads/2019/03/Male-Allyship-Study-Web.pdf.

2. S. I. McClelland and K. J. Holland, "You, Me, or Her: Leaders' Perceptions of Responsibility for Increasing Gender Diversity in STEM Departments," *Psychology of Women Quarterly* 39 (2015): 210–225.

3. Promundo-US, *So, You Want to Be a Male Ally for Gender Equality?*

4. S. J. Gervais and A. L. Hillard, "Confronting Sexism as Persuasion: Effects of a Confrontation's Recipient, Source, Message, and Content," *Journal of Social Issues* 70 (2014): 653–667.

5. H. M. Rasinski and A. M. Czopp, "The Effect of Target Status on Witnesses' Reactions to Confrontations of Bias," *Basic and Applied Social Psychology* 32 (2010): 8–16; R. K. Ratner and D. T. Miller, "The Norm of Self-interest and Its Effects on Social Action," *Journal of Personality and Social Psychology* 81 (2001): 5–16.

6. S. Cihangir, M. Barreto, and N. Ellemers, "Men as Allies against Sexism: The Positive Effect of a Suggestion of Sexism by Male (vs. Female) Sources," *Sage Open* 4 (2014): 2158244014539168.

7. Promundo-US, *So, You Want to Be a Male Ally for Gender Equality?*

8. W. B. Johnson and D. G. Smith, "Lots of Men Are Gender-Equality Allies in Private. Why Not in Public?," *Harvard Business Review*, October 2017.

9. J. M. Darley and B. Latane, "Bystander Intervention in Emergencies: Diffusion of Responsibility," *Journal of Personality and Social Psychology* 8 (1968): 377–383.

10. McClelland and Holland, "You, Me, or Her."

11. C. Kilmartin, "Men as Allies," in *Counseling Women across the Life Span: Empowerment, advocacy, and intervention,* ed. J. Schwarz (New York: Springer, 2017), 225–242.

12. K. Catlin, *Better Allies: Everyday Actions to Create Inclusive, Engaging Workplaces* (San Mateo, CA: Better Allies Press, 2019).

13. Vassallo, T., Levy, E., Madansky, M., Mickell, H., Porter, B., Leas, M., & Oberweis, J. (2016). Elephant in the Valley. Women in Tech. https://www.elephantinthevalley.com.

14. M. Johns, T. Schmader, and A. Martens, "Knowing Is Half the Battle: Teaching Stereotype Threat as a Means of Improving Women's Math Performance," *Psychological Science* 16 (2005): 175–179.

15. R. K. Mallett, T. E. Ford, and J. A. Woodzicka, "What Did He Mean by That? Humor Decreases Attributions of Sexism and Confrontation of Sexist Jokes," *Sex Roles* 75 (2016): 272–284.

16. K. Bennhold, "Another Side of #MeToo: Male Managers Fearful of Mentoring Women," *New York Times*, January 27, 2019, https://www.nytimes.com/2019/01/27/world/europe/metoo-backlash-gender-equality-davos-men.html.

17. J. L. Berdahl, P. Glick, and M. Cooper, "How Masculinity Contests Undermine Organizations, and What to Do about It," *Harvard Business Review*, November 2018.

18. C. Kilmartin et al., "A Behavior Intervention to Reduce Sexism in College Men," *Gender Issues* 32 (2015): 97–110.

19. F. Mols et al., "Why a Nudge Is Not Enough: A Social Identity Critique of Governance by Stealth," *European Journal of Political Research* 54 (2015): 81–98.

20. S. J. Gervais and A. L. Hillard, "Confronting Sexism as Persuasion: Effects of a Confrontation's Recipient, Source, Message, and Context," *Journal of Social Issues* 70

(2014): 653–667; W. B. Johnson and D. G. Smith, "Where Are the Male Allies in U.S. Politics?," *Harvard Business Review*, September 2018.

21. A. M. Czopp, M. J. Monteith, and A. Y. Mark, "Standing Up for Change: Reducing Bias through Interpersonal Confrontation," *Journal of Personality and Social Psychology* 90 (2006): 784–803.

22. H. J. Scarsella, "Story Time: I'm at the Airport . . . ," Facebook, September 2018, https://www.facebook.com/yourprivilegeisshowing/posts/2149647662024229.

23. Center for WorkLife Law, "Bias Interrupters: Small Steps, Big Change," 2016, https://biasinterrupters.org/.

24. American Bar Association, "You Can't Change What You Can't See: Interrupting Racial and Gender Bias in the Legal Profession," October-November 2018, https://www.americanbar.org/groups/diversity/women/publications/perspectives/2018/october-november/new-you-cant-change-what-you-cant-see-interrupting-racial--gender-bias-the-legal-profession/.

25. J. C. Williams and R. Dempsey, *What Works for Women at Work*, rev. ed. (New York: New York University Press, 2018).

26. S. K. Johnson, D. R. Hekman, and E. T. Chan, "If There's Only One Woman in Your Candidate Pool, There's Statistically No Chance She'll Be Hired," *Harvard Business Review*, April 26, 2016.

27. S. Cheng et al., "Calling on Male Allies to Promote Gender Equity in IO Psychology," *Industrial and Organizational Psychology* 11 (2018): 389–398.

28. S. Granger, "Want to Be an Ally to Women at Work? Here Are Five Things Men in Tech Have Been Doing," Slate.com, January 2018, https://slate.com/human-interest/2018/01/want-to-be-an-ally-to-women-at-work-five-things-men-in-tech-have-been-doing.html.

29. C. L. Anicha, A. Burnett, and C. Bilen-Green, "Men Faculty Gender-Equity Advocates: A Qualitative Analysis of Theory and Praxis," *Journal of Men's Studies* 23 (2015): 21–43.

Chapter 7

1. K. Catlin, *Better Allies: Everyday Actions to Create Inclusive, Engaging Workplaces* (San Mateo, CA: Better Allies Press, 2019).

2. C. F. Karpowitz, T. Mendelberg, and L. Shaker, "Gender Inequality in Deliberative Participation," *American Political Science Review* 106 (2012): 533–547.

3. J. B. Evans et al., "Gender and the Evaluation of Humor at Work," *Journal of Applied Psychology* (2019), https://psycnet.apa.org/doiLanding?doi=10.1037%2Fapl0000395.

4. J. Bennett*Feminist Fight Club: A Survival Manual for a Sexist Workplace* (New York: Harper Collins, 2016).

5. J. Smith-Lovin and C. Brod, "Interruptions in Group Discussions: The Effects of Gender and Group Composition," *American Sociological Review* 54 (1989): 424–435.

6. T. Jacobi and D. Schweers, "Justice Interrupted: The Effect of Gender, Ideology and Seniority at Supreme Court Oral Arguments," Northwestern Law and Economics Research Paper, 17-03, 2017, https://papers.ssrn.com/sol3/papers.cfm?abstract_id=2933016.

7. Bennett, *Feminist Fight Club*.

8. E. J. McClean et al., "The Social Consequences of Voice: An Examination of Voice Type and Gender on Status and Subsequent Leader Emergence," *Academy of Management Journal* 61 (2018), https://journals.aom.org/doi/abs/10.5465/amj.2016.0148.

9. D. Proudfoot, A. C. Kay, and C. Z. Koval, "A Gender Bias in the Attribution of Creativity: Archival and Experimental Evidence for the Perceived Association between Masculinity and Creative Thinking," *Psychological Science* 26 (2015): 1751–1761.

10. Bennett, *Feminist Fight Club.*

11. L. Babcock et al., "Gender Differences in Accepting and Receiving Requests for Tasks with Low Promotability," *American Economic Review* 107 (2017): 714–747.

12. Ibid.

13. American Bar Association, "You Can't Change What You Can't See: Interrupting Racial and Gender Bias in the Legal Profession," 2018, https://www.americanbar .org/groups/diversity/women/initiatives_awards/bias-interrupters/; Babcock et al., "Gender Differences in Accepting and Receiving Requests for Tasks with Low Promotability."

14. K. O'Meara et al., "Asked More Often: Gender differences in Faculty Workload in Research Universities and the Work Interactions That Shape Them," *American Educational Research Journal* 54 (2017): 1154–1186.

15. Babcock et al., "Gender Differences in Accepting and Receiving Requests for Tasks with Low Promotability."

Chapter 8

1. H. Ibarra, N. M. Carter, and C. Silva, "Why Men Still Get More Promotions Than Women," *Harvard Business Review*, September 2010.

2. A. Ramaswami et al., "Gender, Mentoring, and Career Success: The Importance of Organizational Context," *Personnel Psychology* 63 (2010): 385–405.

3. Ernst & Young, *Shaping the Future Together: Male Champions for Gender Equity: Experiences, Drivers and Lessons Learned*, 2014, 6.

4. W. B. Johnson and D. G. Smith, *Athena Rising: How and Why Men Should Mentor Women* (Boston: Harvard Business Review Press, 2016).

5. J. Green, "Manager's Pick Mini-me Protégés of the Same Race, Gender," *Bloomberg*, January 8, 2019, https://www.bloomberg.com/news/articles/2019-01-08/ managers-pick-mini-me-proteges-of-same-gender-race-in-new-study.

6. A. Grant, "Men Are Afraid to Mentor Women: Here's What You Can Do about It," LinkedIn, February 2018, https://www.linkedin.com/pulse/men-afraid-mentor -women-heres-what-we-can-do-adam-grant/.

7. J. M. Madera et al., "Raising Doubt in Letters of Recommendation for Academia: Gender Differences and Their Impact," *Journal of Business Psychology* 34 (2019): 287–303.

8. B. R. Ragins, "Diversity and Workplace Mentoring Relationships: A Review and Positive Social Capital Approach," in *The Blackwell Handbook of Mentoring: A Multiple Perspectives Approach*, eds. T. D. Allen and L. T. Eby (Malden, MA: Blackwell, 2007), 281–300.

9. Johnson and Smith, *Athena Rising.*

10. W. B. Johnson and C. R. Ridley, *The Elements of Mentoring*, 3rd ed. (New York: St. Martin's Press, 2018).

11. B. R. Ragins, B. Townsend, and M. Mattis, "Gender Gap in the Executive Suite: CEOs and Female Executives Report on Breaking the Glass Ceiling," *Academy of Management Perspectives* 12 (1998): 28–42.

12. R. A. Brands and I. Fernandez-Mateo, "How Negative Recruitment Experiences Shape Women's Decisions to Compete for Executive Roles," *Administrative Science Quarterly* 62 (2017): 405–442; K. S. Lyness and D. E. Thompson, "Climbing the Corporate

Ladder: Do Female and Male Executives Follow the Same Route?," *Journal of Applied Psychology* 85 (2000): 86–101; Ragins et al., "Gender Gap in the Executive Suite."

13. Brands and Fernandez-Mateo, "How Negative Recruitment Experiences."

14. Ragins et al., "Gender Gap in the Executive Suite."

15. Lyness and Thompson, "Climbing the Corporate Ladder."

16. D. G. Smith and W. B. Johnson, "Male Mentors Shouldn't Hesitate to Challenge Their Female Mentees," *Harvard Business Review*, March 2017.

17. K. Cooper, "Preparing Men to Support Women in Leadership Positions," LinkedIn, August 2017, https://www.linkedin.com/pulse/grooming-men-support -women-leadership-positions-kristen-cooper/.

18. A. H. Eagly and L. L. Carli, *Through the Labyrinth: The Truth about How Women Become Leaders* (Boston: Harvard Business Review Press, 2007).

Chapter 9

1. E. H. Chang et al., "The Mixed Effects of Online Diversity Training," *Proceedings of the National Academy of Sciences* 116, no. 16 (2019): 7778–7783; F. Dobbin and A. Kalev, "Why Diversity Programs Fail and What Works Better," *Harvard Business Review*, July–August 2016, 52–60.

2. A. T. Wynn, "Pathways toward Change: Ideologies and Gender Equality in a Silicon Valley Technology Company," *Gender & Society* 2019, https://doi.org/10.1177/0891243219876271.

3. I. Bohnet, *What Works: Gender Equality by Design* (Cambridge, MA: Harvard University Press, 2016).

4. Australian Broadcasting Corporation, "Chief of Army David Morrison Tells Troops to Respect Women or 'Get Out,'" June 14, 2013, https://www.abc.net.au/news/2013-06-14/chief-of-army-fires-broadside-at-army-over-email-allegations/4753208.

5. 3percentmovement.com, "100 Things You Can Do Right Now to Drive the 3% Number Upward," https://www.3percentmovement.com/sites/default/files/resources/100things_0.pdf.

6. A. Kalev, F. Dobbin, and E. Kelly, "Best Practices or Best Guesses? Assessing the Efficacy of Corporate Affirmative Action and Diversity Policies," *American Sociological Review* 71, no. 4 (2006): 589–617.

7. S. I. McClelland and K. J. Holland, "You, Me, or Her: Leaders' Perceptions of Responsibility for Increasing Gender Diversity in STEM Departments," *Psychology of Women Quarterly* 39, no. 2 (2015): 210–225.

8. R. B. Gunderman, "Why Do Some People Succeed Where Others Fail? Implications for Education," *Radiology* 226, no. 1 (2003): 29–31.

9. C. Lawrence et al., "The Design of Everyday Men: A New Lens for Gender Equality Progress," *Deloitte Insights*, 2019, https://www2.deloitte.com/content/dam/insights/us/articles/ca1671_design-of-everyday-men/DI_The-design-of-everyday-men.pdf.

10. Ibid.

11. N. Greenfieldboyce, "Academic Science Rethinks All-Too-White 'Dude Walls' of Honor," NPR.org, August 25, 2019, https://www.npr.org/sections/health-shots/2019/08/25/749886989/academic-science-rethinks-all-too-white-dude-walls-of-honor; E. Fitzsousa, N. Anderson, and A. Reisman, "This Institution Was Never Meant for Me": The Impact of Institutional Historical Portraiture on Medical Students," *Journal of General Internal Medicine* (2019): 1–2.

12. G. Morse, "Designing a Bias-Free Organization," *Harvard Business Review*, July–August 2016, 15–23.

13. E. J. Castilla, "Accounting for the Gap: A Firm Study Manipulating Organizational Accountability and Transparency in Pay Decisions," *Organization Science* 26, no. 2 (2015): 311–333.

14. Kalev et al., "Best Practices or Best Guesses?"

15. C. Lawrence, "The Design of Everyday Men."

16. Ibid.

17. C. Lawrence, "The Design of Everyday Men"; H. Boushey, *Finding Time* (Cambridge, MA: Harvard University Press, 2016).

18. K. Goetz, "How 3M Gave Everyone Days Off and Created an Innovation Dynamo," *Fast Company*, February 1, 2011, https://www.fastcompany.com/1663137/how-3m-gave-everyone-days-off-and-created-an-innovation-dynamo.

19. 3percentmovement.com, "100 Things You Can Do Right Now."

20. Ibid.

21. Ibid.

22. E. U. Cascio, "Public Investments in Child Care," in *Driving Growth through Women's Economic Participation*, eds. D. W. Schanzenback and R. Nunn (Washington, DC: Brookings Institution, 2017), 123–142.

23. J. N. Laditka and S. B. Laditka, "Adult Children Helping Older Parents: Variations in Likelihood and Hours by Gender, Race, and Family Role," *Research on Aging* 23, no. 4 (2001): 429–456.

24. R. Fry, "The Share of Americans Living without a Partner Has Increased, Especially among Young Adults," Pew Research Center, October 11, 2017, https://www.pewresearch.org/fact-tank/2017/10/11/the-share-of-americans-living-without-a-partner-has-increased-especially-among-young-adults/.

25. US Census Bureau, "Unmarried and Single Americans Week: September 16-22, 2018," US Census Bureau, September 22, 2018, https://www.census.gov/newsroom/stories/2018/unmarried-single-americans-week.html.

26. N. Sarkisian and N. Gerstel, "Does Singlehood Isolate or Integrate? Examining the Link between Marital Status and Ties to Kin, Friends, and Neighbors," *Journal of Social and Personal Relationships* 33, no. 3 (2016): 361–384.

27. 3percentmovement.com, "Are We There Yet? The Road to Pay Equity in Advertising," 2018, https://www.3percentmovement.com/sites/default/files/resources/3PC_PPE_4-2-2019.pdf.

Chapter 10

1. Forté Foundation, "The Tool Kit: Starting a Male Ally Group," Forté Foundation, 2016, http://www.fortefoundation.org/site/PageServer?pagename=allies_toolkit_corporate.

2. R. Bhide, "Engaging Men in Diversity, the Science of Effective Inclusion" (master's thesis, Columbia University, 2016).

3. R. Bhide, "The Person Factor, Male Allies and the Formula for Success," LinkedIn, February 22, 2017, https://www.linkedin.com/pulse/person-factor-male-allies-formula-success-rachana-bhide/.

4. F. Gino, "Rebel Talent: Why It Pays to Break the Rules at Work and in Life," (New York: Dey Street Books, 2018); D. Meyerson and M. Tompkins, "Tempered Radicals as Institutional Change Agents: The Case of Advancing Gender Equity at the University of Michigan," *Harvard Journal of Law & Gender* 30 (2007): 303.

5. Forté, "The Tool Kit."

6. Ibid.

7. Ibid.

8. Our Secure Future, "Mobilizing Men as Partners for Women, Peace and Security Charter, Our Secure Future," March 20, 2019, https://oursecurefuture.org/sites/default/files/3_20_19_charter.pdf.

9. Forté, "The Tool Kit"; ibid.

10. C. Lawrence et al., "The Design of Everyday Men: A New Lens for Gender Equality Progress," *Deloitte Insights*, 2019, https://www2.deloitte.com/content/dam/insights/us/articles/ca1671_design-of-everyday-men/DI_The-design-of-everyday-men.pdf.

11. Ibid.

12. Forté, "The Tool Kit."

13. K. A. Gonzalez, E. D. Riggle, and S. S. Rostosky, "Cultivating Positive Feelings and Attitudes: A Path to Prejudice Reduction and Ally Behavior," *Translational Issues in Psychological Science* 1, no. 4 (2015): 372–381; M. Taschler and K. West, "Contact with Counter-stereotypical Women Predicts Less Sexism, Less Rape Myth Acceptance, Less Intention to Rape (in Men) and Less Projected Enjoyment of Rape (in Women)," *Sex Roles* 76, no. 7-8 (2017): 473–484.

14. J. W. Kunstman et al., "Feeling in with the Outgroup: Outgroup Acceptance and the Internalization of the Motivation to Respond without Prejudice," *Journal of Personality and Social Psychology* 105, no. 3 (2013): 443–457.

15. L. Droogendyk et al., "Acting in Solidarity: Cross-group Contact between Disadvantaged Group Members and Advantaged Group Allies," *Journal of Social Issues* 72, no. 2 (2016): 315–334.

16. Ibid.

17. C. L. Anicha, A. Burnett, and C. Bilen-Green, "Men Faculty Gender-Equity Advocates: A Qualitative Analysis of Theory and Praxis," *Journal of Men's Studies* 23, no. 1 (2015): 21–43.

Conclusion

1. Council on Foreign Relations, January 5, 2018, https://www.cfr.org/interactive/womens-participation-in-peace-processes ; V. Hudson et al., *Sex and World Peace* (New York: Columbia University Press, 2012).

2. A. Hegewisch and H. Hartmann, "The Gender Wage Gap: 2018," (Washington, DC: Institute for Women's Policy Research, 2019); J. Woetzel, A. Madgavkar, K. Ellingrud, E. Labaye, S. Devillard, E. Kutcher, J. Manyika, R. Dobbs and M. Krishnan, "The Power of Parity: How Advancing Women's Equality Can Add $12 Trillion to Global Growth," McKinsey Global Institute, September 2015. https://www.mckinsey.com/~/media/McKinsey/Featured%20Insights/Employment%20and%20Growth/How%20advancing%20womens%20equality%20can%20add%2012%20trillion%20to%20global%20growth/MGI%20Power%20of%20parity_Full%20report_September%202015.ashx.

3. M. Adjei, "Women's Participation in Peace Processes: A Review of Literature," *Journal of Peace Education* 16, no. 2 (2019): 133–154; V. M. Hudson, B. Ballif-Spanvill, M. Caprioli and C. F. Emmett, *Sex and World Peace*, (New York: Columbia University Press, 2012).

Index

Acknowledgments

Allies need allies and we've been fortunate to have them in spades. Because allyship starts at home and is defined through everyday interactions with important women in our lives, we want to start by acknowledging the support of our partners, Erica and Laura. In the process of writing two books together over the past six years, they have held us accountable, provided valuable feedback, and saved us from ourselves too many times to count—albeit with a few eye rolls and a bit of humor to keep us grounded. Our ally journey has developed into a true friendship of families that is integral to our messaging and work. Thanks Erica and Laura for all your love, support, and encouragement.

In addition to our partners, several women and men have been there for us—through thick and thin—as colleagues, confidants, and fierce advocates. Starting with *Athena Rising* and now through the hard work of writing *Good Guys*, these are some of our constant allies: Shannon Johnson, Judith Rosenstein, Lisen Stromberg, and Joe Thomas. Thank you all for your inspiration and personifying what it means to be an ally.

This book could never have been written without the generous contributions of fifty-nine women, each of them thought leaders and luminaries across a broad range of professions and organizations. All of them offered generous, unvarnished reflections on their experiences with men in the workplace—the good, bad, and ugly—with an explicit focus on what great male allyship looks like and what they wished men knew about showing up for women at work. Many of them nominated men who'd been especially effective allies. Twenty-nine of those men also consented to interviews, and their humble reflections about the art of allyship—including some of their failures and missteps along the way—provided essential intelligence as we framed the ally actions in *Good Guys*. Our sincerest thanks to each of you.

Finally, we owe a debt of gratitude to our brilliant and creative editor at Harvard Business Review Press, Courtney Cashman. Courtney tells us the truth, holds our feet to the fire, and makes our writing sing. We are also grateful to several other members of the remarkable HBR team, including Victoria Desmond, Lindsey Dietrich, Erika Heilman, Jeff Kehoe, Felicia Sinusas, and Alicyn Zall.

About the Authors

David G. Smith is associate professor of sociology in the College of Leadership and Ethics at the US Naval War College. A former navy pilot, Smith led diverse organizations of women and men culminating in command of a squadron in combat and flew more than three thousand hours over thirty years, including combat missions in Iraq and Afghanistan. He is the recipient of the Charles H. Coates Commemorative Award for Research in Military Sociology from the University of Maryland, College Park. As a sociologist trained in military sociology and social psychology, he focuses his research in gender, work, and family issues including gender bias in performance evaluations, dual-career families, military families, women in the military, and retention of women. Smith is the coauthor of *Athena Rising: How and Why Men Should Mentor Women* and numerous journal articles and book chapters that focus on gender, families, and the workplace.

W. Brad Johnson is professor of psychology in the Department of Leadership, Ethics and Law at the United States Naval Academy, and a faculty associate in the Graduate School of Education at Johns Hopkins University. A clinical psychologist and former officer in the navy's Medical Service Corps, Dr. Johnson served as a psychologist at Bethesda Naval Hospital and the Medical Clinic at Pearl Harbor where he was the division head for psychology. He is a recipient of the Johns Hopkins University Teaching Excellence Award and has received distinguished mentor awards from the National Institutes of Health and the American Psychological Association. Johnson is the author of numerous publications including thirteen books, in the areas of mentoring, professional ethics, and counseling. Other recent books include *Athena Rising: How and Why Men Should Mentor Women*, *The Elements of Mentoring* (3rd ed.), *On Being a Mentor* (2nd ed.), and other books on mentoring.